Sacred Humanism without Miracles

ALSO BY ROY G. SALTMAN

*The History and Politics of Voting Technology:
In Quest of Integrity and Public Confidence (2006)*

Sacred Humanism without Miracles

Responding to the New Atheists

Roy G. Saltman

palgrave
macmillan

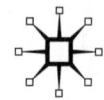

SACRED HUMANISM WITHOUT MIRACLES
Copyright © Roy G. Saltman, 2012

All rights reserved.

First published in 2012 by PALGRAVE MACMILLAN® in the United States—a division of St. Martin's Press LLC, 175 Fifth Avenue, New York, NY 10010.

Where this book is distributed in the UK, Europe and the rest of the world, this is by Palgrave Macmillan, a division of Macmillan Publishers Limited, registered in England, company number 785998, of Houndmills, Basingstoke, Hampshire RG21 6XS.

Palgrave Macmillan is the global academic imprint of the above companies and has companies and representatives throughout the world.

Palgrave® and Macmillan® are registered trademarks in the United States, the United Kingdom, Europe and other countries.

ISBN: 978-1-137-00361-4

Library of Congress Cataloging-in-Publication Data

Saltman, Roy G.
  Sacred humanism without miracles: responding to the New Atheists / Roy G. Saltman.
    p. cm.
  Includes bibliographical references (p.) and index.
  ISBN 978-1-137-00361-4
  1. Humanism, Religious. 2. Atheism. 3. Miracles. I. Title.
  BL2747.6.S25 2012
  211'.6—dc23   2011044514

A catalogue record of the book is available from the British Library.

Design by Scribe Inc.

First edition: May 2012

10 9 8 7 6 5 4 3 2 1

Printed in the United States of America.

For those who strive for amity among religions

and for

David, Eve, and Steven

No father could be more proud

Contents

About the Author		ix
1	Worldviews in Conflict	1
2	Our Physical Universe: Beyond Belief	39
3	Religion: Origins, Interpretations, and Current Practices	75
4	Religion and the State: A Tyrannous Alliance	117
5	Contemporary Interreligious Conflicts	163
6	Acting on Sacred Values in a Scientific Age	197
References		249
Index		255

About the Author

Roy G. Saltman was born in New York City in the early 1930s as the only child of Jewish parents. Told at age six that "you killed our God," he was deeply affected by the widespread interreligious hostility of the times. There was significant discrimination in employment and housing, and quotas for Jews in college admissions. Significant types of discrimination by religion (as well as by race, which was considerably more severe) were made unlawful under the federal Civil Rights Act of 1964. This book is the result of decades of observation and reflection.

Strongly advised to choose engineering as a career in which work would be widely available, he obtained a master's degree at MIT in 1955. Then he began full-time employment in the burgeoning field of computers, designing them for military applications at Sperry Gyroscope Company and applying them for industrial process control at IBM. Finding the private sector stifling, in 1969 he joined the US agency now called the National Institute of Standards and Technology (NIST). He remained there, as a computer scientist, until retirement in 1996. In the course of his working career, he earned an advanced engineering degree from Columbia University and a master's degree in public administration from American University.

NIST scientists consult for other agencies of the federal government, and Saltman was able to carry out valuable research and analysis in the field of computer use in voting technology for the auditing arm of Congress known then as the General Accounting Office. His report, *Effective Use of Computing Technology in Vote-Tallying*, published in 1975, was well received. It was republished with the designation SP500-30 in 1978 in a series available for referencing. When a private foundation wanted additional work done on the same subject, it gave a grant to NIST for Saltman to continue his research. He authored a second report, *Accuracy, Integrity, and Security in Computerized Vote-Tallying* (SP500-158), in 1988. That report identified difficulties in the use of prescored punch cards as ballots and recommended their replacement. They were used in Florida and in other large states. His warning went unheeded.

A quiet retirement as a volunteer docent at a major city art museum was interrupted by the contentious election for president (Bush versus Gore) in Florida in 2000. His second report was introduced into the record in the Florida lawsuit *Gore v. Harris*. As one of the very few persons to have objective knowledge of the technical issues of the voting system being used, he found himself in demand for the next few years as a speaker, consultant, and expert witness in court cases. He testified to a Congressional committee in connection with debate leading to adoption of the Help America Vote Act of 2002. Urged to write a book about the issue, he did so, but not just about the immediate situation. His capability to think broadly about the interaction of multiple subjects, and to undertake research in a variety of issues by reviewing many available studies, enabled him to write *The History and Politics of Voting Technology*, published by Palgrave Macmillan in 2006. This ability has served him well again.

Saltman maintains a strong interest in religions and cultures, both ancient and modern. To satisfy his thirst for knowledge, he has traveled extensively, to many countries in every inhabited continent. Now a widower, he remains in close contact with his three children and his three stepchildren. They have enhanced his life with eight grandchildren and possibly another.

January 2012

CHAPTER 1

WORLDVIEWS IN CONFLICT

TRADITIONAL ADHERENTS OF ONE OF THE ABRAHAMIC religions—Christianity, Islam, and Judaism—maintain a God-centered conception of the universe. They receive and absorb information on how to live from their respective holy books and religious leaders. As a result, these believers know exactly who God is—a supernatural male. "He" created the Earth and all life on it, and "He" may intervene to answer prayers from the faithful who ask for specific events to happen. Furthermore, the theology that informs these folk states that each human has a soul that does not die with the body.

On the opposite pole are people who are certain that there is nothing in our universe but the physical world. These atheists, as well as some agnostics, believe that life on Earth began without the intervention of any supernatural force, and that evolution by natural selection eventually resulted in human beings many millennia later. The results of research by scientists, such as astrophysicists, biologists, and geologists, provide the information that sustains the views of these individuals. Furthermore, atheists generally believe that there is no afterlife, nor any sort of Spiritual World; agnostics are not certain.

True believers and absolute atheists have this in common: they are literalists with regard to holy scriptures. The believers cite chapter and verse to buttress their views. Combative atheists cite chapters and verses to identify contradictions between them. They also identify violations of physical laws and point out parts of the texts that are inconsistent with the liberal morality and cultural norms of today's western Europe and North America. Both groups are rigid; they demand agreement with unprovable propositions about the supernatural and excoriate those who dissent.

For example, the story in Genesis about the seven days of creation and about Adam and Eve and the talking serpent is understood by many people to be a creation myth. Humans who have grown up to be discerning adults can appreciate that the function of this myth is to provide a vehicle for discourse about various ways of living. True believers, as well as uncompromising belief-haters, do not understand the allegorical nature of the story. Those persons who treat the myth literally, whether they believe it or totally discount it without understanding its function, are together in the class of humans who fail to understand an elementary intellectual distinction.

An example of this failure is in an advertisement mailed by the magazine *Free Inquiry* to attract new subscribers. The mailing included a statement by Richard Dawkins, who identifies himself as an FRS (Fellow of the Royal Society). He is one of the New Atheists discussed later, and his statement begins this way: "If you live in America, the chances are good that your next door neighbor believes the following: the Inventor of the laws of physics and Programmer of the DNA code decided to enter the uterus of a Jewish virgin, got himself born, then deliberately had himself tortured and executed because he couldn't think of a better way to forgive the theft of an apple, committed at the instigation of a talking snake."

A conclusion one may draw is that Dawkins really believes that my neighbors (and yours) have a limited capacity to make an elementary intellectual distinction. Is this a case of the pot calling the kettle black?

There may be many interpretations of a particular creation myth, and each explanation may yield a different worldview. That is, the interpretation sets a tone for how humans are to see themselves and how each is to act toward everyone else. For example, a stress on "original sin" and its effect on humans living today ("in Adam's fall, we sinned all") puts a heavy burden of guilt on people and may make them feel unworthy a priori. The implications of that teaching are significant for the future lives of impressionable students.

On the other hand, a stress on the statement from Genesis 1:27, 28, "And God created man in His own image, in the image of God created He him; male and female created He them. And God blessed them," may be employed to provide a totally different orientation. (For the source of Hebrew Bible quotations, see *The Holy Scriptures* in the References chapter.) One does not have to believe in God literally to adopt a humanistic worldview that can be elucidated from the meaning of this text.

The process of interpreting such passages in the Hebrew Bible is a longstanding practice in the Jewish religion in order to make the text meaningful for the contemporary era. (The same issue of interpretation is a major function of the US Supreme Court as it adapts the Constitution, tersely written over 200 years ago, to respond to a current question.) An interpretation of the Hebrew Bible carried out by Jewish scholars is called a *midrash* (plural *midrashim*), and there could be many *midrashim* for the same passage, each produced by a different scholar. Christian exegetes have carried out interpretations also, to demonstrate, for example, that the events of Jesus's ministry were predicted. Much more will be said in this book about this concept, in light of the view of both atheists and fundamentalists that their particular reading of the plain text is the only possible understanding.

In Search of a Middle Way

Is there a rational center between uncompromising religious belief and arrogant, know-it-all disbelief? British author Karen Armstrong, in *The Case for God* (2009), discerns the dilemma of those who "feel uncomfortably caught between two sets of extremists: religious fundamentalists, whose belligerent piety they find alienating, on the one hand, and militant atheists calling for the wholesale extermination of religion, on the other" (321).

Armstrong (b. 1944) has previously written several highly informative books on religion, including *A History of God* (1993). A significant statement in *The Case for God* is that "In most premodern cultures, there were two recognized ways of thinking, speaking, and acquiring knowledge. The Greeks called them *mythos* and *logos* . . .

Logos ('reason') . . . was essential to the survival of our species. But it had its limitations: It could not assuage human grief or find ultimate meaning in life's struggles. For that people turned to *mythos* or myth" (xi).

An important theme in *The Case for God* is that there have been widely different definitions of God, from the earliest times to the present, even among persons of the same nominal religion. In Armstrong's view, the current deep chasm between believers and atheists has its origin in the change in outlook that began with the Renaissance in the fifteenth century. Western society began to develop a civilization increasingly responsive to the discoveries of science based on observations of the physical world. The effect on religion was that "*Logos* achieved such spectacular results that myth was discredited and the scientific method was thought to be the only reliable means of attaining truth. This would make religion difficult, if not impossible" (xv).

One function of religion is to assist us to step outside ourselves and actually experience the transcendent. In times past, according to Armstrong, holy scriptures were interpreted in a mythic sense, improving the likelihood of the experience. Trying to achieve closeness with the transcendent by describing or analyzing it, rather than experiencing it, may not be possible. It cannot be fully articulated, as humans are limited by earthbound language. Intellectualization, inherent in the scientific method, may further distance us.

Attempts to define the transcendent have proceeded since ancient times. "God Is Beyond Comprehension" is the title of a section included in *Oneness: Great Principles Shared by All Religions* (rev. ed. 2002) by Jeffrey Moses. Statements expressing this idea from six of the great religions are listed (122–3). Maimonides (1138–204), the Jewish sage of medieval times, wrote in *The Guide of the Perplexed* that one could only define God by negative attributes, that is, by what was not true, not by what was true. He was born in Muslim Spain but lived and wrote in Egypt for much of his life, where he was significantly influenced by Islamic thought. Muslim philosophers of that era also recognized the limited ability of humans to define the transcendent. The fact that both the

Jewish and Muslim religions forbid the physical representation of the deity or the prophets in pictures or statues is indicative of their views on this issue. Such a representation would be limiting of a fuller understanding, and would constitute a tendency toward idol-worship.

Whether or not Armstrong's view about the impact of the scientific method is correct, the literalist approach to holy writings is in vogue at this time. In particular, the New Testament is seen by some believers as a textbook similar to one that might be found in a class in physics, or perhaps like a handbook of beliefs and recipes for action, such as the Little Red Book of Mao Tse-Tung. Similarly, Muslim *jihadis* seem to be adopting specific statements in the Koran to justify their violence, while ignoring other passages that could provide the opposite interpretation. Jewish supporters of settlements in the Occupied Territories (West Bank) cite biblical passages about the God-given land to buttress their views (e.g., see Genesis 15:18). Their atheist opponents, also reading the texts literally and comparing them to scientific treatises, see them as nonrational, useless, or even destructive, from their point of view.

The Modern Dilemma and Its Analysis

It appears that Karen Armstrong would prefer the premodern, more spiritual, less rational interpretation of religion, and not that of our scientific age. Unfortunately, it is highly unlikely that people who have been educated with late-twentieth-century methods, and who have lived with all the accouterments of advanced technology based on scientific research, can revert to attitudes of the Middle Ages.

The implication of results of scientific investigations of recent centuries is clear: the universe operates on every level, from the atomic to the cosmic, only by physical laws that were established when the universe began. The most recent variable conditions on the Earth have favored the development of life-forms, leading to the evolution of humans, but also causing events dangerous to humans, such as droughts, floods, earthquakes, tsunamis, and epidemics.

This new rational understanding of natural change has affected the basis that many people have used to regulate the way they live.

A statement by a Protestant evangelical leader that Hurricane Katrina of 2005 was "God's wrath over societal tolerance of homosexuality" and a "judgment on the wickedness and decadence of New Orleans" seems ludicrous to those who fully understand the implications of scientific discoveries. In late April 2011, when destructive tornadoes killed about three hundred people in an area of the South where evangelical Christianity is extremely strong, no such pronouncements were made. Natural disasters are not God's revenge or admonitions; rather, they are the result of processes regulated by the fundamental laws of physics operative in our universe.

Furthermore, the Earth doesn't have unlimited resources; they must be managed, even more so than earlier, in the light of recent significant population growth and industrialization. If the availability of sources of sustenance as well as natural disasters are not God's work, what about the sacred values by which we live? Religion, with its core buttressed by miracles, has told adherents how to select their sacred values. Without miracles, religious imperatives are questionable because the basis of religion is devalued. Without miracles, is nothing sacred? And if there is a sacred aspect to human life, how is it to be discovered and applied? These are the questions pursued here.

The remainder of this chapter elaborates on the meaning of the sacred and the impact on religion in the absence of miracles. Additionally, the origin of Christianity as a synthesis of Judaism and paganism, along with its debt to its church–state alliance, are discussed. The New Atheists are introduced, and their baseless claim that moderate religion leads to fanaticism is countered. Chapter 2 reviews the results of scientific research that has led us to understand both the origin of the universe and the operation of physical laws that have yielded the evolution of humans on planet Earth. Chapter 3 provides a discussion of religion, including its function, its analysis by a number of important theorists, its relationship to culture, and reasons for its continuation. Chapter 4 describes the violence and suffering historically generated by state-supported religion. Chapter 5 concerns the contemporary worldwide turmoil fostered by extreme variants of religious practice. Finally, in Chapter 6, the issue of sacred values that can be established independently of supernatural command is addressed. This chapter also undertakes a review of seven international convocations, held over the period 1933 to 2009, in which some of these values have been identified. It is asserted that sacred humanism, also called "humanism with sacred values," is the rational middle ground between religion and a value-free atheism. Persons with this lifestance aim to improve the world; actions consistent with that purpose are delineated.

THE GRECO-ROMAN ERA

Ideas and actions of the period from 400 BCE ("before the Common Era") to 400 CE ("of the Common Era") affect much of what we think and do today. This era may be considered to have begun at about the time that Socrates was condemned to death and Plato started to write philosophical works. Later in the period, the pagan Romans conquered the Greeks, who had developed stories about semidivine heroes called "demigods," as well as the Jews, who had evolved monotheism. The era would end with Christianity, defined by a revised Nicene Creed, as the state religion of the Roman empire, with both paganism and Christian "heresies" proscribed.

With the conquests of Alexander the Great in the late fourth century BCE, Greek culture spread most strongly throughout the lands bounded by the eastern half of the Mediterranean Sea. This culture included Greek language and customs, as well as schools of its philosophers. For example, the ideas of the philosopher Epicurus (341–270 BCE) were widely disseminated, including the concept that the gods existed but that they did not interfere in the affairs of humans. In a reaction against Hellenism, "*apikouros*" (Epicurean) became a pejorative used by some Jews throughout the Greco-Roman world against nonpietistic individuals who were too closely associated with worldly attitudes and modes of living. The

Jews of Judea were successful in battling the forces of the Greco-Syrian monarch Antiochus IV Epiphanes, beginning in 167 BCE, leading to their temporary independence commemorated in the festival of Hanukkah, but were not so fortunate after being overrun by Roman legions under Pompey in 63 BCE.

Christianity began in the first century CE at a time when the Roman empire was at the height of its power. The Mediterranean Sea was a Roman lake. Rome's power, enforced by its unequaled military legions, did not ensure that its subject peoples were always content. Many revolts were attempted. For example, the Jews rose up in 66 CE in their home country, but the result was their defeat, the destruction of the holy temple in Jerusalem in 70 CE, and death or slavery for many of the losers. According to Martin Gilbert in *The Dent Atlas of Jewish History* (1993), other Jewish revolts against Rome that failed occurred in 115–17 CE in Cyrenaica (in today's Libya), Egypt, Cyprus, and Mesopotamia (now Iraq). Another failed revolt, the Bar Kochba rebellion, occurred in 132–35 CE, in Judea itself. After this final revolt was suppressed by Emperor Hadrian, Judea was renamed Syria Palaestina by the Romans. Jerusalem became Aelia Capitolina, and Jews were forbidden to live there. If nothing succeeds like success, then nothing fails like failure. The devastating military defeats in the homeland of Judaism must have had a significant outcome in conversions to the new religion by "God-fearers." These were persons in the Diaspora who were sympathetic to Judaism and participated in some of its rites and festivals, but were not actually Jews.

One interpretation of Christian theology is that it is a synthesis of two disparate lines of religious thought: monotheistic Judaism and Greco-Roman polytheism. This borrowing and synthesis is not unique. The story of Noah in the Hebrew Bible appears to have been adapted from flood myths of earlier civilizations in Mesopotamia. The Koran, according to some experts, contains borrowings from the works of the two older monotheisms.

The development of Christianity owes much to the Roman admiration of Greek culture. The Romans may have defeated the Greeks, but they adopted much of the Greek pantheon of gods and heroes. Greek architecture, as well as copies of their statues, decorated Roman villas. New Roman cities established in conquered territories (such as Jerash, now in Jordan) mirrored Greek designs, with public temples, libraries, baths, and theaters. The Greek language was still in wide use as the lingua franca in the lands bordering the eastern Mediterranean. The Hebrew Bible was translated into Greek in stages in the third and second centuries BCE; the translation was called the *Septuagint*. Greek was the original language of the New Testament. Christianity's triune godhead—the Father, the Son, and the Holy Spirit—is claimed to be really one God. This apparent attempt to be simultaneously monotheistic and polytheistic puzzles many nonadherents as confusing and inconsistent. In addition, consider the following description: *A certain man was the son of a god and a mortal woman, although he had a nominal human father. As an adult, he performed a number of wondrous feats. He died a horrible and painful death, but became immortal.*

This account fits both the Greek hero Heracles (called Hercules in the Roman world) and the crucified Jew, Jesus. Heracles was born to a mortal woman, Alcmene; his real father was Zeus, the most powerful of the immortal Olympian gods. However, Heracles had a mortal father, Amphitryon, in the same sense that Jesus had a mortal father, Joseph. Heracles performed 12 wondrous labors. Jesus carried out many miracles, such as turning water into wine, raising Lazarus and the daughter of Jairus from the dead, walking on water, driving out demons that possessed humans, and healing blind and paralyzed individuals.

Heracles died when he was given a poisoned tunic to wear; it burned his skin and painfully tore away his flesh when he tried to remove it. He asked his companions to build a bonfire around him, to allow him to die. According to the description of Sofia Souli in *Greek Mythology* (2007), "When the flames had begun to rise high, thunder was heard, lightning flashed, and a cloud descended to take Heracles into the sky. So it came about that he joined the immortals and ascended to Olympus . . ." (80).

Another "remarkable man," who was born about the time of Jesus but lived until old age, was Apollonius of Tyana, according to New Testament scholar Bart D. Ehrman (b. 1955). (Tyana is in Cappadocia, in present-day central Turkey, but was then a part of the Greek world.) Speaking as the instructor in the video course *The Historical Jesus* (2000), Ehrman notes that Apollonius was born under circumstances similar to Jesus, in that an angelic visitor announced his conception to his mother, telling her that her infant would be divine. His birth was accompanied by miraculous signs and wonders. As a child, Apollonius was religiously precocious, far beyond what clerical leaders thought possible. As an adult, he became an itinerant preacher; he healed the sick, drove out demons, and raised individuals from the dead. A story told about Apollonius, in which he forced a devil to depart a man, is quite similar to the story told about Jesus in Luke 8:26–39. Apollonius told listeners that they were not tied to this material world, but could live a more spiritual life, just as Jesus told similar groups. Apollonius attracted disciples who were certain that he was not of this world. However, he raised the ire of powerful individuals who charged him with crimes and brought him before Roman authorities (actually, the Roman emperor Domitian, in about 96 CE). Unlike Jesus, he was acquitted and he returned home. After he died and supposedly ascended to heaven, his disciples were sure that they saw him alive. Later, books were written about him, from which we have gleaned much biographical information.

Other heroes of legend, such as Theseus from Greek myth and Rama, hero of the Hindu epic *Ramayana*, have similar parentage to those of the individuals already discussed, that is, a male god and a mortal woman (Theseus was the son of Poseidon; Rama's mother was magically impregnated by the god Vishnu). As noted above, they are called demigods. Contemporary individuals in the Greco-Roman world seemed to need a similar parentage to be thought of as powerful and respected. After Alexander conquered Egypt, it was recognized that its god Amon had powers and functions similar to those of the Greek god Zeus. Alexander was worshipped as the divine son of Amon-Zeus. Later, as the Roman leader Octavian was preparing to assume the role of emperor in 27 BCE with the new name Augustus, the myth was promoted that he was the son of the god Apollo, who had mated with his mortal mother, Atia. Later, he would be referred to as the "Savior of the World." Thus the idea that Jesus was the Son of God (in a special sense that did not apply to mortals) was hardly strange either to believers in Greco-Roman polytheism or to nonbelievers familiar with it. It is known that followers of Jesus and those of Apollonius of Tyana met during the second century CE and argued about which one had powers that came from God (or the gods) and which one was a mere mortal.

The story of Jesus, involving a painful death, resurrection, and subsequent immortality, is too well known to require a repetition here. Note that many of Jesus's miracles relate to the immediate concerns of ordinary humans, for example, sickness and death. Along with Jewish ethics, which also were lacking in Greek myths, these aspects of Christianity must have been appealing to the masses. These concepts are missing in the efforts of Heracles. However, to the Jews of that time who were devoted to their own theology, the idea of the corporeality of God was anathema. As a result, Christianity achieved its first successes, not among the Jews, but among the Greek-speaking Gentiles of the eastern Mediterranean basin. The triumph of Christianity over competitive belief-systems, such as that held by followers of Apollonius of Tyana, is owed to the Roman emperor Constantine, whose mother, Helena, was a devoted Christian.

A world-altering battle occurred in 312 CE, in which the old religion battled the new. At Milvian Bridge near the city of Rome, the armies of Constantine and Maxentius fought for control of the empire. Maxentius associated himself with the demigod Hercules, while Constantine had seen a vision (or had a dream) telling him to have faith in the cross, symbol of the suffering of the demigod Jesus. Of course, we know that Constantine was victorious, and Maxentius drowned in Rome's Tiber River. Pagan religions and Christian "heresies" within the Roman empire soon followed Maxentius's example, although more slowly and with decree-based pressure from a hostile, state-run religion. That religion, with specific beliefs firmly established, would achieve its absolute dominance just before 400 CE.

The rejection of Christianity by many Jews, even the continuation of their very existence, has been a source of Christian hostility continually expressed over the centuries. In a recent conversation between a Christian and a Jew while jointly visiting the sixteenth-century cathedral of Cusco, Peru, the Christian asked, innocently, "Why do the Jews persist?" The Christian did not appear to appreciate that the question, posed with the verb "persist" as if the Jews were just weeds in a lawn to which much herbicide has been applied, reflected teachings of the disparagement of Jews many centuries old. There had been the issue among early Christian theologians whether the Jews should be eliminated immediately or allowed to "persist" so that they might be converted. The view that it must be "either-or" rather than "live and let live" was a long-lived theme that only recently has seemed to dissipate. According to Paula Fredriksen, scholar of ancient Christianity, the orthodox bishop of Antioch, John Chrysostom (347–407 CE), asked his congregation in 387, "Don't you understand that if the Jews' way of life is true, then ours must be false?" (Fredriksen and Reinhartz 2002, 30).

From that point, Christianity would hold sway, unchallenged, for three centuries. Then a new religion, Islam, would arise and become strong enough to contest Christian hegemony throughout the Mediterranean region.

Religion and the State

In classical Greece and Rome, support of the state's deities was required by law. Atheism was punishable by death. Nevertheless, atheistic documents exist from the sixth century BCE. It has been recorded that Xenophanes, a Greek philosopher of that period, said that if cows and horses had hands, then horses would draw the forms of gods like horses; cows would draw them like cows. Socrates, the famous gadfly whose views and methods of dialogue were discussed by Plato, was sentenced to death in 399 BCE. One of the charges against him was impiety, or not acknowledging the gods of the city, an accusation of atheism as it was then defined.

In ancient Rome, Jews and Christians were called atheists because they refused to sacrifice to the gods of the state. Jews were given an exception to the requirement for sacrificing, because their religion was very old. Christians, belonging to a new religion, were not exempt; they were subject to arrest and could face the death penalty. That changed when Constantine became emperor in the early fourth century CE; he made Christianity legal. In 380 CE, emperors Theodosius I of the East and Gratian of the West, with the Edict of Thessalonica, made Christianity the official religion of the empire. Not until 1791 CE, the date of adoption of the First Amendment to the US Constitution, would there be true separation of church and state in any country in the Western world.

Theodosius ordered many pagan temples destroyed and prohibited the public performance of pagan worship and sacrifices. The prohibition included ancient Greek, Roman, and Egyptian religions, as well as any other pagan religions whose devotees came under control of the new Christian empire. (Judaism was permitted, as it was not pagan.) Examples of destruction or defacement of sacred statues and wall-incised line-sculptures of other religions may still be seen throughout the areas under Christian control at that time. The 2001 destruction of Buddhist statues in Afghanistan by Taliban extremists is hardly a new departure in human activity.

With the general adoption of this new faith by European monarchies by the end of the Dark Ages, Christians did unto others what was done to them. Jews became second-class, restricted in their daily movements and in the types of work in which they could engage. Muslims, in control of countries to the east and south of Europe after the eighth century, were the enemy against whom many battles were fought. Atheists continued to risk death by speaking out; heretics risked a similar fate. It would not be until the eighteenth century, which included the French and American revolutions, that espousal of atheism or of an unapproved religion began to be possible without fear of criminal charges or violent attack.

In recognition of the history of the entanglement of religion and government, the Framers of the US Constitution (in force by

1789) did not accept the common European arrangement. In a revolutionary idea for its time, they attempted to eliminate the direct influence of religion on the operation of government. They made no mention of God in the Constitution (except, beyond the body of the document, in a final note that the signatures were affixed "in the Year of our Lord one thousand seven hundred and Eighty seven"). They wrote, in Article VI, paragraph 3, that "no religious Test shall ever be required as a Qualification to any Office or public Trust under the United States."

This text was considered initially to apply only to the federal government and not to the states. The First Amendment, adopted with nine others as the Bill of Rights in 1791, states that "Congress shall make no law respecting an establishment of religion, or prohibiting the free exercise thereof."

In the federal republic, the application of the Bill of Rights to the states was not certain at first. A US Supreme Court decision in 1925 called *Gitlow v. New York* was a significant step toward Bill of Rights' coverage of state law as well as federal. Subsequent decisions have expanded this understanding. Since the First Amendment requires freedom of speech, no penalties can be assessed by the federal or any state government on any person for favoring atheism or any particular religion in speech, whether written or verbal.

However, several states of the United States retain provisions in their constitutions limiting office-holding to persons who believe in God, but any attempt to enforce these requirements at this time is likely to be unsuccessful. An article in the February 2010 issue of the official magazine of Americans United for Separation of Church and State discussed the history of state requirements for religious oaths of office. The article pointed out that "a 1961 US Supreme Court decision struck down such religious tests." The case, *Torcaso v. Watkins*, was originally filed in Maryland in 1960 by Roy Torcaso (1911–2007), who was denied a license to become a notary public because he refused to take a religious oath of office. Although the Maryland Supreme Court upheld the denial, the unanimous opinion of the top federal court overturned the Maryland decision. The opinion, written by Justice Hugo Black, stated that "We repeat and again reaffirm that neither a State nor the Federal Government can constitutionally force a person 'to profess belief or disbelief in any religion.'"

In 2009, religious extremists in North Carolina were outraged that a certain city councilman in that state had failed to take a religious oath of office. They called for his ouster. However, no lawsuit challenging his accession to office has been filed. The law on this subject is clear.

THE NEW ATHEISTS

One unexpected but interesting consequence of the attacks of September 11, 2001, on the Pentagon and New York City's World Trade Center was that several books touting atheism were written. The fact that the assaults were carried out by Islamic *jihadis* was one of the motivating factors for these New Atheists. They are given this special name because their attitude has been highly aggressive. According to an article on CNN.com by Simon Hooper, "What the New Atheists share is a belief that religion should not simply be tolerated but should be countered, criticized and exposed by rational argument wherever its influence arises."

British zoologist Richard Dawkins (b. 1941), professor of the Public Understanding of Science at Oxford University, is one of the New Atheists. Dawkins provided a useful definition in his book *The God Delusion* (2006). He wrote that "An atheist . . . is somebody who believes there is nothing beyond the natural, physical world, no supernatural creative intelligence lurking behind the observable universe, no soul that outlasts the body and no miracles—except in the sense of natural phenomena that we don't yet understand" (14).

Another New Atheist book is *god Is Not Great: How Religion Poisons Everything* (2007), by journalist Christopher Hitchens. With an attitude similar to that of Dawkins. Hitchens (b. 1949) saw religion as an institution that fosters ignorance and violence and should be totally eliminated. Unfortunately, Hitchens will not be able to respond to statements made in this book as he passed away in December 2011. A third horseman of the atheist posse is Sam Harris (b. 1967). His book, *The End of Faith* (2006) has a similar theme. "There is no God," shout Dawkins, Hitchens, and Harris, in effect, from nearly every page of their respective books.

It appears that all three of the New Atheists so far identified were raised in a Protestant Christian milieu. Yet their works demonstrate only the most superficial knowledge of any religion or denomination. Dawkins's current religion appears to be evolution and his god Darwin. Hitchens stated that "my particular atheism is a Protestant atheism" (11). Harris may decry the attacks of the *jihadis*, but he evidences no knowledge of Islam in general. Their knowledge of Judaism is similarly close to zero, despite the fact that Hitchens admitted that his mother was Jewish (11), and it is reported in an online biography that Sam Harris's mother was Jewish, also. They should have been embarrassed about their significant gaps in knowledge, considering the subject of their treatises, yet they demonstrated no contrition.

Hitchens revealed also that his second marriage was performed by a rabbi who happened to be homosexual, and he noted that such conduct would have resulted in stoning to death if the prescriptions of the Hebrew Bible were carried out. What Hitchens failed to appreciate is that Judaism, unlike some Protestant sects, does not treat all biblical language as a requirement to be literally followed. It is an understanding by many Jews that each generation must interpret the holy scriptures for themselves, in light of the changed mores of current civilization. Judaism, along with nearly every Christian denomination, does not allow a man to have more than one wife, though it clearly was approved for the patriarchs in the Bible. Nor does Judaism now countenance stoning to death for the wide variety of sins for which that punishment was a biblical remedy. The abject failure of Hitchens's rabbi was not that he did not carry out the commandment to "be fruitful and multiply," but that he carried out a marriage ceremony for someone so ignorant of the religion into which he married.

The New Atheists, in another of the many demonstrations of their ignorance, almost always refer to the Hebrew Bible as the Old Testament. In the Christian version, the books are *not* presented in the same order as in the original Hebrew, nor necessarily with the identical translations. The use of the term "Old Testament" indicates an acceptance of Christian theology with regard to Judaism. The term is often used by authors writing from a Christian perspective, even if they appear to have adopted atheism, for example Robert A. Hinde, author of *Why Gods Persist* (2nd ed., 2010). In the one place where Christopher Hitchens referred to the "Hebrew Bible," he equated it with the Pentateuch (102). *Wrong!* The Pentateuch is only one of the three parts of the Hebrew Bible. These parts are: (1) the Law, that is, the five books of Moses (sometimes called the Pentateuch), *plus* (2) the Prophets, which includes the books of the prophets, such as Isaiah, as well as Joshua, Judges, the two Samuels, and the two Kings, *plus* (3) the Writings. The latter includes such books as Job, Psalms, and Ecclesiastes. The term "Hebrew Bible" is used by unbiased, non-Jewish scholars, for example Bart D. Ehrman in *God's Problem* (2008).

When Jesus states in Matthew 7:12 that "Therefore all things whatever ye would that men should do to you, do ye even so to them: for this is the law and the prophets," two of the three primary divisions of the Hebrew Bible are being cited. (For the source of New Testament quotations, see *The Holy Bible* in the References chapter.) Since Christians do not divide their Old Testament in this manner, the reference in this verse is not obvious to those who have only the barest minimal knowledge of religion. Jesus is stating here a similar interpretation given the Jewish religion by the Jewish sage Hillel the Elder (ca. 110 BCE–ca. 10 CE); its essence is the Golden Rule. Certainly, it is a good guide to apply in interpersonal relations, whether one follows the teachings of Hillel or of Jesus or, for that matter, of the Buddha. See, in Chapter 6, "The Charter for Compassion *of 2009.*"

No Miracles versus No God

The assertion that there is no God is a much more sweeping conclusion than simply asserting the nonoccurrence of miracles. The idea that God does not exist is not a defense of science; it is a theological statement. Richard Dawkins, who finds no proper function for theologians, correctly defends evolution as a scientific fact because there is much real evidence to support it. He rightly attacks Creationism and Intelligent Design because there are no scientific facts to back up those concepts. Certainly, there is no scientific evidence that there is a God, but similarly there is no scientific evidence that no God exists. In his blunt and angry atheistic stance, Dawkins has gone way beyond scientific knowledge into mere opinion. His opinion deserves no more weight than that of any true believer.

The statement that there are no miracles, the premise of this book, is not the same as saying that there is no God. The limited assertion made here is equivalent to stating that the physical laws of the universe are never violated. That is, everything that occurs in the universe, including on Earth, is consistent with those physical laws. To restate the proposition in an alternate form, no supernatural force directly intervenes by violating physical laws on Earth or anywhere else in this universe. This view is similar to that of Epicurus of some two millennia ago. In fact, the claim is that there has been no such intervention from the time of the formation of the universe through the present. Furthermore, there will be no miracles for the indefinite future until it no longer matters because there will be no beings on this Earth capable of cogitating about it.

In the black/white thinking of the New Atheists, belief or disbelief in God is the single issue of concern. In *The God Delusion*, Richard Dawkins fills seven pages with vehement castigation of "agnostics," people who are not sure. This unnecessary vitriol occurs because Dawkins lumps two independent issues together and fails to distinguish between them. Once it is understood that no miracles occur, the question of whether God exists is immaterial (pun intended), at least for happenings in life on Earth. *If the concept of no miracles is accepted, there is no conflict between religion and science.* The view put forth here is naturalism rather than agnosticism. Earth is the real world in which physical laws explain everything concerning the movement of matter. With regard to a possible Spiritual World, nothing can be explained, as no scientifically derived evidence of it exists now or is likely to exist in the future.

The elimination of miracles from possibility is sufficient to strongly limit the credibility of religious pronouncements about the physical world. It also forces religion to compete with nonreligious rational arguments about ethics and human conduct. By insisting that God doesn't exist, the writings of the New Atheists seem to imply, additionally, that spiritual thinking of any type, to quote Dawkins's title, is "delusional"; nonsense.

Humans have an enormous capacity for imagination. This application of abstract thinking has been responsible for progress, because it considers, among other things, what might be instead of what is. Furthermore, imagination has resulted in the arts: music, poetry, drama, literature, painting, sculpture, and other forms. The arts are extremely valuable for enriching human culture, for providing a respite from daily cares, and for providing mechanisms for self-expression and self-understanding. Imagination has also resulted in philosophical and speculative thinking and writings, including those about our personal relationship with the Infinite. These are certainly "spiritual" concerns. Free speech must allow such speculations, as long as one particular belief is not forced on others who disagree. State power must never assign criminality to thoughts, but only to certain actions that may have varying degrees of criminality under the rule of law.

One implication of the no-miracles dictum is that there will be no supernatural Day of Judgment or End of Days. No Messiah has come, and one will not come in the future. If human life on Earth ends abruptly, it will be due to a natural cause or to human self-destruction. Possible natural causes include effects of a large asteroid striking the Earth, or a devastating volcanic eruption due to a geologic "hot spot" condition such as the caldera existing beneath Yellowstone National Park, or life-destroying radiation coming from the explosion of a nearby "white dwarf" star as it becomes a supernova. Astrophysicists have discovered that such a star exists about 3,260 light-years away (not far by cosmic standards). Self-destruction could result from the use of nuclear or biological weapons, from new mutations of deadly microorganisms that have become totally resistant to human-developed control measures, or from some type of uncontrolled pollution, leakage of atomic radiation, or global temperature change caused by human activity. If none of those events occurs beforehand, changes in the sun's output of light and heat, due to its aging and becoming a "red giant" star, might cause the end of human life in about five billion years.

Another implication of miracle nonexistence is that prayer has no effect in bringing forth the result prayed for. Dawkins has reported (63) a statistically valid experiment in which some sick people were prayed for and knew it, other sick people were prayed for and didn't know it, while a third group of identified sick people were not prayed for and didn't know it. The results, reported in the *American Heart Journal* of April 2006 in an article by Herbert Benson, MD, et al., were that "there was no difference [in outcomes] between those patients who were prayed for and those who were not." Additionally, "those who knew they had been the beneficiaries of prayer suffered significantly more complications than those who did not." The fact that there were religiously oriented people who expected the result of the experiment to support the efficacy of prayer demonstrates the depth of magical thinking among individuals of genus *homo,* species *sapiens,* subspecies *sapiens*—that is, we humans.

It is a rational supposition, though, that prayer may have value for the person *doing* the praying and for any co-congregants involved in that process. Prayer may bring more courage, fortitude, and community solidarity, all of which make religion helpful to people and provide reasons for its continued use. Abraham Joshua Heschel (1907–72) described it poetically:

> Prayer can water an arid soul,
> mend a broken heart,
> repair a weakened will.

THE IMPACT OF NO MIRACLES ON THE ABRAHAMIC RELIGIONS

ON JUDAISM

While the basis of Judaism is God's revelation to Moses at Sinai, miracles were closely associated with the exodus from Egypt. Examples of these are the implementation of the ten plagues, the parting and subsequent closing of the sea in the saving of the Israelites from

Pharaoh's army, and the delivery of food and water to the Israelites in the desert. The Passover, with its seder or holy meal that celebrates the Exodus, is perhaps the most widely celebrated holiday among modern Jews. But Judaism is not, for many non-Orthodox Jews, dependent on belief. Many do not believe in the actual occurrence of these miracles. For them, the message of the religion is political freedom, religious freedom, and important ethical requirements, as well as solidarity with other families in their community with whom they share a common heritage.

As an indication of a recent change in perspective, all the denominations except the Orthodox now have women rabbis. In addition, the more-liberal movements have made God gender-neutral, that is, the pronouns "He" and "Lord" are no longer used in English translation of traditional prayers. In one instance, the translation of what should be literally "King of the World" is rendered as "Sovereign of Existence." The Hebrew *Adonai* (Lord) is simply not translated; *Adonai* is used in the English text.

On Christianity

If there are no miracles, the implications for Christianity are serious. It is a religion of belief in miracles. The Nicene Creed of 325 CE, and also the Creed of Constantinople of 381 CE, includes beliefs that Jesus, "the only begotten Son of God," was made incarnate, suffered and died, was resurrected ("the third day he rose again"), and ascended into heaven. Additionally, persons named as saints of the Roman Catholic Church must have carried out specific miracles. A miracle that used to be important to Christians is mentioned in the text of Joshua 10:12 and following verses concerning the movement of the sun. This text was used by the Roman Catholic Church during the Renaissance and later to enforce belief in an Earth-centered model of our solar system, despite growing scientific evidence, based on observations of the sky, that demonstrated its incorrectness. Certain avenues of scientific research, as well as family planning and healthy outcomes in sexual intercourse, have been held back in deference to conservative Christian theological views. It may yet be that, in the current century, many persons who nominally call themselves Christians will understand the miracles to be symbolic. For such people, the important message of their religion is not the actual occurrence of the miracles but how to live one's life in the right way, how to be courageous in the face of challenges and difficulties, and how to face death with calmness and equanimity.

Christianity, like Judaism, has had to address the issue of female clergy in recent times, although Christian theology appears to require that God be male. According to data released by the Hartford Institute for Religion Research, in 15 mainline and conservative Protestant denominations, about 12 percent of clergy are female. There are currently no female clergy in the Church of Jesus Christ of Latter-day Saints (the Mormon Church) or in the Roman Catholic Church.

Efforts by doubters to maintain a relationship to the transcendent through the Roman Catholic denomination may have been hurt by the revelations of scandalous cover-ups in several countries of priests' sexual abuse of young people. In the United States, widespread negative publicity has resulted from revelations of immoral conduct by some well-known Protestant pastors who preached against the same type of activity that they secretly practiced. In 2002, a pastor in Bremerton, Washington, was convicted of murdering his wife in 1997 after the woman with whom he was having an affair at the time finally revealed the plot. (Judaism is not immune. Also in 2002, a previously respected rabbi in Cherry Hill, New Jersey, was convicted of hiring two men to murder his wife.)

A possible positive outcome of these situations may be that clergy in the West will no longer be treated with more deference than that given to laity. Religious organizations, despite their aura of holiness, are staffed by humans who are subject to the same emotional appetites as the rest of us. Law enforcement, supposedly serving all the people, has the duty to protect the public from predators or others who violate criminal statutes, not exempting those who use their religious affiliation as a cover. I fervently hope that deference to the ordained personnel of religious groups will no longer apply in law enforcement in any nation. Additionally, national and international religious bodies must cooperate with local law enforcement. In 2011, a report was released in Ireland revealing that actions constituting obstruction of justice or "cover-ups" by international and national religious authorities had prevented adequate prosecution of sexual misconduct by priests in the Diocese of Cloyne. In a democracy, national secular law must supersede religious dicta on issues of public health and safety and certainly on issues of criminality. *The New York Times* summarized the problem in its editorial of July 15, 2011, stating that "the Vatican has blatantly resisted the idea that civil law must trump church rules in confronting criminal acts" (A20).

ON ISLAM

In Islam, the essential happening was Muhammad's receipt of revelations from Allah through the angel Gabriel. Revelations are not miracles, as defined here, since they do not, by themselves, cause changes in the physical world. Thus Islam is not primarily dependent on miracles although there is a belief in a certain night journey of Muhammad. The Prophet is said to have flown from Mecca to Jerusalem on a winged horse and then ascended to heaven from the rock now enclosed by the Dome of the Rock. Like Judaism, Islam is a religion of practice more than of belief. Still, it has yet to accept female clergy.

Muslims accept the Hebrew Bible and the New Testament as prior revelations, although they believe them to be incomplete and misguided. Since God is all-powerful, Muslims believe that Allah did not need to rest on the seventh day of creation. In the Koran, the aborted sacrifice of Isaac by Abraham in the Hebrew Bible is replaced by a similar action (Sura 37:100–107) with a different child. Muslims interpret the text to refer to Ishmael, Isaac's half-brother and the ancestor of the Arabs. Furthermore, for Muslims, Jesus of the New Testament is not the Messiah but only a prophet. In many Muslim-majority countries, there continues to be a close relationship between the state and the religion. Islam is the "official" religion of Iran, Pakistan, and Bangladesh, as well as many Arab countries. Until recent times, Christians and Jews were permitted to live and work in Islamic countries only because they were "people of the book." Before the advent of more secularized government, they were second-class residents called *dhimmis,* required to pay a special tax. This situation is elaborated on in Chapter 4.

The Physical World and the Spiritual World

A necessary outcome of acceptance of the nonexistence of miracles is a greater separation of the physical world from the Spiritual World. Possibly the Spiritual World could be equated with the human-invented entity called heaven, but in view of the widely existing tendency now to discuss the value of "spirituality," using the term "Spiritual World" seems more appropriate. Humans who believe in such worlds communicate with them through their minds and, for some, the communication is two-way. We know that electrical activity in the brain due to deep meditation can be identified and sensed; see *Why God Won't Go Away: Brain Science and the Biology of Belief* (2001) by Andrew Newberg, Eugene D'Aquili, and Vince Rause. (The first part of this title is an overreach. The change in brain functioning in meditation does not imply the existence of a deity.)

A possible counterargument by believers to the assertion of the nonoccurrence of miracles is the claim that God does not act at the present time by violating physical law. In this scenario, "He" (again using the anthropomorphic view of religious traditionalists) influences the minds of people who then take the actions requested, for example, "God told me to choose the priesthood as my profession." The claim that a revelation or a personal communication came from the Spiritual World cannot be disproved. Spiritual Worlds may be imaginary, or they may be real. Certainly, nonbelievers may scoff, and denounce beliefs in communication with a Spiritual World as delusional, but they have no physical evidence to support their claims. It is generally not possible to argue rationally against such a belief. Only if a spiritual communication informs the believer to carry out acts that are unlawful, or dangerous to the self or to others, could a concerned outsider have any reasonable cause to interfere, that is, to notify the believer's close family or authorities, or to urge the believer to seek psychiatric treatment.

Similarly to revelations, the beliefs of religious people in the immortality of the soul, in heavens and hells, and in reincarnation (if the identical DNA is not required) may be professed without any violations of physical laws. Whether humans have souls and whether an afterlife exists are other questions for which no final answers are possible. In Hamlet's famous soliloquy (Act 3, Scene 1), Shakespeare described death with his marvelous literary flair: "The undiscovered country from whose bourn no traveler returns." No more than that need be said.

Certain individuals with a scientific worldview have been courageous in their efforts to push religion back from the intrusion of its theology into the scientific understanding of the physical world. It has been a long struggle, beginning with efforts in Christian Europe by such individuals as Copernicus and Galileo. Now it is necessary to push the New Atheists back from claiming truths in fields in which they have no facts. It cannot be known whether a Spiritual World exists in reality, but we know that it exists as belief in the minds of many millions of people. It may be that each person has his or her own Spiritual World or a sense of the Infinite that is outside of intellectual discourse. For example, members of the Religious Society of Friends (Quakers) believe that God continues to talk to people today; at a Quaker meeting, any congregant may speak if "moved by the Spirit." What evidence do the New Atheists have that will counter this belief? Shouting at believers that their views are irrational will not change their minds. Belief in a Spiritual World is beyond rational thinking; it cannot be countered with a mathematics-like, deductive argument.

Similarly, we may also speculate about the origin of human creativity. How did our early ancestors decide to create stone tools, learn to make fire, and conceive of religious ideas? In Chapter 3, the concept is pursued that religion is fundamental to human culture. Did the cerebral genius of Leonardo da Vinci, Shakespeare, Mozart, Einstein, and other artists, writers, and scientists come as a result of evolution or from some supernatural deity? Certainly, believers are of the opinion that the revelations received by their prophets are from the Spiritual World. Possibly other forms of creativity are, also. (Note below the quote from Einstein about the "intuitive mind.") Perhaps, one day, the answer to these questions will be known, but we have no assured evidence at this time, one way or the other.

Profane versus Sacred; Sacred versus Holy

Academicians who have analyzed religion, such as philosophers, anthropologists, and sociologists, have noted that one method of analysis is to divide all aspects of life into two mutually exclusive categories: the sacred and the profane, as set out in, for example, *The Sacred and the Profane* (1959) by Mircea Eliade (a theorist of religion whose ideas are discussed in Chapter 3). The sacred, as used there, generally includes any aspect of life relating to religion, such as rituals; artifacts; special days; special topography such as mountaintops, rivers, and caves; specially constructed edifices; and persons undertaking special roles. The term "holy" is often used as a synonym for "sacred" when applied to matters of religion. See, for example, *The Idea of the Holy* (1923) by Lutheran theologian Rudolf Otto (1869–1937), originally written in German. Etymologically, "holy" has a northern European origin, while "sacred" derives from Latin.

An early example of the use of "sacred" in a secular context is from the oath required to be taken by the young men of ancient Athens when they reached the age of 18. One requirement was "We will fight for the ideals and Sacred Things of the City both alone and with many."

The connection of "sacred" with "ideals" indicates a broader meaning than only the supernatural. In a statement originally written in English, the same usage may be seen. The last sentence of the US Declaration of Independence is as follows: "And for the support of this declaration, with firm Reliance on the Protection of Divine Providence, we mutually pledge to each other our lives, our Fortunes, and our sacred Honor." Another example is the following, "possibly or probably by [Albert] Einstein," according to *The Ultimate Quotable Einstein* (2011), Alice Calaprice, editor: "The intuitive mind is a sacred gift and the rational mind is a faithful servant. We have created a society that honors the servant and has forgotten the gift" (477).

The choice of "sacred" in the title of this book, rather than "holy," was deliberate. "Holy" is used to specify an artifact, action, or belief whose source is religious. "Sacred" is used in this presentation to indicate the highest and most important values that humans hold, regardless of their source. Among the New Atheists, only Sam Harris applies the term. He states: "There is clearly a sacred dimension to our existence and coming to terms with it could well be the highest purpose of human life. But we will find that it requires no faith in untestable propositions . . . for us to do this" (*The End of Faith*, 16).

The first sentence of this quotation is certainly consistent with the outlook here. However, the idea that the "sacred dimension" can be determined without reference to "untestable propositions" suggests an enormous naïveté. Life would be much less interesting if every ethical issue could be entirely solved by scientific experiment or mathematical analysis. Certainly, it is possible now to collect data and make statistical analyses that might support small changes to criminal law, for example, in order to ensure more-equal treatment of perpetrators who commit the same crime. Similarly, cost-benefit analysis might be used to provide an answer to what amount of monetary compensation is to be received by the families of those killed in an accident from a negligent perpetrator judged responsible for the deaths. Unfortunately, use of techniques such as statistics or cost-benefit analysis in ethical considerations often requires quantitative valuation of a human life, a very subjective judgment. We elect legislators, appoint judges, and empanel members of juries, all of them human beings, to make the most important decisions for us in the public sphere. The possibility that they could be replaced by mathematicians and computer programmers, using solely their technical skills, is simply laughable.

Harris proposes no immediate solution to the problems that his book delineates. After stating that religion is not a rational enterprise [agreed!], his final conclusion is that "reason, spirituality and ethics" must be brought together in a "rational approach to our deepest personal concerns." That's all that is said; no further actions or plans are proposed.

Daniel C. Dennett, professor of philosophy at Tufts University and also an atheist, has presented a less aggressively hostile analysis of religion in his book *Breaking the Spell* (2006). He writes about the sacred as follows: "I have sacred values—in the same sense that I feel vaguely guilty even thinking about whether they are defensible and would never consider abandoning them (I like to think!) in the course of solving a moral dilemma. My sacred values are obvious and quite ecumenical: democracy, justice, life, love and truth (in alphabetical order)" (23).

In this quotation, Dennett cites not his actual sacred values but rather relevant subjects from which particular values might be chosen. He goes no further toward explication. For example, he does not say what his values are for "life." Even today very serious debates are being conducted about when human life begins and when it ends. What does Dennett believe? Similarly, on the subject of criminal justice, issues include the morality and efficacy of the death penalty and differences in representational quality between those who can pay and those who cannot. Where does Dennett come down? Another form of justice is social justice. To what extent should government, private organizations, and non-needy individuals ensure care and assistance for the elderly, poor, handicapped, and unemployed? What is Dennett's view? He certainly favors democracy in theory, but to what extent does secrecy of government operations, differences in financial resources that fund political campaigns, and manipulation of the press by government flacks reduce its quality? Furthermore, "love" and "truth" are terms that are widely used, sometimes with great sophistry or with a deliberate attempt to deceive. As a philosopher, Dennett certainly knows the difficulty both in defining terms and in the selection of conditions for moral decision-making in specific instances. He makes no attempt to do so in his book, which therefore provides no assistance in a quest for the sacred.

THE NEW ATHEISTS AND "RELIGIOUS MODERATION"

Among the allegations made in these and other New Atheist books is that religious moderation, meaning the typical observances of most of the world's population, is a primary cause of the violence perpetrated by religious extremists. For example, Sam Harris states in *The End of Faith* that "Religious moderates are in large part responsible for the religious conflict in our world, because their beliefs provide the context in which scriptural literalism and religious violence can never be adequately opposed" (45).

The hubris of Sam Harris in this regard is clear. He knows God's views as well as any fundamentalist preacher. He writes: "'respect' for other faiths, or for the views of unbelievers, is not an attitude that God endorses" (13). He later says, "religious moderation appears to be nothing more than an unwillingness to fully submit to God's laws" (21).

Dawkins echoes this view in *The God Delusion*: "even mild and moderate religion helps to provide the climate of faith in which extremism naturally flourishes" (303).

Other documents, besides holy texts, have been used to justify extremism and violence. The works of social philosopher Karl Marx (1818–83), including *The Communist Manifesto* (1848) and the first volume of *Das Kapital* (1867), were used as the intellectual basis for Communism. This messianic movement, after gaining power in Russia, repressed all religions and claimed that its adoption would lead eventually to an end to war and national boundaries, a kind of secular End of Days. Instead, its results included totalitarian government, starvation for millions in the Soviet Union as a result of farm collectivization, suppression of civil rights, many deportations to gulags in Siberia, and the establishment of puppet regimes with a similar agenda in countries under its control. At the height of their influence, Communists in America cited the following statement in the Declaration of Independence to justify their aims: "whenever any Form of Government becomes destructive . . . , it is the Right of the People to alter or abolish it."

The function to which a text will be put cannot be determined in advance. In the future, some obscure writing that seems innocuous to most readers may be used as the underpinning of a new religion or of another secular but authoritarian and violent movement. Are the New Atheists calling for censorship in which all potential publications would be subject to review so as to weed out any that might contribute to future conflict or to some preposterous ideology? Having very little foresight beyond their immediate goal of venting their views, the New Atheists do not consider the longer-term implications of what they propose.

THE UNBEARABLE LIGHTNESS OF NONBEING

The quest for the sacred begins in this world without miracles. The following true anecdote is an example of religious moderation, tolerance, and cooperation, in which the sacred plays a role. (Names have been changed or eliminated for privacy.) The task of determining whether the events described will contribute to future fanaticism is left to the reader.

Susan Lamston died at home on a Thursday evening, not long ago. It was only three weeks earlier that she and her husband, Gary, learned of her serious illness. She had started to stumble as she walked. Gary took her to be examined by her primary care physician in the pleasant suburb in which they lived, and that doctor had her admitted to the local county general hospital. MRI scans were taken; a brain tumor was discovered. She needed to be sent to a center of expertise for possible brain surgery and, fortunately, there were two such complexes in the heart of the metropolitan area, just 40 minutes away. Due to bed availability, she was transported to the State University Medical Center. The tumor was inoperable, it was determined; the tumor was too close to the brain stem. She was returned the next day to the home that she and Gary had shared for 20 years.

Susan was well known to her oncologist. He had treated her for breast cancer for the previous seven years, and had overseen her two mastectomies during that time. She had been administered the prescribed amounts of chemotherapy following her operations. However, for several months preceding her death, preventative medication had been stopped, as her heart had started to be affected. After her brief trip to the university medical center, the oncologist, together with a radiologist, prescribed ten sessions of radiation therapy over two weeks.

While the radiation therapy was ongoing, Gary realized that he and Susan had not made necessary arrangements for end-of-life situations; they were both over 70. Their marriage was the second for both. Each had been previously married to their first spouses in a Jewish ceremony, which was followed by a civil divorce more than 25 years later. Both had children from their initial marriages.

Susan had not completed a will, although she had made an initial stab at it. Gary brought their lawyer to her bedside, and he prepared a will in accordance with discussions that they had previously had. She signed it on probably the last day that it was truthful that she was of "sound mind," as the will specified. The shakiness of her signature was clear. She also signed a Power of Attorney document that permitted Gary to pay her bills. Gary asked Susan whom she wished to officiate at her funeral, and she replied with the name of a particular rabbi. This individual, now retired but still living in the area, had been the spiritual leader of her congregation.

Additionally, the pair had not purchased grave lots, and certainly no casket had been purchased "pre-need." While Susan was being cared for by a nurse's aide, Gary visited the office of the nearby multidenominational cemetery and purchased side-by-side grave lots in the Jewish section. Gary went also to a Jewish funeral establishment in the metropolitan area for the purpose of purchasing a casket and arranging for the soon-to-be needed services of that organization. As carrying out the latter tasks for a loved one can be a highly emotional process, Gary was fortunate to be accompanied by a good friend who happened to be a well-respected psychologist and grief counselor.

The radiation treatments appeared to have no positive effect; Susan continued to decline in ability to function. At the end of the radiation treatments on a Friday that turned out to be six days before her death, the oncologist admitted that improvement was rarely seen in people over 70. He explained that the brain tumor, as were also liver and spine tumors that had occurred concurrently, was a metastasis of the breast cancer. The stopping of the preventative medication was not a factor in the existence of her brain tumor, the oncologist said, because that medication cannot go to the brain.

Gary should contact the local hospice organization, he recommended, and he submitted the necessary paperwork to enable the organization's engagement at no out-of-pocket cost. When Gary and Susan returned home after that final radiation, Susan was already incapable of caring for herself. She was heavy enough in weight that when she needed to be undressed and put back in bed, Gary couldn't do it by himself. He tried, but Susan slipped to the floor from the couch where she had been sitting, and he couldn't pick her up. At first, Gary didn't know what to do; there was no one else to help him at that moment. Susan and Gary lived by themselves in a four-bedroom house that once had been filled with children and their friends. With a sudden inspiration, he called 911 and explained the situation. Soon, two county emergency medical technicians arrived, undressed Susan, slipped her nightgown on her, and put her in bed. Gary was thankful and appreciative of the quick response.

The hospice organization sent a nurse to visit Susan soon after being alerted by the oncologist. She had come sometime over the weekend, and returned on Tuesday. After she left the second time, she consulted with a physician on call with the organization. Later that day, she called back and suggested that Susan's family should arrive "sooner rather than later." Immediately, Gary notified Susan's three adult children; they arrived from their several homes, hundreds of miles away, as promptly as possible. They stayed at the parental home from Wednesday through Sunday. Susan's breathing became more and more labored and, at 10:23 p.m. on Thursday, it suddenly stopped. Present at her bedside were Gary, all her children, and a daughter-in-law. The latter was an experienced epidemiologist, was aware of the signs of impending demise, and had called the family together at the appropriate time. They had their arms around each other as she died. Gary had never before seen anyone die while he watched.

After they composed themselves, Gary proposed a toast to Susan's life. He found a bottle of wine and enough glasses for each of them, and they all joined in. Then he called the hospice nurse, and she came and verified the death. After that, the funeral home was called. They sent two men with a hearse. As they lifted the body, it seemed to Gary like a rag doll. It was not the lively, vital person that he knew: one who was in comfortable control teaching a class of skeptical college students and responding with helpful suggestions to the life-difficulties of social work clients. If it is true that each human has a soul, then certainly her soul had departed. What remained of her was only the unbearable lightness of nonbeing.

The men put the body in a body bag and transferred it to a gurney. They rolled the gurney through the front door and onto the driveway, placed it in the hearse, and drove away. Gary would not see Susan again in life, but he would have, in the next few weeks, several nightmares involving death. After those latter experiences, he would better understand the need, in some cultures, for the propitiation of the spirits of the dead.

The Sacred Is Invoked and Is Sensed

A reform Jewish funeral was held that Sunday, with the burial immediately following. It has been typical Jewish practice to hold a funeral and burial within 24 hours of death, but that could not occur in this situation. In this case, before 24 hours were up, the Sabbath began, and funerals are not held then. The funeral was attended by individuals of varying religions, including friends, colleagues, students, and even some social-work clients, in addition to the family. Eulogies were given, and the usual prayers invoking God's name were recited. These included the 23rd Psalm and the *Kaddish*. The latter is the Jewish prayer for the deceased, though it simply praises God.

At the burial, similar prayers were offered, and the casket containing the body was lowered into the ground in an already prepared space. Mourners threw clods of earth onto it, in a gesture that signifies participation in the ritual and acceptance that the dead person is truly gone. That was a symbolic good-bye from each person whose hands had thrown earth down upon the casket. A student of Susan's, who knew of her Boston origins and fondness for the Red Sox, added some soil (with Gary's assent to her request) that she said had been "liberated" from the area around home plate of Fenway Park.

Each of us experiences the death of a friend or relative in the light of our personal history with that person. Gary said that he regretted not including Susan's canoe paddle as grave goods, a concept that would have resonated with many an ancient culture. Susan had used the paddle, which still hangs in their garage, in her work as a waterfront instructor years ago in Maine summer camps. It was symbolic of happy times, about which she often spoke.

The events of the day moved Gary profoundly. As the body was lowered into the ground, a sense of the sacred was with him. Philosophers of religion would call it a hierophany. The presence of the sacred is important to many thoughtful and educated people, even in a secular world extensively informed by science.

What has been described so far about Susan's decline, death, and burial is unremarkable in a prosperous, well-governed area of a First World, fully developed country. With the rule of law in place, the legal documents that were drawn up would be honored according to regulations put into law. Gary's travels in his own car to various establishments followed roads that were safe and well paved. Travel proceeded without harassment. No one demanded bribes to carry out expected duties. With a clear separation of church and state, there was no official state religion whose rites needed to be carried out or even recognized. Furthermore, the tolerance and even friendliness of different religious denominations made it possible for the funeral to be held in a community building owned cooperatively by several religious congregations, Christian and Jewish.

Decisions about Susan's medical care proceeded according to modern medical practice. The benefits of medical science, and its limitations, are appreciated and accepted by almost everyone in a First World country; the few exceptions are often reported with incredulity. Failure to give a child appropriate medical care may subject the caregivers to criminal prosecution. In a "primitive" society, that is, a nonliterate one in which the scientific explanation of the physical laws of the universe is ignored or not understood, it might have been believed that Susan had carried out some action that made the gods angry, or that a shaman had put a spell on her. Instead, no person proposed that, rather than having modern medical treatments, prayer sessions should be held or that she could be cured with "a laying-on of hands" by a faith healer.

Medical appointments for Susan were easily made, in light of the serious and pressing nature of the situation. Trained physicians, nurses, technicians, and administrators were on duty. Medical interventions were carried out in a professional manner in sanitary and not overcrowded facilities instrumented with much useful technology. Both Susan and Gary had monetary resources and health insurance, which smoothed the process at every step.

THE CONTRADICTORY NATURE OF THE HUMAN CONDITION

Notable about the entire process that ended with her burial was that Susan had told Gary privately on several occasions that she did not believe in God. She admitted to being scared that certain individuals would find out. That was unlikely because she retained a strong cultural attachment to Judaism, even though she did not personally observe the Orthodox dietary and Sabbath restrictions. She was knowledgeable about the rituals, and knew the essential prayers in Hebrew far better than Gary did. She had requested that a rabbi officiate; a Jewish funeral and burial were both appropriate and desired. Her family would have been puzzled, if not hurt, if something else had transpired. Nevertheless, the plain texts of the prayers seemed hollow, perhaps even unbelievable, to those with nonexistent or agnostic beliefs.

Her fear of discovery was due to the type of students she taught and the organizations with which she was associated. After getting her PhD in social work at the state university, she obtained a tenure-track position at a public university of a different state. (She had obtained a master's degree in social work many years earlier.) The small city in which her teaching position was located was about two hundred miles from home, in rural surroundings. Susan had an apartment there for use during the fall and spring terms. She returned home on weekends, or Gary drove out to keep her company. Her students there, as well as the faculty, were overwhelmingly white Protestant, and some students were fundamentalist. Although social work is a secular profession, she was seen as a representative of the Jewish community, as many Jews are in a non-Jewish milieu. On occasion, she needed to explain the faith, in particular Jewish beliefs about Jesus. After seven years of teaching, she received tenure but had to retire almost immediately thereafter owing to health reasons.

With her breast cancer in remission, she taught social work as adjunct faculty in the pastoral counseling program of a Jesuit-sponsored university. The faculty was extremely welcoming, and her Jewish religion was easily accepted and respected. Most of the faculty and students were Roman Catholic, although persons of other faiths were also there. There was no religious indoctrination, proselytization, or discrimination. Again, she had concern that her lack of belief would be revealed, to the expected consternation of the faculty and student body, but that never happened.

Faculty and students of the Department of Pastoral Counseling held a memorial service for her about two weeks after she died. They printed a booklet, stating that Susan had been "born into eternal life"—certainly not a Jewish idea. The school held another memorial service a year later honoring several faculty members, including Susan, who had died over that period. If their rituals employed their own concepts, symbols, and procedures, Gary thought that was perfectly fine. They were on their own home grounds; their means of expression were genuine and heartfelt. The intent of their ceremonies was clear, regardless of the particular religion in which it was expressed: they cherished Susan and her contributions, and were immeasurably saddened by her loss.

Gary had *shiva* services (rites of mourning) held at his home the week after the burial, led by the Reform Jewish congregation to which he belonged. The next week, after the mourners were gone, the house seemed empty and eerily quiet. Life went on for everyone else as if nothing had happened. This apparent lack of concern seemed selfish to Gary; after all, *his wife had died*. Not only did he note the apparent unconcern of other people, but he realized that the physical universe was totally indifferent to Susan's passing. The sun continued to rise and set as the Earth turned on its axis. The moon continued in its sequence of phases. As the Earth continued to revolve, fall turned into winter and then into spring. Tulip bulbs that Susan planted the previous year came up and bloomed, even though she was not there to enjoy them. To Gary, the blooms were one more reminder of Susan. He was sad and felt a hole in his being. As a cultural Jew with views similar to Susan's nonbelief, he nevertheless hosted a traditional grave-unveiling ceremony with her children within a year after she died, and lit a commemorative *Yahrzeit* candle on the anniversary of her death.

CHAPTER 2

OUR PHYSICAL UNIVERSE

BEYOND BELIEF

THE PURPOSE OF THIS CHAPTER IS TO distill, into about twelve thousand words, the results of many thousands of hours of research and millions of words of publications. This extensive body of work, summarized here, has been carried out by numerous scientific specialists of the cosmos, the Earth, and the plants and animals that have lived on Earth. The intent is to emphasize that the current status of humanity on this planet has occurred only through operation of physical laws of the universe. Furthermore, the recognition that humankind achieved its wondrous development out of the singularity that, billions of years ago, was the entire universe compressed into a single ball of enormous energy, may help provide an understanding of the sacred. This exposition is preceded by a discussion of myths of creation that prescientific cultures devised.

HUMANKIND'S LONGSTANDING CURIOSITY

Among the celestial objects that can be seen without a telescope, our sun and moon are the most obvious. The sun cannot be stared at for very long with the naked eye. (In fact, "staring at the sun" has been used as an analogy to discussing death; see Chapter 3.) We can easily look at the moon, however, and wonder what is happening on our nearest celestial neighbor.

Many years ago, soon after sunset, a little boy asked his father, "Who turned the light on in the moon?" He was curious about the fact that, in the daytime, the moon appears pasty white, while at night it appears luminous. This change from day to night seemed similar to his experience looking at a window shade from the street. In the daytime, a white shade drawn behind a window appears pasty like the moon, whereas at night, if a light is turned on in the room, the luminosity can be seen through a translucent shade. Analogizing, as reported in this example, may be a hallmark of human intelligence.

The little boy who asked about the moon's luminosity was not aware that the phenomenon had been investigated by researchers a very long time ago. Among those individuals in ancient times who studied the issue were the Greek philosopher Anaxagoras (fifth century BCE), Chinese astronomers of the Han dynasty (second century BCE), and an Indian astronomer, Aryabhata (fifth century CE). Each of them separately concluded that the moon shines with the reflected light of the sun but, during the day, the luminosity is masked by the ambient light.

George Smoot (b. 1945), as a child, was similarly curious about the moon. He noted, while driving with his parents, that regardless of how the car turned, the moon seemed to keep following them. His parents gave young George a simplified explanation of this condition, which only further fired his imagination. Smoot continued with his interest and expanded it, eventually earning a PhD in astrophysics and the 2006 Nobel Prize in physics. Some of his work is cited below.

Creation Myths

The creation myth of Judaism, briefly discussed in Chapter 1, is written in Genesis 1 and 2 of the Hebrew Bible. It was later adopted by Christianity. The myth continues, to this day, to be defended by some fundamentalist churches as a true presentation of the founding of the world. We do not typically refer to our religion as myth. However, a statement by researcher of myths Joseph Campbell (1904–87), reported in *Thou Art That: Transforming Religious Metaphor* (2001), is highly pertinent at this point. That book, a compendium of some previously unpublished writings and presentations by Campbell, includes the transcript of a 1979 interview by Eugene Kennedy. Campbell is asked, "How would you define mythology here?" and he responds: "My favorite definition of mythology: other people's religion. My favorite definition of religion: misunderstanding of mythology" (111).

Campbell wrote extensively on mythology and comparative religion. His books include *The Masks of God* (four volumes, 1962–68). He was interviewed over a significant number of hours by Bill Moyers for public television, and the series ran in 1988. A book of the interviews, titled *The Power of Myth* (1988), was published soon after.

Creation myths are stories that describe the origins of the physical world, a subject about which early peoples knew nothing in a factual sense. This type of myth may concern the origin of the universe and the various objects in our solar system, as well as the topography of the Earth and the life-forms that inhabit it. Each creation myth covers at least some of these subjects, if not all of them. Every culture that has ever been investigated has been found to have a religion, and nearly every religion has a creation myth that is integral to it. Each creation myth provides part of the basis for the worldview of the culture with which it is associated. The common worldview benefits internal cohesion within the culture. To members of a prescientific culture, the creation myth may be internalized as an unquestioned certainty, whereas outsiders may think it strange or even nonsensical.

Many compendia of creation myths are available. The Judeo-Christian myth is written in a holy book. The myths of other cultures may be oral, passed on to each successive generation. Each myth is different in specifics, although there are common themes. Five types have been classified:

- *Creation out of nothing* by the thought, word, dream, or bodily fluid of a supernatural being; the story in Genesis is of this type.
- *Creation by a diver*, such as a bird or amphibian, that plunges to the bottom of a primordial ocean to bring up sand or mud that develops into land. The Huron Indians of North America have such a myth.

- *Creation by the dismemberment of a primordial being.* An example is the myth of the peoples of ancient Mesopotamia. In that story, the goddess Tiamat is dismembered by the god Marduk, who becomes the chief god of Babylon. The descriptive document, called *Enuma Elish*, is named from its first two words. A copy of this myth, written in Old Babylonian cuneiform, was found in the library of Ashurbanipal, king of the Neo-Assyrian empire, 668–627 BCE. The library was discovered during excavations at Nineveh near present-day Mosul, Iraq.
- *Creation by the splitting of a primordial unity,* such as the cracking of a cosmic egg or replacing chaos by an organized universe. A myth from China is of this type. The myth concerns P'an Ku, who is hatched from a cosmic egg. Half the shell is above him as the sky and the other half is below him as the Earth. He grows taller each day for eighteen thousand years, gradually pushing them apart until they reach their appointed places. Then P'an Ku disintegrates; his limbs become the mountains, his blood the rivers, his breath the wind, and his voice the thunder. His two eyes are the sun and moon. People are formed from parasites on his body.
- *Emergence* in which the progenitors reach the present world after passing through a series of other worlds or metamorphoses. The myth of the Navaho Indians of North America is of this type, as is the myth of their neighbors, the Hopi. The Hopi myth is particularly interesting, as it involves a female creation principle, Spider Woman. The Hopi continue to employ the primacy of matrilineal descent as a method of social organization.

Other themes in creation myths have been found. For example, several myths in various parts of the world employ the concept of the divine (or hero) twins, such as Castor and Pollux. The myth of the Maya, people of southeast Mexico and adjacent countries, uses this theme. The story is recorded in the *Popul Vuh,* a book of a particular group of Maya called the Kekchi or Quiche. In this myth, First Father, Hun Hunahpu, is walking past the entrance to a cave when the Lords of Xibalba, the gods of the underworld, call to him from inside. (Spanish has no "sh" sound, as in "should" or "shall." An "x" is used often to represent that sound.) The gods tell him to enter the cave and play the Maya ball game with them. He goes in, but the gods behead him and hang his severed head from a tree. Shortly thereafter, a daughter of one of the gods stops in front of the hanging head, which spits into her hand. She becomes pregnant from this interaction and gives birth to twin boys, Hunahpu and Xbalanque. After many adventures and their final defeat of the Lords of the Underworld, the twins become the sun and the moon.

Changing Conceptions of the Universe

Until the Renaissance brought new ideas, the Western world accepted, with only one minor alteration, the arrangement of celestial objects described by Greek philosopher Aristotle in the fourth century BCE. His model was not inconsistent with the Christian interpretation of Genesis 1 and 2, nor with its interpretation of particular verses in the biblical book of Joshua concerning the sun's movement.

Aristotle's universe consisted of a number of concentric and transparent crystalline spheres, with the Earth at the center. Each of the innermost spheres, rotating at its own unique and constant speed, carried one celestial object. In sequence from the Earth, these spheres carried the moon, Mercury, Venus, the sun, Mars, Jupiter, and Saturn. (Other objects in our solar system were unknown.) Outer spheres carried the stars, and an outermost sphere was the province of the Prime Mover, Aristotle's concept of a godlike function that (or who) keeps everything going. Of course, for Christianity, the Prime Mover was equated with its God.

This model was unsatisfactory for those who analyzed planetary motions two millennia ago in the Roman empire. The fact that the planets appear to reverse direction for a time could not be explained. A modification, involving the addition of smaller circles called "epicycles" attached to each planetary sphere, attempted to explain retrograde planetary motion. Epicycles do not exist; they were a fiction that attempted to make a mathematical model fit actual observations. This model of the universe with the Earth at its center, surrounded by Aristotle's concentric spheres, modified by epicycles to explain planetary motion, was described in 150 CE in a document called the Almagest. The author was an Egyptian astronomer with Roman citizenship named Claudius Ptolemy. Its concept would not be challenged in the West for 1,400 years.

The correct arrangement of the solar system, with the sun at its center, was actually proposed by a Greek astronomer, Aristarchus of Samos, in about 200 BCE. However, his views were questioned with concerns that demonstrated a lack of understanding of physical laws. Specifically, if the Earth is rotating on its axis, why don't objects fly off, and why don't flying creatures fall behind? Furthermore, if the Earth is revolving around the sun, then why doesn't the same star seen six months later, when the Earth is on the other side of the sun, appear at a slightly different position? (This change in position, seen from a different viewpoint, is called "parallax.") The first two questions could not be answered authoritatively until the seventeenth century. The third question could not be answered until it was understood that the stars were so far away that parallax, although existing, was too small to be observed without more precise instrumentation.

In 1543, Nicolaus Copernicus of Poland (1473–1543), a man of several disparate competencies, made public a treatise he had written titled *On the Revolutions of Heavenly Spheres*. The work proposed a sun-centered model of our solar system, with the Earth correctly positioned as third from the sun. It was submitted for publication when the author knew he was dying, ensuring that he would not have to face the opposition of certain highly placed clergy and others believing the literal truth of Joshua 10:12–15. In that text, the sun moves around the Earth except when ordered to stand still. His work might have brought the wrath of the Inquisition upon him, as it did to Italian scientist Galileo Galilei (1564–1642), after the latter published his support of heliocentrism in 1632. Through his telescope, Galileo had seen the planet Venus in phases, as we see phases of the moon. The position of Venus in the sky when "full" is consistent only with a sun-centered solar system.

Copernicus's understanding, while revolutionary for his time, was not fully correct. His model retained the concept of circular motion and constant speed of the planets, thereby requiring the retention of epicycles. Actually, the planets' speeds vary with their distance from the sun as they orbit around it; their path is elliptical, not circular. The elliptical nature of planetary orbits was discovered by German scientist Johannes Kepler (1571–1610), from data supplied to him by his employer, Danish astronomer Tycho Brahe (1546–1601), while working in Prague. An important milestone in science was the work by English mathematician and scientist Isaac Newton (1642–1727) that showed convincingly that the physical laws of motion are universal. They apply on Earth and they apply also to motions of planets and moons around their respective central celestial bodies. It was Newton's Three Laws of Motion, included in his *Principia Mathematica* (Mathematical Principles) of 1687, that made clear why objects don't fly off the moving Earth and why flying birds don't fall behind.

THE MILKY WAY GALAXY

One of many groupings of stars in the universe is the Milky Way galaxy, which includes our solar system. It is seen with the naked eye as the band of light that encircles a good part of the night sky; it has been written about certainly since the fifth century BCE. Ancient observers speculated about its composition. The astronomer known as Alhazen (965–1037 CE) ended questions about its nearness by attempting to measure its parallax. He concluded that, since he could not find any parallax, the Milky Way was not in the atmosphere, but was very far away. Alhazen (also known as Ibn al-Haytham), a devout Muslim born in Basra (then in Persia, now in Iraq), worked primarily in Cairo. He was one of the very first individuals who, accurately, could be called a scientist, since he based his views on careful observations of the physical world.

In 1610, Galileo determined with his telescope that the Milky Way consisted of a vast number of extremely faint stars. At some point, probably in the late eighteenth century, astronomers began to understand that the sun was not the center of the universe, but was only a star in the Milky Way galaxy. William Herschel (1738–1822), born in a German state but living in England, determined in 1785 that the galaxy, to a first approximation, is in the shape of a disk. (The Milky Way is the galaxy seen on edge.) He correctly placed our solar system within the galaxy but, incorrectly, near its center. He also discovered the planet Uranus.

Through the early years of the twentieth century, conventional wisdom held that our galaxy was almost the total extent of the universe. American astronomer Edwin Hubble (1889–1953) made discoveries that changed that view. Hubble examined a small, glowing area in the sky called the Andromeda nebula, and determined that it was much further away than stars in our galaxy. According to George Smoot, author of *Wrinkles in Time: Witness to the Birth of the Universe* (2007/1993), Hubble discovered that the nebula was actually another galaxy, measuring it as 800 thousand light-years away, ten times the typical distance to stars within our galaxy. (A light-year is the distance that light can travel in an Earth-year.) Hubble was incorrect in his measurement; actually the Andromeda galaxy is 2.5 million light-years away.

Light: Its Transmission, Speed, and Bending

The fact that light travels at a finite speed, and not at an infinite speed, is an essential piece of knowledge necessary for modern understanding of the universe. Its actual value is required to associate quantitative values with distances in the cosmos. As one might suspect, Aristotle had an opinion on this subject; his view implied an infinite speed of light. He was wrong. Muslim scientists of the Middle Ages understood that the speed of light was finite, beginning with Alhazen's *Optics*, completed around 1021. In the West, both Johannes Kepler and French philosopher Rene Descartes (1596–1650) believed that the speed of light was infinite, demonstrating that science in the Islamic world was more advanced in that time period.

By 1676, French astronomers, viewing the moons of Jupiter as they revolve about the planet, came to the conclusion that light had a finite speed, although their initial number was more than

20 percent lower than the actual value. Other French scientists, working in the mid-nineteenth century, achieved better accuracy. In 1879, Albert Michelson (1852–1931), in an experiment performed at the US Naval Academy, achieved a highly accurate result: an estimated 299,940 kilometers per second in a vacuum. Michelson was awarded the 1907 Nobel Prize in physics, the first American to receive a Nobel in the sciences. Later experiments using electronic equipment have determined the speed of light with higher precision.

Modern understanding of the universe began with the 1916 publication of a technical journal article by Albert Einstein (1879–1955) titled "A General Theory of Relativity." Einstein, born in Germany and employed for a time by the Swiss patent office, came to the United States before World War II. A Jew, he emigrated as a result of the official Nazi policy in the 1930s of demonizing Jews and not allowing them to work in the professions. (Hitler did not order what he called "the final solution to the Jewish question" until a few weeks after his initially successful invasion of the Soviet Union on June 22, 1941.) Einstein's model required that light traveling in a straight line at a finite speed would be bent as it passed close to a large mass. The fact that light bends indicates that it consists of particles with some mass, even if each is extremely tiny. Actually, a Newtonian view of the cosmos results also in a bent light beam in the same circumstances, but Einstein's results require a bend twice as great. This prediction was verified initially by studies of starlight that must pass very close to the sun to reach us. The studies were done during total eclipses so that pictures could be taken without sunlight's overwhelming the photos. Comparisons were made with the same area of the sky during nighttime. The first eclipse employed for this research occurred over the South Atlantic Ocean in 1919. Two observation stations were used, one near the African coast and one near the Brazilian coast. The results from both stations verified Einstein's prediction. However, there continued to be considerable skepticism in scientific circles about Einstein's theory after this first experiment. Subsequent studies with greater attention to experimental details and more precise equipment have continued to demonstrate the correctness of Einstein's work.

THE EXPANDING UNIVERSE AND THE BIG BANG

A significant conclusion from Einstein's theory is that the universe must be either expanding or contracting; it is not static. Initially, Einstein did not wish to believe the implications of his equations. He added a "cosmological constant" that would counter the dynamic quality of the universe otherwise indicated. Later, he realized that this modification was incorrect, as it became clear from other research that the universe is actually expanding.

A quantitative understanding of the size and age of the universe began to be possible when the concept of the Doppler shift began to be used to analyze light coming from stars. Named after Austrian scientist Christian Doppler (1803–53), the term indicates a change in the various frequencies of a spectrum of sound or light as the source of the emission comes toward a receiver or recedes from it. A single frequency in a source of sound or light approaching the receiver will appear to be higher than its actual value (a "blue shift" for light), and a frequency in a source receding from the receiver will appear lower than its actual value (a "red shift" for light). Humans can listen for the Doppler shift when a railroad engine or a truck on a freeway sounds its horn as it passes by. The concept for stars was developed by American astronomer Vesto Slipher (1875–1969) at Lowell Observatory in Flagstaff, Arizona. It began to be applied in the decade that began in 1910.

The technique developed by Slipher was applied extensively by Hubble at the Mount Wilson observatory near Los Angeles. Hubble's data of 1931 showed that there is, in most cases, a nearly linear correlation between the distance of a galaxy from our own and the velocity with which it is receding from us. This correlation is true for almost all galaxies. One prominent exception is Andromeda, a relatively close galaxy that is approaching rather than receding. It is part of a "local group" of galaxies that includes our Milky Way.

The implication of Hubble's findings is that the universe had a beginning, has been expanding, and continues to expand. That is, there existed an initial, extremely dense, extremely small "singularity" consisting of all the matter in the universe tightly compacted at an immensely high temperature. At a finite time in the past, this singularity exploded, in what has been called the "Big Bang," into the universe that we see today. We observe (with optical and radio telescopes) many galaxies with their stars, including objects such as quasars and black holes; other agglomerations of matter such as planets, moons, asteroids, and comets; and large, free-floating clouds of mostly hydrogen and helium.

The Big Bang hypothesis was controversial when first proposed, and it was strongly opposed by several respected scientists who believed in a "steady-state" universe. In fact, the name "Big Bang" was given to the concept by one of its opponents, but the name has been accepted and it has stuck. The steady-state hypothesis, not viable any longer, implied that the universe had no beginning. A requirement of the "steady-state" hypothesis is that matter has been created ex nihilo, that is, out of nothing, and continues to be created. Even if the steady-state hypothesis is incorrect, there remains the question of where the matter came from that exploded in the Big Bang. "Why is there any matter at all?" is a fundamental question, probably unanswerable. Even if the matter of the Big Bang resulted from the collapse and coming together of all the matter in a previous universe, the question is simply put back to an earlier time, but not answered.

In 1948, Ralph Alpher (1921–2007) and Robert Herman (1914–97), both with the Johns Hopkins Applied Physics Laboratory, wrote a seminal paper about the Big Bang. They were aided in their effort by physicist George Gamow (1904–68), born in Russia but an immigrant to the United States and teaching at an American university. Gamow was well known through his books that popularized science, employing a fictional "Mr. Tompkins." Alpher and Herman wrote that, if the Big Bang occurred, the universe would have begun at a temperature of many millions of degrees, but by now, its temperature should have dropped to just a few degrees above absolute zero. At present, they wrote, the universe should be bathed in faint background radiation—an echo of that primordial event—at a frequency corresponding, by scientific theory, to the current temperature of outer space. Their research built on earlier work on thermodynamics by German physicist Max Planck (1858–1947).

Following the publication of the Alpher/Herman paper, there were no immediate efforts to verify the existence of the background radiation. However, in 1964, the presence of the radiation was discovered by accident, by Arno Penzias (b. 1933) and Robert Wilson (b. 1936), two electronics scientists at Bell Laboratories in northern New Jersey. They were doing research on radio astronomy and satellite communications. The radiation was observed in their equipment because it was in the microwave range in which they were working. At first, they thought it was some sort of static or interference, and attempted to adjust their equipment to eliminate it. They were unsuccessful. Not sure of the implications, they reported their findings to experts at nearby Princeton University and, after a telephone discussion, realized that they had sensed the cosmic microwave background (CMB) radiation. Penzias and Wilson received the Nobel Prize for their work. Further analysis of this radiation from more recent sensings has demonstrated that it corresponds to a temperature of 2.725 degrees Celsius above absolute zero. It occurs in a spectrum of frequencies, with the highest power at 160.2 gigahertz, equivalent to a wavelength of 0.19 centimeters. (A cycle per second is now called a "hertz," and a "gigahertz" is a unit of 1 billion hertz, named after German physicist Heinrich Hertz (1857–94), who significantly extended the theory of electromagnetic propagation.)

The CMB radiation, to an approximation, appears uniform in all directions. If that were completely true, then the universe would consist of matter uniformly distributed. However, we know that matter in the universe is arranged quite unevenly, that is, it has clumped. Stars have formed, constituting a "clumping" of gaseous matter. There are many galaxies, each consisting of stars closer to each other than they are to stars in other galaxies. Between galaxies, there is much empty space. Some galaxies have larger numbers of stars and others have fewer. Furthermore, there are areas of the universe where there are many galaxies and other areas where there are few of them. Research carried out by George Smoot and associates determined that there are actually very small "wrinkles," or perturbations, in the cosmic background radiation, probably due to quantum mechanical effects that occurred soon after the Big Bang. These wrinkles caused the universe's nonuniformity as it expanded. Smoot earned his Nobel Prize for this work.

THE AGE, SIZE, AND EXTENT OF THE UNIVERSE

The numbers that specify significant parameters of our universe are simply immense. They are, to use a phrase that seems appropriate in this context, beyond belief. The incomprehensibility of these extremely large numbers creates difficulties in acceptance by ordinary folks who have had no exposure to scientific thinking or to rational experimentation with aspects of the physical world. It is not surprising that such people are prey for purveyors of fundamentalist religion or to fantastic concepts based on science fiction.

The age of the universe is currently estimated to be 13.73 billion years (where a billion equals one thousand million), based on observations of the CMB radiation by space-based electronic equipment called the Wilkinson Microwave Anisotropy Probe. If humans existed from the beginning of the universe, and each human generation was, on the average, 25 years, the number of generations from the Big Bang until now would be about 550 million. Even when the somewhat lower ages of our solar system and the first life on Earth are discussed, it will be seen that the relevant numbers still remain far outside of the time horizon of typical humans.

The number of stars in the universe is estimated to be 10 to the 21st power. The number of galaxies in the universe is about 100 billion or 10 to the 11th power. These two figures imply that the average number of stars per galaxy is 10 billion (10 to the 10th power). Smaller galaxies may have 10 million stars (10 to the 7th power), while larger ones may have one trillion stars (10 to the 12th power). Our galaxy is estimated to contain about 200 billion (2×10 to the 11th power) stars.

The size of the universe now is about 93 billion light-years across. In comparison, the Milky Way galaxy, roughly circular, is about

0.1 million light-years in diameter. That is, the extent of the universe is almost one million times the size of our galaxy.

Formation of our Solar System

It is generally agreed by astrophysicists that our sun was not born with the Big Bang or soon after. In fact, it was born about 9.18 billion years following the Big Bang; that is, after roughly two-thirds of the time had elapsed between the Big Bang and now. There were stars formed soon after the beginning of the universe, and these consisted primarily of only the elements with the lowest atomic weights, that is, hydrogen and helium. (An atom of a chemical element consists of a nucleus of protons and neutrons, surrounded by electrons. The number of electrons must equal the number of protons for the atom to have a neutral charge. The atomic weight of an element equals the sum of the number of protons and neutrons in the nucleus of its atoms. Ordinary hydrogen has just one proton and no neutrons in its nucleus, and has one electron in orbit around it.)

A star forms by the collapse of a cloud of primarily hydrogen, which begins to swirl around a center, and eventually becomes dense and hot enough for the process of nuclear fusion to begin. It is nuclear fusion that generates a star's light and heat by converting hydrogen into helium. The theory of nuclear fusion was explained by physicist Hans Bethe (1906–2005). Like Einstein, he emigrated from Germany to America in the 1930s because of the Nazi policy toward Jews and descendants of Jews. He had lost his university employment because his mother was Jewish.

Stars have a cycle of birth and death. A very old star may become a "white dwarf" as it ages and, as a supernova, may explode at the end of its life. It may have been the residue from an explosion of an old star that formed the sun about 4.6 billion years ago. As the gas that formed the sun began to swirl around a center and condense, some of the material formed rings. Material in some of the rings came together to form planets. The Earth was formed about 4.56 billion years ago.

The Earth contains, in smaller or larger quantities, all the naturally formed chemical elements. Elements heavier than hydrogen and helium—for example, carbon, oxygen, silicon, iron, and uranium—were not formed in the Big Bang; they were formed by the nuclear fusion activities of active stars. This process was described by English astrophysicist Fred Hoyle (1915–2001) and his colleagues. Thus the material that formed the sun and other objects in our solar system must have come from the chemical processes of another star.

As the Earth grew by accretion of material, it became hot enough to melt metals. Due to their greater densities, these metals sank to the center of the Earth and became its core. The core is primarily made of iron and nickel, and it is the source of the Earth's magnetic field. Soon after the Earth began to form, a well-accepted theory is that it was impacted by another somewhat smaller planet, also just beginning to develop. Much of the debris from this collision remained in orbit around the Earth and formed the moon. The collision may have been the source of the tilt of the Earth's axis of 23.5 degrees, which causes the seasons. Rocks brought back from the moon by the Apollo astronauts have been dated at 4.527 billion years, about 33 million years younger than the Earth.

Dating of the solar system is possible by using the fact that unstable isotopes of uranium and thorium will decay over millions of years into isotopes of lead, an element having a slightly smaller atomic weight. (Each isotope of a chemical element has atoms with the same number of protons but a different number of neutrons.) The time during which half of a uranium or thorium isotope will decay into lead (called the half-life) is known. In meteorites that contain no uranium or thorium the relative abundance of the four isotopes of lead can be measured. In material on the Earth containing lead that did not fall as a meteorite, radioactive decay of uranium and thorium will have increased the percentages of three of the four isotopes of lead. A comparison of the percentages of the lead isotopes in appropriate meteorites with the percentages in Earth-originated lead has been used to determine the age of the Earth.

Development of Biological Knowledge

Cells

The discussion that follows on the development of life would not be possible without the knowledge resulting from centuries of biological research. Of particular importance is the development of cell theory, made possible by advances in microscopy beginning in mid-seventeenth-century Europe. The first observation of a live cell under a microscope occurred in 1674. The observer was Anton van Leeuwenhoek (1632–1723). He described a particular type of algae and, in addition, probably saw bacteria. The observations and interpretations of a number of scientists over the next three centuries resulted in the latest tenets of cell theory. These are:

- The cell is the fundamental unit of structure and function in living organisms.
- All cells arise from preexisting cells by division.
- Metabolism and biochemistry, constituting energy flow, occur within cells.
- Cells contain hereditary information (DNA) that is passed from cell to cell during cell division.
- All cells are basically the same in chemical composition in organisms of similar species.
- All known living things are made up of one or more cells.
- Some organisms are made up of only one cell.

There are two kinds of cells:

- *Prokaryotes*: These cells lack a nucleus. Archaea and bacteria are two domains of prokaryotes.
- *Eukaryotes*: These have distinct nuclei bound by a nuclear membrane and membrane-bound organelles. They also possess organized chromosomes that store genetic material.

The former classification of living things into plants, animals, and other minor categories has been replaced by a tripartite classification of archaea, bacteria, and eukaryotes. That is, all living things are made up of one of the three types of elementary cells.

Inheritance

The mechanism of inheritance was unknown in the nineteenth century, but research had begun. In 1866, monk Gregor Mendel (1822–84) had completed a series of experiments with pea plants. He was able to show that certain traits in the peas, such as their shape or color, were inherited in different packages. These packages are what we now call genes. In 1868, the compound called nucleic acid was isolated from the nuclei of cells. However, the relationship of nucleic acid to genes was unknown until an experiment in 1944 demonstrated that a disease-carrying agent, when transferred from one type of bacteria to another, would continue the disease into the next generation in the second type. The agent transferred was nucleic acid.

By the late 1940s, researchers were aware that DNA, an acronym for **d**eoxyribo**n**ucleic **a**cid, was most likely the carrier of inheritance. They knew also that DNA included particular amounts of four chemicals, named adenine, thymine, guanine, and cytosine (usually represented as A, T, G and C), but the connections within the molecule were unknown. With the help of Rosalind Franklin (1920–58) and Maurice Wilkins (1916–2004), whose use of X-ray diffraction techniques provided significant assistance, Francis Crick (1916–2004) and James Watson (b. 1928) were able to determine the double-helix form of DNA in 1953. The two strands of the double-helix are connected in a ladderlike arrangement in which A, T, G, and C form the rungs of the "ladder." A simpler molecule, RNA, standing for **r**ibo**n**ucleic **a**cid, has been identified, also, and various forms of it are also active in the inheritance process.

Beginning of Life I:
First Formation of Organic Molecules

The Earth contains an atmosphere. This is due to its sufficiently large gravitational field that keeps gases floating near its surface from drifting into outer space. The moon, by contrast, has no atmosphere because its gravity is not strong enough. The initial atmosphere of Earth consisted primarily of carbon dioxide, nitrogen, and water vapor; ammonia and methane were present also. This composition was determined as a result of analyses of volcanic emissions and the gases observed when minerals from deep in the Earth are heated to extreme temperatures. It has been established also that the initial atmosphere of the Earth had no free oxygen. (Oxygen in carbon dioxide or water vapor is not free; it is combined, respectively, with carbon or hydrogen.) In contrast to what might be expected, research has shown that the lack of free oxygen was necessary for the initial formation of organic molecules. If there were free oxygen, organic molecules could not have formed.

All animals and plants require the employment of organic molecules in their metabolic processes. (That is why these molecules are called "organic.") These molecules consist of atoms of carbon, combined with atoms of hydrogen, oxygen, and nitrogen. Sometimes, these molecules may also include atoms of sulfur or phosphorus. According to T. R. E. (Richard) Southwood in *The Story of Life* (2003), "if energy is applied to solutions with mixtures of various inorganic compounds containing the elements carbon, nitrogen, oxygen and hydrogen, then a wide-range of simple organic compounds (amino acids, fatty acids and sugars, such as glucose) is produced" (10).

Energy that was applied to the young Earth to form organic molecules came from volcanoes and impacts of asteroids, meteorites, and cosmic rays. Furthermore, it has been determined that organic molecules are formed in space, and that about 10 percent of comet debris and other particles that fall on the Earth are organic.

BEGINNING OF LIFE II: FIRST FORMATION OF LIFE-FORMS

Around 3.9 billion years ago, the Earth was bombarded for a period of time by a large number of comets, meteors, and perhaps even larger space objects. These entities were primarily debris from the formation of the solar system. They deposited water on the Earth in the form of ice, which, very quickly, formed water vapor in the atmosphere above the extremely hot surface. Water vapor had also resulted from significant volcanic activity. Meanwhile, the Earth was slowly cooling after the end of the process of accretion of material and the formation of its core. Once the surface of the Earth cooled below 100 degrees Celsius, about 3.8 billion years ago, the water vapor condensed and fell as rain. Oceans began to be created. Runoff from the Earth's rocks, containing dissolved minerals, provided the oceans with their salty components. In addition, the oceans were rich in iron at that time, in part due to volcanic eruptions that brought up iron from far below the surface.

The earliest forms of life on Earth were prokaryotes. There is fossil evidence for their existence at about 3.4 billion years ago, and they thrived in an oxygen-free environment. The evidence for all other creatures cited later is similarly from the fossil record. Prokaryotes lived in the oceans and possibly on land, but not on their surfaces. There was considerable ultraviolet radiation from the sun impacting the Earth's surface at that time, and there was no ozone layer to restrain it. The radiation prevented life from forming on or very close to the surface. Prokaryotes continue to live among us as bacteria. They are found within our bodies, as well as in environments that are hostile to humans, such as hot geyser pools and Antarctic ice.

There are three primary requirements for the formation and continuation of bacterial life. First, each cell must have an outer membrane, a cell wall or "skin" that separates the cell from the outside world; it allows food to enter, prevents unwanted substances from entering, and permits waste products to depart. Second, each cell must have a metabolic system, which converts incoming food into nourishment and generates waste. Third, some of the cells, if not all, must have the ability for self-replication, that is, for reproduction of offspring.

The sequence in which the three requirements developed is not fully known, nor are the mechanisms through which bacteria initially developed from organic molecules. Considerable research continues on these topics. With regard to the development of membranes, it is known that lipids were important in their creation. Lipids are a broad class of naturally occurring organic molecules, including fats, waxes, and various kinds of glycerides; they contribute significantly to the formation of cell membranes in currently living life-forms. For the process of metabolism, cells may have used a nonorganic method initially. Eventually prokaryotes must have developed the process of converting glucose, one of the available organic molecules, into a chemical called adenosine triphosphate (ATP) through "glycolysis." This process continues to be used by most organisms today. For self-replication, the initial use of the "messenger" form of RNA has been proposed. RNA is still in use in organisms, but this early use would have been before DNA had evolved. Some scientists say that "we live in an RNA world."

Beginning of Life III:
The Oxygen "Catastrophe"

One variety of prokaryotes that lived in the oceans has been named cyanobacteria; it evolved, at latest, by about 3 billion years ago. This variety was the first organism to use photosynthesis as a means of sustaining itself, which means that it employed light from the sun as a catalyst in its metabolic process. With the aid of sunlight, cyanobacteria combine water and carbon dioxide to produce energy needed for nourishment, and they generate free oxygen as a waste product. At first, the free oxygen combined with the iron in the oceans and formed iron oxide, which precipitated to the ocean floors. These deposits are well documented. Eventually, the oceans were cleansed of all free iron. Some uncombined oxygen remained in the oceans, and the remainder began to seep into the atmosphere. As a result, oxygen began to kill off species of prokaryotes that did not use oxygen in their metabolism; oxygen was severely toxic to them. Many varieties of prokaryotes went extinct. Those able to survive lived far underground or in close proximity to thermal vents under the oceans. (The Earth's core was still very hot.) Newer forms of prokaryotes evolved to begin to use oxygen, that is, they were aerobic, and these types generated carbon dioxide as a waste product. The composition of the atmosphere changed with the increase in both carbon dioxide and oxygen.

There is evidence that, when oxygen began to leak into the atmosphere, it eliminated the methane that was there, by combining with it to form a different substance. Methane is a "greenhouse" gas and was causing the heat of the sun to be retained in the atmosphere. With the methane gone, the heat dissipated and the temperature of the Earth's surface plummeted. The first Ice Age began, and the entire Earth may have been covered with ice, resulting in the first "snowball Earth." Eventually, the heat produced from volcanic vents, as well as the carbon dioxide (another "greenhouse" gas) generated by aerobic bacteria, reversed the process, reliquefying the oceans.

The "oxygen catastrophe" occurred about 2.5 billion years ago. That situation was not the end of the importance of cyanobacteria. In succeeding millennia, they would evolve to join together with a plantlike organism in a process called "endosymbiosis." In this process, the cyanobacteria were "swallowed" by the other organism and became part of its internal mechanism. This combination formed the basis of all plant life, in which, during daytime, carbon dioxide is used as an input and oxygen is the waste product. Eventually, animals would evolve to use oxygen as one of their necessary inputs and to generate carbon dioxide as a waste product. Thus the two major forms of living creatures have complementary metabolic processes.

Beginning of Life IV: First Formation of Cells with Nuclei

The evolution of cells with nuclei (eukaryotic cells) was an enormous advance. The nucleus contains the genetic material that directs all the cell's activities. In addition, eukaryotic cells contain mitochondria, which produce energy for the cell. Research has shown that eukaryotes arose by endosymbiosis. All these cells contain components derived from two and, in green plants, three bacteria.

An extremely important capability of eukaryotic cells is the ability to reproduce sexually through a process called meiosis. Prokaryotic cells, such as bacteria, reproduce asexually, with a different process called mitosis. In the latter process, the DNA of the cell is first replicated, that is, a twin is produced. Then each twin moves to opposite sides of the cell. When the cell divides, each twin remains with one of the new cells. Thus each new cell has the same DNA as the parent cell.

In meiosis (sexual reproduction), the first step is that the DNA of the sex cell is replicated, that is, a twin is produced (as in mitosis). Then the twins may exchange some DNA in a special process called "crossing over." After that, the two new sets of DNA move to opposite sides of the cell and the cell divides. Now there are two new daughter cells, but the process is not yet complete. A second cell division occurs, but the DNA is not replicated as a precursor. As a result, there are four daughter sex cells, each containing half the necessary DNA. Due to the special nature of the "crossing over" process, each of the four daughter cells may have a slightly different set of DNA than the parent cell. If any one of the cells is joined in sexual reproduction with an appropriate cell from an external source, the correct amount of DNA will be in the new fertilized cell. As Southwood states about this process, "sex in plants and animals ensures that every individual of a species will differ slightly and evolution occurs by selection within almost infinite variety. Meiosis therefore provides the potential for the evolution of very many different types of organism and we might expect therefore that its development must have led to a step change in the rate of evolution" (27).

The oldest fossils said to be from single-celled eukaryotic organisms (called protists) have been dated at 2.1 billion years ago, but more numerous fossils of that type are dated at about 1.7 billion years ago.

Beginning of Life V:
First Formation of Multicelled Organisms

Animals and plants are multicellular. Scientists postulate that most animals evolved in the seas and oceans, in an oxygenated environment, where sunlight provided energy. Bacteria and algae, one-celled creatures, were their sources of food. Thus the predatory nature of the food chain had begun. The earliest and simplest type of animal has two concentric layers of cells in a globular form with a single cavity in the center. Sponges are an example of this type of organism. The cavity provides the space for the metabolic functions. The next advance was an animal with three concentric layers of cells with two cavities. The first cavity is inside all three layers and the second cavity appears between the middle layer and innermost layer. The second cavity provides the space for digestive and circulatory organs.

Another possible environment for animals is totally different. This situation occurs in the vicinity of hydrothermal vents in the oceans. The source of energy is not light, but heat; sulfur and hydrogen are used for respiration. Animals living in this environment are totally anaerobic; that is, they do not use oxygen. These vents were discovered in 1977, and many new species of primitive animal life, such as formerly unknown worms and barnacles, were found.

Status of the Earth, One Billion Years Ago

At one billion years ago, when the first multicelled organisms had just begun to evolve, more than 92 percent of the time interval from the Big Bang until now had elapsed. In addition, more than three-quarters of the time period from the formation of the Earth until now had already occurred. At about one billion years ago, the Earth's surface was divided into just two contiguous areas of opposite type: a single ocean and a single supercontinent that has been named Rodinia. The knowledge that this occurred is derived from the theory of plate tectonics, a science only developed since the 1960s but that owes its beginning to pioneering German climatologist and meteorologist Alfred Wegener (1880–1930). Wegener's groundbreaking book (pun intended), *The Origin of Continents and Oceans*, was published in 1915.

Tectonic Plates

Wegener and later researchers have determined that the Earth's entire surface is divided into seven or eight major tectonic plates (the number depends on definitions) and many smaller ones. These plates form the Earth's lithosphere, which includes its crust and the uppermost part of the next lower layer, called the mantle. Some of the larger plates carry continents. In the center of the Earth is its core, and the mantle exists between the core and the crust. The lithosphere is hard and rigid, and rides over a weaker, hotter, and deeper part of the mantle. Many geologic activities occur along the boundaries between plates. These occurrences include earthquakes, volcanic eruptions, mountain-building, and oceanic-trench formation. The plates may move laterally up to a maximum of 10 centimeters (about 4 inches) per year. For example, the North Atlantic Ocean is widening about 2.5 centimeters (approximately 1 inch) per year due to the activities of neighboring tectonic plates at their boundary in the middle of the ocean.

Neoproterozoic Era: One Billion to 540 Million Years Ago

Names for durations of time in the history of the Earth have begun to be used in a standardized manner by geologists, paleontologists, and other scientists. The longest durations used here are called eras, although eras may be combined into longer time spans called eons. Eras are divided into durations called periods, and the latter are divided into epochs. An era beginning one billion years ago called the Neoproterozoic was a time of significant evolution of plants and animals, given that their basic building blocks were in place. In identifying numerical dates up to one billion years ago, the units mya (millions of years ago) and kya (thousands of years ago, where k stands for kilo) will be used. As various centers of expertise employ slightly different dates, the dates used here may differ slightly from dates cited elsewhere.

In the first period of the Neoproterozoic era, the Tonian (1000–860 mya), the supercontinent Rodinia began to break into two parts. These new supercontinents are named Gondwana and Laurasia. Positions of the land masses with respect to the Earth's poles were not the same then as they are now. As the tectonic plates move in time, land masses that were near the poles in earlier times may be near the equator now, and vice versa. During the Cryogenian period (860–630 mya), the second of the three periods of this era, there were at least two more formations and reversals of a "snowball Earth" condition.

In the final period, the Ediacaran (630–540 mya), there were three groups of animals that have been seen in the fossil record. All of them lived in the ocean. Examples of the first group looked like jellyfish, that is, they were round with several "arms." An individual of the second group looked like a large leaf, anchored to the sea floor by its "stem." Members of the third were wormlike. (See Southwood, fig. 4.2, p. 40.)

Paleozoic Era: 540 to 248 mya

The Paleozoic era era occupies more than half the time from its beginning to the present day. At the start of this era, the diversity of animal forms increased significantly. This increase has been designated the Cambrian Explosion, after the name of the first of six periods in this era, the Cambrian (540–490 mya). The animals that evolved at the beginning of this era had developed skeletons, but not the kind possessed by fish, birds, or mammals. These were exoskeletons, that is, they were on the outside of the animals, not the inside. The exoskeleton promotes the development of claws as well as biting and grinding mouths, such as employed by crabs, and drilling mouthparts, such as those used by snails.

The evolution of the exoskeleton required that animals absorb certain minerals, without which the exoskeleton could not exist. The process is called biomineralization, and these minerals include calcium carbonate or calcium phosphate. The availability of this calcium-based personal equipment facilitated a predatory lifestyle, which would be a standard manner of living for many creatures. The food chain, in which smaller and less-developed animals are prey for larger or stronger ones, is a common way of living for animal life on our planet. Until the middle of this era, all the creatures that existed lived in aquatic environments.

A particular type of animal with an exoskeleton that first appears in the fossil record at the beginning of the Paleozoic era and disappears near its end is called a trilobite. These creatures belong in the phylum (a primary division of animals) Arthropoda, which includes crabs, insects, and spiders. It had a shape something like a horseshoe crab, with antenna at its front, many sideways-facing appendages along its sides, and a tail at the rear. Like all animals with exoskeletons, it molted. The trilobite had eyes with many facets. The lens of the trilobite's eye was, similarly, made of a calcium compound.

Another important type of animal that begins to appear in the early Paleozoic era is a chordate. All animals with vertebra, that is, those that have backbones, are members of the phylum Chordata. Those found in this era have been classified as an early type of fish. It had no jaws, and a living descendent today is the lamprey. An important source of these fossils has been a particular location in China. That location, as well as the Burgess Shale in British Columbia, Canada, is a rich lode for fossils that has added extensively to our knowledge of ancient life. Another fact deduced from such sources is that there was an extinction of many species during the second period of the Paleozoic era called the Ordovician (490–443 mya).

Jawed fishes are first found in the third period, the Silurian (443–417 mya), and many different types of fish dominate the fourth period, the Devonian (417–354 mya). A particular type of fish, the lobe-finned, had a muscular lobe at the base of each of its fins. It lived in shallow water and its descendants evolved limbs from its fins, enabling it to walk along the bottom of the aqueous body in which it was living. Later, it would evolve to live on land. It is the ancestor of all amphibians, reptiles, birds, and mammals.

Some plant-life began to colonize the land in the Silurian, continuing the same process through the Devonian. In the latter period, the level of oxygen in the atmosphere started to increase and it became high enough to create a strong ozone layer. This layer prevents much of the sun's life-destroying ultraviolet radiation from reaching the surface of the Earth. Therefore, life on land became possible for animals. The first animals to venture forth to breathe oxygen directly from the air were arthropods, such as spiders and mites. Amphibians, which mix life on land with life in the water, began to evolve. Amphibians lay their eggs in water, and can breathe under water as well as on land.

By the beginning of the fifth period, the Carboniferous (354–290 mya), plant-life had spread throughout the world. There were large numbers of varieties, including shrubby growths and tall trees. Mayflies and dragonflies, which lay their eggs in water, were common. Also in the Carboniferous, reptiles evolved. Land reptiles differ from amphibians in that they lay their eggs on land in hard shells and they cannot breathe under water.

In the sixth period, the Permian (290–248 mya), a single supercontinent named Pangaea reformed. Again, there was a single world ocean, as there had been when Rodinia formed. On land, insects evolved into forms that they would retain to the present time. Reptiles underwent a significant evolutionary development. There were reptiles that were either carnivorous or herbivorous. In addition, reptiles may be distinguished by groupings according to a certain feature of the skull, according to Southwood (100–101). One particular form of this feature has resulted in tortoises and turtles. A second form exists in mammals as their descendants, and a third form occurred first in dinosaurs and then in birds.

At the end of the Permian period, which was also the end of the Paleozoic era, there was a significant extinction of many species, possibly more than 90 percent of all of them. Both land-based and water-based species suffered. The cause of the extinction is believed to be an eruption of lava consisting of molten basalt from the Earth's mantle that continued for about one million years. An enormous amount of fiery rock was spewed out, and this occurred about 248 mya; effects on the world climate were disastrous. The eruption was located in an area of Siberia. There is evidence that there were two such eruptions; a preceding one occurred about 256 mya, centered in southwestern China.

MESOZOIC ERA: 248 TO 65 MYA

There are three periods in the Mesozoic era: the Triassic, the Jurassic, and the Cretaceous. The supercontinent Pangaea did not break up until the end of the Triassic (248–206 mya), and the lack of a sea barrier before that time allowed both plants and animals to extend their ranges to whatever locations the climate would permit. Ferns were an important plant and spread widely. Conifers (such as pines) were trees widely dispersed in the Triassic. Other trees of that era that exist today were the royal palms and the ginkgo biloba. Both of these species of trees have individuals that are single-sex. Transfer of pollen from male royal palms to female royal palms was achieved by a certain type of insect, possibly the earliest example of pollination by this method. In the Triassic, dinosaurs evolved on land, and were small compared to those found in the Jurassic. In addition, marine dinosaurs are found in this first period, including icthyosaurs and plesiosaurs. All dinosaurs are a type of reptile.

In the Jurassic (206–144 mya), reptiles that fly are found. Later, the first bird, archaeopteryx, evolved. Dinosaurs existed in a large number of varieties. Some of these are huge and ferocious, as many of us know from popularization. Others are only herbivorous (plant-eating). New amphibians, such as frogs, toads, and salamanders, are found. The first mammals, small shrewlike animals, occur in the fossil record. They likely evolved from a type of reptile called a cynodont.

In the Cretaceous era (144–65 mya), dinosaurs and other large reptiles are the dominant land animals. They occupy all the land areas that will become the future continents. However, at the end of the Cretaceous, several mass extinctions occur, including all land and marine dinosaurs. With regard to the tectonic plates, Pangaea has split into several parts, and the continents that we know today are beginning to form

Cenozoic Era: 65 mya to the Present

The Cenozoic era is usually divided into two periods. The first period, the Tertiary, has five epochs, called Paleocene, Eocene, Oligocene, Miocene, and Pliocene. The second and current period of the Cenozoic era is named the Quaternary. It has two epochs, the Pleistocene and the Holocene. The latter is current.

In the Paleocene epoch (65–55 mya), mammalian life diversified. Earliest forms include ungulates (hoofed animals), primates, rodents, and carnivores. In the Eocene (55–34 mya), further differentiation resulted in horses, rhinoceroses, and camels. Among the primates, ancestors of the lemurs split off. Whales returned to the ocean, having evolved from a terrestrial meat-eating ungulate.

With regard to the continents, by the end of the Eocene, Antarctica and Australia have separated and Antarctica is moving toward the South Pole. India, which had been separate from the rest of Asia, is moving toward a collision with the larger land mass. When it joins with Asia, an outcome will be an uplift of the Himalaya Mountains to their lofty condition that exists now. Similarly, Africa and South America have separated and the Atlantic Ocean, although narrow at the very beginning of this era, will continue to widen to the situation we know today. In the Oligocene epoch (34–24 mya), further development of mammalian forms resulted in such animals as pigs and elephants. Primates appear in North America. Antarctica has reached the South Pole and begins its glaciation. The Mediterranean Sea is all that remains of an ocean that separated Europe from Africa.

In the Miocene epoch (24–5 mya), the earliest form of mastodon existed. It has been discovered in fossils in North America. Many modern birds are found. In the evolution of hominoids, the line of primates that will become gibbons, orangutans, and more human-related species called hominids, the use of the thumb for gripping develops and is an important step. The separation of the hominids from gibbons and orangutans occurs in the middle Miocene, about 11 mya. Late in the Miocene, about 7–5 mya, the hominid line diverges three ways: into groups that will eventually become gorillas, chimpanzees, and primates that will begin to walk upright. Grasslands replace many forests in several continents in this epoch. The presence of these grasslands is cited by anthropologists as an impetus for the ancestors of humans to stand up on the hind legs. Without the protection of trees, these primates needed greater height to spot the presence of enemies or other dangers, and to locate game to be hunted. In addition, it appears that walking upright is more energy-efficient than walking on all fours.

In the Pliocene epoch (5–1.8 mya), the last epoch of the Tertiary period, australopithecines, a particular hominid among whose descendants will be genus *Homo*, begins to develop in Africa. Several different species of australopithecines have been found, including *Australopithecus afarensis*, a particular skeleton of which has been nicknamed "Lucy." In this epoch, the land bridge (isthmus of

Panama) formed between North and South America. A significant interchange of animal types occurred between the two continents. However, in North America, rhinoceroses became extinct.

In the Pleistocene (1.8 mya–10 kya), the first epoch of the Quaternary period, there were several "Ice Ages." Ice sheets and glaciers advanced and retreated four or five times. The northern oceans were frozen during these periods. The last Ice Age maximum was about 18 kya. Since then, the climate has warmed, but not linearly. There have been intervals of returning coldness. In this epoch, there was further development of large mammals, such as woolly mammoth, woolly rhinoceros, musk ox, moose, reindeer, and mastodon. The "woolly" forms and the mastodon died out at the end of the epoch. In the Holocene (10 kya to the present), human culture has resulted in the extinction of a number of animal species.

EVOLUTION AND DEVELOPMENT OF *HOMO SAPIENS SAPIENS* (HUMANS)

An early species of genus *Homo*, called *Homo habilis*, is found in Africa beginning at about 2.6 mya. It is probably a descendent of the gracile form of austropithecines. A different form, called robust, eventually died out. *H. habilis* continues to be found until about 1.6 mya. Another species of genus *Homo* that begins to be found as early as 1.8 mya is *Homo ergaster*; it continues to be discovered until about 500 kya. A species with a different name, *Homo erectus*, appears on later research to be the same as *H. ergaster*. The *H. erectus/ergaster* species has been found in China and Java, as well as in Africa, and may have continued to exist in the Far East until perhaps 25 kya.

The earliest stone axes made by genus *Homo*, probably by hammering one piece of stone against another, date to the earliest years of *H. habilis* and are of a type called Oldowan. There is evidence that members of *H. habilis* carried these tools around over some distance for the purpose of using them in other locations. A type of hand tool used by genus *Homo* from 1.8 mya to just a few hundred kya is called Acheulean. Some of these tools were intended for cutting, because opposite faces were chipped so as to provide a sharp edge.

It has been determined that chimpanzees use tools also, but they do not use one tool to make another tool, and they do not carry tools very far to use them. It has been determined that humans and chimpanzees have about 98 percent of their DNA in common, but no chimpanzee has ever made a fire; nor has any other tool-using animal other than genus *Homo*. The Greek myth of Prometheus, in which fire is given to humankind, is indicative of that culture's understanding of the importance of this invention to future human development.

Modern humans are classified, for anthropological purposes, as genus *Homo,* species *sapiens,* subspecies *sapiens*—that is, *Homo sapiens sapiens*. The origin of *H. sapiens sapiens* is in east Africa about 200–100 kya, according to a view widely held among anthropologists. Analyses of DNA components of currently living persons show that some humans left east Africa before 100 kya. In their first journey, they probably crossed the Red Sea at its southern end to what is now Yemen. Then they migrated east, followed the coast of the Indian Ocean, eventually reaching India, Indonesia, and Australia. Other humans, when they left Africa, traversed the Middle East to the east and continued past the Caspian Sea, turning north into central Asia. Then some trekked further east to Mongolia, Siberia, and China, while others turned west to Europe. The first settlers of North America probably crossed the Bering Strait when the sea level was low and there was a land bridge between Siberia and Alaska, or they followed the southern edge of the ice sheet in boats from Asia. The Americas were first reached about 18 kya.

The tool kits of early modern humans, dated from 40 kya, show a more complex set than Acheulean. Then humans began to use other materials for tools besides stone, for example, bone or wood, and they began to make arrowheads to be used with bows. Additionally, humans began to make decorative objects, started weaving and making pottery, drew the now-famous pictures on the interior walls of caves in southwestern Europe, and buried their dead with ceremonial goods.

Neanderthals

Given that name because the first example of its skull was found in the Neander Valley in Germany, Neanderthals are closely related to modern humans. Their classification is *Homo sapiens neanderthalensis*. They are another subspecies of *Homo sapiens* because it has been shown that they interbred with early modern humans and produced viable offspring. According to recent research, between 1 and 4 percent of the human genome in Europe and Asia has Neanderthal genes. Much of this research has been carried out in Germany at the Max Planck Institute for Evolutionary Anthropology. Fossils of Neanderthals have been dated to about 300–35 kya; they have been found in many areas of Europe, in central Asia, and in Israel. Artifacts consistent with their living patterns have been dated to 28.5 kya in Russia, in the northern Ural Mountains at the Europe/Asia boundary.

Neanderthals were hunters. They made stone tools of a type called Mousterian. These were more elaborate than Acheulean, but not as accomplished as those of contemporaneous humans. At about 100 kya, Neanderthals were living in a cave on Mount Carmel near Haifa, Israel, while humans were living in a nearby cave. Similar nearby habitations have been noted in southwestern Europe, down to 35 kya. A reasonable supposition now is that they disappeared through interbreeding with humans. Red hair has been cited as a trait obtained from Neanderthals. It is not known whether Neanderthals could speak in words, but they apparently had the same necessary bone in the throat, called the hyoid. They buried their dead in particular positions with some grave goods, possibly indicating some religious beliefs.

Homo Floresiensis

Quite recently, bones of a group of individuals of genus *Homo* were found on the island of Flores, east of Bali in Indonesia. It has been reported that partial skeletons of nine individuals were discovered, including one complete cranium. The remains were dated to between 18 and 13 kya. Also recovered were stone tools. These were "from archaeological horizons ranging from 94 to 13 kya," according to reports. There has been considerable controversy whether these individuals, who were of extremely short stature with certain differences compared to bones of modern humans, represented a separate species, identified as *Homo floresiensis*, or were modern humans with diseases or exaggerated traits. Modern humans living today in the vicinity of the find are also of short stature. According to a 2009 study by Stony Brook University Medical Center in New York State, the skeletons are from a separate species, and are not members of *H. sapiens* dwarfed by disease. It is likely that *H. floresiensis* is descended from *H. erectus*.

The Culture of Humans

The preceding brief description, beginning with the birth of the universe with the Big Bang, 13.73 billion years ago, has ended with the physical evolution of *Homo sapiens sapiens* and the recent extinction or disappearance of other forms of genus *Homo*. Evolution has provided the means for allowing humans to develop as cultural beings, but not everything that humans do, categorized below, can be described accurately or completely in Darwinian terms. That would be reductionism carried to an extreme.

The human way of living began while our biologic development was ongoing. Cultural life has been investigated by anthropologist Clifford Geertz, whose findings are extensively discussed in Chapter 3. In *The Interpretation of Cultures* (2000/1973), he wrote: "the transition to the cultural mode of life took the genus *Homo* million years to accomplish; and stretched out in such a manner, it involved not one or a handful of marginal genetic changes, but a long, complex, and closely ordered sequence of them" (47).

Tool-making began about 2 mya and fire-making had begun at about 790 kya, both by ancestral species. The earliest grave arrangements are dated to 100 kya, as mentioned earlier. The first cave art is dated at 32 kya.

The way we live today includes the various emotions felt by individuals, describable in subtle nuances. These include primary emotions that result in actions by the self or that are felt immediately in response to an action of another person, another animal, or the physical world. Examples are surprise, fear, anger, disgust, disappointment, and exaltation. Also, there are secondary emotions felt as a result of a buildup of remembrances of past actions. The latter may have evolved later, and include grief, guilt, love, pride, happiness, contempt, and vengefulness. Possible actions as implementations of feelings include altruism, aggression, kindness, cruelty, and flight.

The way we live today also includes

- the use of language, both oral and written;
- the intricate social relationships of individuals with each other; humans are social animals and live in groups;
- varieties in patterns of settlement, including nomadic hunting/gathering (the first pattern), herding as well as fixed-location agriculture (the next development, after domestication of certain grains and animals), followed by urbanized living;
- highly developed methods of achieving satisfaction of basic needs such as food, clothing, shelter, and medical care, however unevenly distributed;
- development of craftsmanship and its transfer via teaching to new and younger colleagues; later, based on an insatiable thirst to know and understand, the development of knowledge in many fields, both scientific and humanistic, through observation, research, exploration, publications, and symposia, and also the retention of this knowledge and similar transfer;
- development and innovations in technology, with special mention of weapons, energy, biology, medicine, transportation, communications, and computation;
- an extensive program of education starting in childhood (including basic and higher), as well as training and employment in various fields;
- development of transmission of information and ideas, by methods including speeches and lectures, distribution of newspapers, magazines, and books, and presentations and transmission through movies, videos, and electronic media;
- concern with the nonmaterial issues of life, as expressed in ethical studies and philosophy, based on the self-awareness by humans that all of us are fallible, that we all have animal

natures tempered by the demands and restraints of civilization, and that, in the long run, we will all die;
- application of concepts of the supernatural and of Spiritual Worlds that such entities inhabit, and the relationship of humans with them, leading to development of organized religion;
- establishment of rituals and the celebration of holidays, for holy and for secular purposes;
- development of arts and entertainment, including *content-oriented* art, such as literature in the broadest sense, poetry, painting, sculpture, architecture, and design of interiors, clothing, and adornments; *performance-oriented* entertainments, such as dancing, sports, and acrobatics; and activities in any of several media involving *both content and performance*, including story-telling, drama, music, opera, ballet, singing, and comedy;
- development and use of coinage, banking, finance, and associated activities, and use of money as the major instrument of economic exchange, for example, for labor;
- a subculture of widespread economic activity and commercialism, associated with satisfaction of basic and optional needs and assisting in the creation of productive livelihoods for personal satisfaction and minimization of public unrest;
- various levels of production methods, from crafts to mass manufacturing, and associated processes of packaging and distribution;
- establishment of governments, including functions of executive, legislative, judicial, law enforcement, and defense; maintaining the basic infrastructure and some human services; as well as responsibility for recording human statistics and economic statistics, for setting national standards in various areas, and for recording property boundaries, administering a tax system, and establishing elections, and other methods of filling public offices;
- a continuing series of wars among increasingly large groups, including regional and world-size conflicts, as newer transportation, communication, and weapons technologies have made that possible.

CHAPTER 3

RELIGION

ORIGINS, INTERPRETATIONS, AND CURRENT PRACTICES

MANY MILLENNIA AGO, OUR EARLY ANCESTORS BEGAN to make artifacts to serve as tools and as weapons. As was pointed out in Chapter 2, the earliest stone tools have been dated to 2.6 mya; they were discovered at Gona, Ethiopia, in a general area where many other ancient artifacts have been found. These fabricated artifacts were associated with an ancestor species, *Homo habilis*. Later ancestors developed the ability to make fire. A recent archaeological discovery in northern Israel, at a crossing of the Jordan headwaters called *Gesher B'not Ya'aqov* (Bridge of the Daughters of Jacob), provides the earliest evidence of fire-making. It occurred, according to the analysis of the ashes and their context, at 790 kya. Interestingly, this discovery was made by archaeologists from the Hebrew University of Jerusalem. It seems clear that researchers at that Jewish-sponsored center of learning are not required to believe that human life began with Adam and Eve, just 6 kya.

ADVANCED SYMBOLIC THINKING: THE HUMAN DIFFERENCE

Humans, that is, subspecies *Homo sapiens sapiens*, began to evolve around 200 kya. The making of tools and starting fires requires symbolic thinking, as well as memory to remember previous actions so that, through self-learning and the teaching of others, expertise within a human group could be increased and enhanced actions carried out. Fully evolved symbolic thinking is an essential quality of humans not shared by other animals. This characteristic has resulted in communication through language, and that ability has fostered subsequent developments that further distinguish us. An even more complex capability is to figuratively stand outside oneself and objectively analyze a situation in which the self is participating. This advanced symbolic thinking has permitted humans to imagine changes to their environment that they could carry out, to actually implement many of these changes, and also to contemplate their place in the universe. Humans are apparently the only species of animal whose members can envision their own deaths while still healthy, even many years in advance. Religion may have resulted from such ratiocination.

Language requires symbolic thinking, because each noun, serving as a symbol, stands for a thing and each verb, similarly, stands for a particular action. Syntax, a human-developed logical system for communication, allows us to realize a meaning in the sequence of symbols in a sentence. The basic syntax used in a particular language seems to be learned without special training by human children as they acquire speech and process language spoken to them.

The idea of naming things or people (i.e., creating a symbol, verbal or written, for each entity) resonates with humanity as a sacred activity. The Mesopotamian Epic of Creation from perhaps 1700 BCE (briefly mentioned in Chapter 2 as *Enuma Elish*) is included in a compendium called *Myths from Mesopotamia* (1989), translated and edited by Stephanie Dalley. The epic begins as follows:

> When skies above were not yet named
> Nor earth below pronounced by name,
> Apsu the first one, their begetter,
> And maker Tiamat, who bore them all,
> Had mixed their waters together,
> But had not formed pastures nor discovered reed-beds;
> When yet no gods were manifest,
> Nor names pronounced, nor destinies decreed,
> Then gods were born within them.
> Lahmu (and) Lahamu emerged, their names pronounced. (233)

Similarly, in Genesis 2:19, "and whatsoever the man would call every living creature, that was to be the name thereof."

The point is being made that naming, an aspect of symbolic thinking, is a supremely important milestone in human development. Similar to the point made about Genesis 1:27–28 in Chapter 1, this interpretation has been presented here to increase understanding and to make the text relevant to a contemporary issue. There will be more discussion on this subject, particularly in view of the failure of the New Atheists to appreciate that interpretation of ancient texts for modern use characterizes much nonfundamentalist religion. These absolutists, situated on the far left on a scale of opinion about religion, have much in common with fundamentalists, located on the far right. With their rigid ideologies, they have met around the far side of rational thinking.

Religion and the Universe

The Sun

Factual knowledge about the universe began with what could be seen with the naked eye—for example, the locations on the horizon of the rising and setting sun, and the changes in those parameters with the seasons. It became clear to ancient peoples that these changes were cyclical. They realized that, in addition to the daily cycle of the sun, another cyclical unit of time based on the sun existed on Earth. They named it the year (in whatever language they spoke), and noted that its duration could be determined. Similarly, it was seen that the proportion of daylight and darkness in each day changed in the same yearly cycle. The days with the least and most sunlight, which occur at the start of winter and summer respectively, are called the "solstices." The days during which the durations of sunlight and darkness are equal are commonly called the "equinoxes." (More precisely, these dates should be called "equiluxes," but the common usage will serve for this presentation.) These days occur at the beginning of spring and fall.

Communities began to note and even celebrate these special solar events. Early constructions of wood and later ones of stone, such as the well-known Stonehenge on Salisbury plain in England, were built by several prehistoric societies to improve the accuracy of the determination of these special days. They may have been used also for other purposes related to astronomy, religion, or agriculture. The day of the summer solstice, in Sweden called *Midsommer*, still remains a national holiday in that nation, although it has lost any religious association.

The Winter Solstice

Of the four solar-significant times of the year, the winter solstice is the one presenting the most anxiety because, as the date approaches, much living flora appear to be dying and the duration of daylight is reduced. Today, using our current (Gregorian) calendar, the winter solstice occurs around December 21 in the northern hemisphere, but in the distant past, when the Julian calendar was in use, the solstice fell on December 25 in many years. In pagan Rome, the celebration of the winter solstice began on December 17 with the feast of Saturn. This festival was called Saturnalia and it lasted about one week. Saturn, the son of Uranus, the Sky-Father, and Gaia, the Earth-Mother, was the god of agriculture. By the winter solstice, many plants had died and others had gone dormant. It was hoped that, as the days got longer again, resurrection of plant life would occur.

The Jewish festival, originally called the Festival of Lights and later also Hanukkah (meaning "dedication"), was established to be celebrated for eight days, beginning on the 25th day of the month of Kislev. This month begins in the late fall, and occasionally extends past the winter solstice. As discussed in Chapter 1, the holiday was first celebrated in about 164 BCE, some two centuries before the beginning of Christianity. In ancient Jewish literature, theological reasons are given for its establishment on that date, but it is possible that an unstated reason was to create a Jewish competitor to Saturnalia. It is known that Saturnalia was celebrated long before the establishment of Hanukkah. Certainly, the name "Festival of Lights" indicates that the occurrence of the winter solstice was a factor, and the use of the 25th of the month was not likely to be a pure coincidence.

Additionally, the winter solstice was celebrated as the birthday of the god Mithra, who was known to be worshipped in Persia and further east, and in the Roman empire from the first century BCE. This god was supposedly born of a virgin in a stable, attended by shepherds who brought gifts. Mithraism had a large following among Roman soldiers. The winter solstice was also the birthday of *Sol Invictus*, the Unconquerable Sun. This deity was venerated in the Roman empire from the second century CE and was named the official state deity by Emperor Aurelian in 274 CE. The function of *Sol Invictus* was to provide a supreme god that could be worshipped by all the varying cultures within the Roman empire without a clash with local beliefs. The phrase "*Sol Invictus*" was imprinted on Roman coins through the reign of Constantine (ruled 306–37 CE). The current practice in the United States of placing "In God We Trust" on coins is a reestablishment of this pre-Christian custom of a militaristic empire that held many peoples captive. The religions of Mithraism and *Sol Invictus* died out after the promulgation of the edict that declared a particular creed of Christianity to be the only state religion and proscribed all other sects and religions except Judaism. The latter was, at best, grudgingly tolerated and sometimes not; see Chapter 4 for more exposition on this subject.

It is believed by some historians of religion that the winter solstice was chosen as the date to be celebrated as Jesus's birthday, in order to co-opt believers in Mithraism and in *Sol Invictus*. There is no evidence that Jesus was actually born on this date. The New Testament states that shepherds were still tending their flocks in the fields at the time (Luke 2:8), indicating that it was not postharvest. Several early Christian scholars are known to have preferred dates that occurred at other times of the year. For example, Clement of Alexandria (ca. 150–ca. 215 CE), later named a saint in major Christian denominations, believed the correct date was May 20, although he recognized that other scholars had argued for different dates other than December 25, for example, April 18 and May 28. Origen (ca. 185–ca. 254 CE), another Christian scholar, argued that Jesus's birthday should not be celebrated at all, since that was the way that Pharaoh, Herod, and pagan gods were honored.

The Spring Equinox

The most hopeful of the two equinoxes and two solstices is the spring equinox; it promises new life. If Jesus was born on the winter solstice, then he was conceived on or about the previous spring equinox. Roman Catholics celebrate the Feast of the Annunciation of the Blessed Virgin Mary on March 25, the usual date of the spring equinox in the Julian calendar. This festival recognizes the belief by Roman Catholics that, on that date, the angel Gabriel told the Virgin Mary that she was pregnant. It is certainly interesting that the human gestation period of about nine months is the same number of months as the interval between the spring equinox and the winter solstice. Whether this is a coincidence or has an evolutionary basis is a question for other researchers to answer.

In 204 BCE, the religion venerating Cybele, a fertility goddess and *Mater Magna* (Great Mother), was brought to Rome on the recommendation of the Delphic Oracle as well as interpreters of certain prophetic books. At the time, the Romans were carrying out the Second Punic War against the Carthaginians and their general Hannibal. The Romans had suffered defeats, and it was believed that the presence of this goddess would bring good fortune. Good fortune occurred soon thereafter, as the Romans won the war and the next harvest was plentiful. This religion had its origin among the Phrygians, whose home territory is in what is now west-central Turkey (the plain of Anatolia). In the theology of this religion, Cybele had a lover called Attis. He was said to have been born of a virgin birth, and had later died a violent death. Around the time of the spring equinox, days of mourning were held, and then his resurrection by Cybele's magic was announced to the great joy of the celebrants. Tammuz was another god worshipped in the Near and Middle East who died and was resurrected.

The Jewish festival of Passover was designed to occur in the spring. The month in which it was first held was called Abib or Aviv (Exodus 13:4) meaning spring, although the Babylonian name Nisan was later adopted. Passover begins when the moon is full, in the middle of the month that begins after the spring equinox. Certain elements of Passover echo earlier pagan spring festivals. The month of Aviv is specifically called the "first month" in the Hebrew Bible, although, at present, the Jewish New Year, Rosh Hashanah ("head of the year"), is celebrated near the Fall equinox, at the beginning of the "seventh month." History leaves much strange cultural detritus in its wake.

The date of Easter Sunday was originally based on the Jewish Passover but its date was changed so as not to occur at the identical time as its predecessor (see Chapter 4 for more on this issue.) The name Easter comes from the name of the Great Mother Goddess of the Saxon people called Eostre. An ancient word for spring was "Eastre." Other related cultures had a similar goddess with names such as Ostare or Ostara. Adherents believed that, on the spring equinox, she mated with a solar god and had a child that was born nine months later. Thus the child was born on the winter solstice, called Yule by pagan Germans and Scandinavians.

Nowruz (the name has many spelling variants) is a spring equinox and New Year's Day holiday celebrated in Iran and other primarily Muslim countries of central Asia (e.g., Kazakhstan) and the Balkans (e.g., Albania). It is believed that Nowruz had its origin in the Zoroastrian religion. It may have been celebrated for over three thousand years. In Zoroastrian theology, on the day of the spring equinox, the powers of the eternally fighting bull (representing the Earth) and the lion (personifying the Sun) are equal. A Persian scholar of the tenth century CE wrote that it was the belief of the Persians that Nowruz marks the first day when the universe started its motion, that is, it was the birthday of the universe. The concept of the "birthday of the world" is also associated with the Jewish holiday of Rosh Hashanah.

In Iran, the holiday of Nowruz is heralded by a character called Haji Firuz, portrayed by a man wearing a red costume and having painted his visible skin black. Supposedly, black is an ancient Persian symbol of good luck, although it may also have a connection to ancient customs of the religions of India. He symbolizes the rebirth of the Sumerian god of sacrifice Domuzi (equivalent to Tammuz), who was killed at the end of each year and reborn during the festival of the New Year. Haji Firuz sings and dances through the streets with tambourines and trumpets, spreading good cheer. Nowruz lasts 12 days.

The Moon

Another sky phenomenon that could be seen by prehistoric peoples without instruments was the cycle of moon phases. The concept of the month ("moonth") came from the moon's cycle, but the current Gregorian calendar has lost the direct connection. (The number of days in a moon cycle is close to 29.5.) The solar year of about 365.24 days is roughly 11 days longer than 12 moon cycles (354 days). The ancient people of Chaco Canyon, in the southwest United States, developed an advanced knowledge of an actual, multiyear moon cycle (that is little-known even today) in the tenth and eleventh centuries CE, and may have used their knowledge of certain sight lines of moon maximums in building construction, and possibly for rites.

The Jewish and Muslim religious calendars retain the basic moon cycle; months in each of these calendars begin on the day of the new moon. The Jewish calendar adds one lunar leap month every two or three years, adding a total of seven months over 19 years. There are almost exactly 235 lunar months ([19 × 12] +7) in 19 solar years. This addition of seven months keeps the Jewish calendar in rough correspondence with the solar year, enabling retention of a connection with the seasons. Passover is always in the spring, Rosh Hashanah always close to the fall equinox, and Hanukkah always close to the start of winter. In contrast, the Muslim religious year is exactly 12 lunar months totaling 354 days, except that one day is added in each of 11 years over a cycle of 30 years. The result of that arrangement is that there is no permanent relationship between Muslim holidays and particular seasons of the year.

Our Planets, Our Galaxy, and the Constellations

The planets of our solar system that can be seen with the naked eye (Mercury, Venus, Mars, Jupiter, and Saturn) were identified in prehistoric times by their unique motions compared with the stars. Their wanderings in the heavens were followed. For example, the Maya people, discussed further in Chapter 4, followed the movements of Venus, the brightest of the planets, very closely for religious purposes. Other planets, as well as constellations (groupings of stars as seen from Earth, fancifully named), have been used also for astrology, totally without any basis in reality. Other objects that could be seen included the Milky Way, as well as occasional events such as supernovae, eclipses, comets, and meteor trails. Eclipses often resulted in fear among ancient peoples who experienced them, allowing for their exploitation by scheming individuals; meteorites that have fallen to the Earth have sometimes been treated with undeserved reverence.

The Cosmos

Appreciation of the vast extent of the universe increased rapidly after telescopes and then electronic aids were invented and applied, as pointed out in Chapter 2. Accumulated data, obtained through research, actual observation, and analyses, have permitted understanding of the beginning and subsequent expansion of the universe to its current configuration. This new knowledge should have resulted in a general understanding that creation myths are not factual. However, that has not happened among people hypnotized by their religious beliefs. Skeptics and agnostics may still use creation myths as allegories to teach moral lessons, but if creation myths cannot be appreciated as important artifacts of human development then human history is misunderstood. Atheists need to be aware of this implication.

Some Early Spiritual Thinking

The earliest humans most probably had no written language, but even if they did, they didn't record their thoughts on indestructible materials. What we think they believed must be inferred. Evidence of very early religion comes from discoveries of human burials and their grave goods, as well as art found on the walls of caves in France and Spain. The earliest burials with ritual goods have been dated at about 100 kya. In those graves, found in caves in hills overlooking the Israeli coast just south of Haifa, the antlers of a deer were placed in the hands of a dead child, and the mandible of a wild boar was placed in the hands of a dead adult male. In *Uniquely Human* (1991), Philip Lieberman wrote about the people who buried these dead: "Burials with grave goods clearly signify religious practices and concern for the dead that transcends daily life . . . The evidence . . . is consistent with their having possessed cognitive abilities that approach our own" (162, 163).

Lieberman is a chaired professor in the Department of Cognitive and Linguistic Sciences at Brown University. He continues, "If we assume that the minds of our distant ancestors worked like ours, we can take grave goods as evidence for religious beliefs that predicate an afterlife, rebirth, or perhaps even reincarnation" (164).

Anthropologist Roy Rappaport (1926–97) asserted, similarly, that religion began with the beginning of human culture. It is thus innate to the human condition. Rappaport, president of the American Anthropological Association from 1987 to 1989, indicated his views in *Ritual and Religion in the Making of Humanity* (1999). The final manuscript was completed in his last months. He wrote, "Given the central place that religious considerations have occupied in the thoughts and actions of men and women in all times and places, and given the amount of energy, blood, time and wealth that have been spent building temples, supporting priests, sacrificing to gods and killing infidels, it is hard to imagine that religion, as bizarre as some of its manifestations may seem, is not in some way indispensable to the species . . . *religion is as old as language, which is to say precisely as old as humanity*" (1, 2, 16).

The Importance of Death to Religion

It is not just coincidental that the indications of religion among the earliest humans have been found in connection with burials. Death and religion are closely associated. If people didn't die, it is unlikely that religion would exist. Gods don't die; they are immortal, but there are variations: Heracles and Jesus experienced human suffering and death before achieving immortal status; other gods, such as Attis and Tammuz, were killed but resurrected. Mesopotamian goddess Tiamat, although cut in half, was transformed into other eternal entities, heaven and earth. Mythological beings have no need of gods of their own. It was never recorded that Zeus prayed or sacrificed to a higher god; nor has that been written about any other god or goddess that could be named. Immortality *is* the highest level; there is no higher plane of existence. Adopting the concept of French anthropologist Claude Levi-Strauss (1908–2009), mortality and immortality form a fundamental, mutually exclusive, binary pair. In Buddhism, in which there is no prayer to a god, the ultimate goal is nonexistence, that is, an end to the cycle of reincarnations. Nonexistence has a similarity to immortality since, like immortality, it continues forever.

Sociologist Peter L. Berger (b. 1929), writing in *The Sacred Canopy: Elements of a Sociological Theory of Religion* (1967), appears to agree with this concept. He notes that "every human society is, at last resort, men banded together in the face of death" (52).

He connects death to religion with the following statement: "Insofar as the knowledge of death cannot be avoided in any society, legitimations of the social world *in the face of death* are decisive requirements of any society. The importance of religion in such legitimations is obvious" (44).

Anthropologist Bronislaw Malinowski (1894–1942), in his book *Magic, Science and Religion, and Other Essays* (1948), wrote similarly, "Of all sources of religion, the supreme and final crisis of life—death—is of the greatest importance . . . Man has to live his life in the shadow of death, and he who clings to life and enjoys its fullness must dread the menace of its end. And he who is faced by death turns to the promise of life. Death and its denial—Immortality—have always formed, as they form today, the most poignant theme of man's forebodings" (47).

Death is often cited as one of the few events of life that are inescapable. In 1789, the newly adopted Constitution of the United States was being implemented with the election of the first president and members of the first Congress. Benjamin Franklin (1706–90), that stalwart of independence, wrote to a friend about his concern for the success of the new nation. "In this world, nothing is certain but death and taxes," Franklin quipped. This aphorism has been repeated endless times and applied in a multitude of contexts since it was reported in a book of his witty remarks some years after his death.

The assertion here is that the continuation of religion, like death and taxes, is certain. It is likely that New Atheist Christopher

Hitchens probably wished it weren't true, but he agreed nevertheless. He wrote, in *god Is Not Great,* "Religious faith is, precisely *because* we are still evolving creatures, ineradicable. It will never die out, or at least until we get over our fear of death, and of the dark, and the unknown, and of each other" (12).

Hitchens's nomination of "fear of death" as a reason for religion's staying power has merit, in my view. As long as people continue to die, this concern of humans is very unlikely to go away. It is human to be concerned, or anxious, or even fearful, about the eventual extinction of one's self. If death were generally described favorably by healthy adults not persuaded to accept martyrdom, then suicide would not be so strongly opposed nor would it have the reputation of a failure of society. We typically mourn deaths. We are almost never happy to hear of death (except for enemies in wartime), although we are more easily reconciled if the deceased was in great pain or was in such a physical state, such as paralysis or dementia, that there was a very low quality of life. Occasionally, we may be secretly pleased by another's death or misfortune if he or she had engaged in disgraceful conduct, espoused a horrible point-of-view, or was, in some way, a personal enemy. The Germans invented a marvelous word for this emotion: *schadenfreude.*

"Death anxiety," a term with a meaning similar to "fear of death," but put in the context of mental health, has been discussed extensively by Irvin Yalom (b. 1931) in his book *Staring at the Sun* (2008). Yalom is emeritus professor of psychiatry at Stanford University School of Medicine. The title refers to a maxim of seventeenth-century French writer La Rochefoucauld that translates to "neither the sun nor death can be faced straight on." The book reports on a number of therapy sessions that Yalom has had with patients suffering death anxiety. These individuals required treatment because they were panicked and unable to adequately pursue daily life. Yalom philosophizes about the issue. He writes, "Death anxiety is the mother of all religions, which, in one way or another, attempt to temper the anguish of our finitude. God, as formulated transculturally, not only softens the pain of mortality through some vision of everlasting life, but also palliates fearful isolation by offering an eternal presence, and provides a clear blueprint for living a meaningful life" (5).

The recognition of the value of religion by Yalom doesn't mean that he is religious himself. He is not a believer, a fact he makes clear in a report of his interaction with a visitor who is a rabbi. He quotes himself responding to the rabbi as follows: "Your belief . . . is incompatible with the core of my existential vision of humanity as free, mortal, thrown alone and randomly into an uncaring universe . . . Those commodities [that you said were provided by your religion]—meaning, wisdom, morality, living well—are not dependent on a belief in God. And, yes, *of course*, religious belief makes you feel good, comforted, virtuous—that is exactly what religions are intended to do" (193, 194).

Religions Today

Religions that are widely practiced today and have holy literature as well as longstanding traditions include the three Abrahamic faiths with origins in the Middle East; Hinduism and Buddhism from south Asia; Daoism and Confucianism and related traditions of China; and Shinto from Japan. A fine summary of each of these eight may be found in *The Handy Religion Answer Book* (2002) by John Renard. For each, topics included are history and sources; signs and symbols; religious beliefs; membership, community, and diversity; leadership, authority, and organization; holidays and regular observances; and customs and rituals. Another useful text is *The Illustrated World's Religions* (2009) by Huston Smith. This set of descriptions, omitting Shinto but adding some "primal religions," is more interpretive. Smith's writing is eloquent and it demonstrates a deep understanding of the functions of religion as well as the meanings for adherents implied in each one.

Certain aspects of ancient beliefs continue to be kept alive by many people who are also observant of one of the major religions listed above. Pascal Boyer, in *Religion Explained* (2001), points out that "official religion is not the whole of religion." Witches are still suspected of attacks in parts of Europe; in Muslim countries, some people fear desert spirits called *jinn*. Additionally, a concern for the "evil eye" seems to be a preoccupation of some earthy folks who would otherwise declare themselves adherents of Judaism, Christianity, or Islam. One may purchase, in many countries, a small disc-shaped amulet with a bull's-eye on it that is supposed to provide a defense.

It is not uncommon for close relatives or friends of a deceased person to visit the grave and talk to the person as if he or she were still alive. This may occur in any society, whether advanced or still developing. This activity is not considered strange or psychotic by most people, but is recognized as a method of working through grief, a natural and healthy process. None of the Abrahamic religions officially recognizes the practice. The New Atheists make no mention of such a situation but, from the tenor of their writings, one could easily assume that they would consider it "delusional." That would only further demonstrate their disconnect from the reality of the human condition.

Some aboriginal peoples who have been conquered and forced to drop their old religion have tried to make their ancient practices and beliefs fit in with the religion of the conquerors. These attempts have resulted in an amalgamation of sorts. In *Religion: A Humanist Interpretation* (1996), Raymond Firth wrote that an "admixture of traditional folk beliefs and rituals from outside the main doctrinal field of the faithful has been characteristic of many rural Muslim, Christian and Buddhist congregations in the Orient, Europe and elsewhere in the world" (13).

In actions going even further, various aboriginal groups in the Americas are trying to resuscitate their former religions. There are, of course, many ancient religions that have gone extinct, like species of plants and animals. Some of us bemoan the loss of living species, but few seem to be concerned with the loss of indigenous cultures and their associated religions. In fact, missionaries work to snuff them out. Unique religions of nonliterate peoples still exist in remote areas of Asia, Oceania, Africa, and South America. Many of these have been described by ethnologists and cultural anthropologists, who continue to study them today.

Some of the questions that religion seeks to answer are these:

- What is the origin of the universe and of life?
- What supernatural beings exist, and what should be our relationships with them?
- What should be our highest ideals and our forbidden actions?
- What constitutes proper conduct toward oneself, other humans, and other living things?
- What is the meaning of life?
- What happens to us after we die?

These questions have been asked for a long time in many cultures. The *Shvetashvetara Upanishad*, written in India about 300 BCE reported, similarly:

> "Disciples inquire within themselves:
> What is the cause of this universe? Is in Brahman?
> From whence do we come? Why do we live?
> Where shall we at last find rest?
> Under whose command are we bound by the law of happiness and its opposite?"

Every modern religion seems to have its own answers to these questions, and each has developed a complex theology to justify its answers. Each theology generally describes a supernatural existence beyond the physical world, involving God or a pantheon of gods or ancestors and other spirits. It may concern, also, the disposition of souls following death, and, in some cases, descriptions of heaven(s) and hell(s). Serious believers accept the occurrence of miracles (actual interventions of the supernatural in the physical world) that are essential to their specific religious system. Additionally, it has been stated by some apologists for religion that the birth of a baby, or another natural event, is a "miracle." The poetic use of this word is an indication of how human creativity and imagination can be used to muddy the distinction between the physical world and the world of the spirit. It is agreed here that the beginning of new life, as well as the occurrence of death, are sacred events worthy of recognition, celebration, and commemoration. It is for such purposes that religion has been invented and rationally applied.

Religions often require belief in the divine nature of revelations from a Spiritual World to special humans, typically called prophets. These revelations, such as those to Moses and Muhammad, are not miracles, as they do not involve violations of physical laws. Furthermore, according to some theologies, we will be judged after we die, and rewards or punishments await us for eternity, or until a Judgment Day or an End Time. Some religions allow for the possibility of reincarnation and, for each individual, the conditions of the next life (or its avoidance) may depend on certain qualities of the current life. The concept of individual choice in this life affecting the afterlife is a common theme among religions, although theological arguments concerning free will versus predestination have occurred in both Christianity and Islam.

What we can learn from all these is that the sole remaining human subspecies has an extremely wide variety of religious beliefs and practices. It is axiomatic now (as opposed to the views that many educated Europeans and North Americans held before the last third of the twentieth century) that all humans, regardless of culture or ethnicity, have a similar range of basic intelligence. This idea was originally put forward by E. B. Tylor, discussed below. Franz Boas (1858–1942) publicized this view in the United States with regard to whites and African Americans. He made this idea clear in a commencement address to Atlanta University—a black institution—in 1906. Boas, born and educated in Germany but residing in America from 1887 on, has been cited as "the father of American anthropology." Beginning in 1899 at Columbia University, he led the first PhD program in anthropology in the United States.

Emile Durkheim, also discussed below, stated that all religions are legitimate when viewed from inside. There may be consistencies among religions that can lead to universal understandings and acceptance of others. By ignoring commonality and considering specifics only, many believers—percent unknown—conclude that their religion is correct and all others incorrect. As shown in Chapter 4, state-sponsored attempts to change the religion of nonconformists, and to ensure a single religion within an area of political control, have led to significant violence, from the distant past right down to the present.

SOME THEORISTS AND THEIR THEORIES OF RELIGION

In the nineteenth century in Great Britain, there was considerable intellectual ferment concerning the truth of certain Christian teachings. The reputed age of the Earth, claimed by Bishop James Ussher (1581–1656) to be just about six thousand years, based on his analysis of the text of Genesis, began to be seriously doubted as a result of geological findings. Facts discovered included soil strata (layers of different composition) that were found to exist as digging progressed downward from ground level. The strata were shown to be in the same sequence from top to bottom at every location investigated. This arrangement demonstrated a time-sequence of deposition over a wide area. Fossils of extinct species of animals appeared in the strata, demonstrating that the layers were ancient in their origin. Among the important researchers in that field were William Smith (1769–1839), who began to understand geologic history as he dug canals, and Charles Lyell (1797–1875), who was well-educated in the field. In 1859, Charles Darwin (1809–82) published *Origin of Species (1859)*, concerning evolution by natural selection, followed by *The Descent of Man* (1874).

Detailed analyses of non-European religions based on observations began in the second half of the nineteenth century. Much data on early religion theorists is provided by Daniel Pals in *Eight Theories of Religion* (2nd ed., 2006).

E. B. TYLOR

The understanding of human societies, beginning with the earliest ones, was moved forward significantly with the analysis carried out by Edward Burnett Tylor (1832–1917), son of prosperous English Quakers. His interest in the subject was piqued by a trip to Mexico as a young man. Self-taught and without formal higher education (like William Smith, the canal digger), he nevertheless wrote extensively on ethnology (the study of cultures), including his most influential two-volume book, *Primitive Culture* (1871).

He is said by some to be the founder of cultural or social anthropology; his work was eventually recognized academically and, in 1896, he became the first professor of anthropology at the University of Oxford.

Religion is "belief in spiritual beings," according to Tylor. The earliest beliefs held by humans he called "animism," after the Latin *anima* meaning "spirit." Spirits could be seen almost everywhere by early humans, in rocks, trees, rivers, and winds, for example. Similarly, it was held by many early believers that every person and animal had a soul, a type of spirit, independent of the body. Tylor believed that religion had become more complex over time, evolving to a higher form, just as Darwin showed that biological life had evolved. In this very early application of "Social Darwinism" (a name that would later be applied to this concept), polytheistic beliefs were an intermediate step to monotheism, the most recent and (claimed to be) the most advanced form of religion. In the foreseeable future, Tylor reasoned, religion must give way to science, as there is no physical evidence for spirits or souls.

Tylor's writings demonstrate that he was not a believer in Christianity. He believed strongly that all humans, of whatever culture, have the same mental capacity. Their reasoning abilities are the same, even though some are more advanced in developments in technologies than others.

W. Robertson Smith

The Scottish biblical scholar and anthropologist William Robertson Smith (1846–94) learned Latin, Greek, and Hebrew at an early age, and traveled to Arabia to research the customs of desert communities. In the 1880s, he became professor of Arabic at Cambridge University, and later became editor of the *Encyclopedia Britannica*. Among his most important works was *The Religion of the Semites* (1889).

In Arabia, Smith discovered totemism, a system of group living in which each clan of a tribe has its own unique sacred "totem"—most often a particular type of animal but occasionally a type of plant or a physical force. While a function of the clan system is to require that marriages are allowed only between persons of different clans (exogamy), another function is in the treatment of the sacred totem. Members of a clan are not permitted to harm any living example of their totemic symbol, if an animal; they feel an extreme closeness to its species. Clan members may claim descent from it or believe that they and the totem animal have a common origin. Smith surmised that, at certain holy meals, the taboo would be reversed and the totem would be killed and eaten. However, he had no evidence of it. Later researchers of the cultures of aboriginal Australians determined that the holy meal consuming the totem occurred there.

An important concept put forth by Smith was that religion pertains to the common good, not private interest; it expresses a community's public hopes and goals, thereby strengthening the social bonds between its members.

JAMES G. FRAZER

The Golden Bough (1st ed., 1890) was a major part of the life's work of James George Frazer (1854–1941), a Scotsman born in Glasgow. His book would go through a number of expansions and abridgments through the first decades of the twentieth century. It is an enormous compendium of beliefs, myths, and rituals of many nonliterate cultures throughout the world. Frazer obtained his data from missionaries, diplomats, explorers, merchants, and other travelers, although he himself remained in his quarters at Cambridge University in England.

Frazer's view of the progression of belief from magic to religion to science was similar to that of Tylor. Additionally, he introduced the concept of "survivals." He pointed out that the saying of a blessing when someone sneezes is a "survival" of a pagan belief continuing in Christian culture, as is the use of Easter eggs and Christmas trees. Similarly, religion itself is a "survival" in the age of science, according to Frazer.

SIGMUND FREUD

The founder of psychoanalysis, Sigmund Freud (1856–1939), is best known for his theory of the unconscious mind and the idea of the

Oedipus complex. He was born in Moravia to a Jewish family. His province of birth, then in the Austro-Hungarian empire, is now part of the Czech Republic. While still a boy, he moved with his family to Vienna, the empire's capital; he remained there for almost all his life. Following the *Anschluss* (annexation) of Austria to Nazi Germany in 1938, he fled Vienna for London, where he died of cancer.

As a young man, he studied at the University of Vienna and became a physician. He undertook neurological research on the brain, but encounters with physicians Josef Breuer (1842–1925) in Vienna and Jean-Martin Charcot (1825–93) in Paris led him into psychological concerns instead. Both Breuer and Charcot were involved in that field. In later life, Freud began to be interested in the psychological origins of religion, a subject about which he had strong views. He was an avowed atheist and believed that religion was the "universal obsessional neurosis of humanity." He claimed to examine religion scientifically, that is, without any bias, and he used his tools of psychoanalysis against it. Thus it is not surprising that Christopher Hitchens cited Freud eight times in *god Is Not Great* and, in four of those eight citations, Freud's book *The Future of an Illusion* (1927) is mentioned. None of Freud's other works are cited by the New Atheists.

Freud wrote three books on the subject of religion. The first was *Totem and Taboo* (1913). In this book, Freud adopts the view, common at the time, that totemism was the earliest form of religion. He connects the holy killing of the totem animal to the relationship of a male child to his father. He wrote, "Psychoanalysis has revealed to us that the totem animal is really a substitute for the father, and this really explains the contradiction that it is usually forbidden to kill the totem animal, that the killing results in a holiday and that the animal is killed and yet mourned" (182).

In his interpretation of religion, Freud understands "the father" in the above quote to be a substitute for God. Indeed, in Christianity, Father is often used as a name for God; it is stated that Jesus called God "Abba," meaning Father in Aramaic, the language he spoke. Thus Freud is able to associate his views with those of James G. Frazer, whom he quotes as stating that "the Christian communion has absorbed within itself a sacrament which is doubtless far older than Christianity" (199, 200). In the communion, the body and blood of Christ are symbolically eaten by participants at the service.

In *The Future of an Illusion,* Freud extends this line of thought, comparing the need for religion to a child's need for a protective father who may be, also, a stern and frightening figure. Here, Freud asserts that when the grown-up adult realizes that he can never do without protection against strange powers, "he creates for himself the gods whom he dreads, whom he seeks to propitiate, and whom he nevertheless entrusts with his own protection" (30).

The "illusion" in the book's title refers to Freud's view that some of the basic ideas of Western religion, that is, those that concern the afterlife and the power of God, are merely wishes amounting to self-deception.

Freud completed *Moses and Monotheism* (1939) in London, just before he died. His assertions about the origin of monotheism with Egyptian pharaoh Akhenaten as well as his statements about Moses's origin and career are not accepted today by any serious scholar. It is correct that "Moses" is an Egyptian name, as Freud states, but that is not proof that Moses was an Egyptian, as Freud claimed. "Sigmund" is not a Hebrew name, either; its use indicates a process of assimilation to a majority culture. In the Bible, the name "Moses" was given to the child by the Egyptian princess who drew him out of the river. In this final book, Freud softened his stance on the value of belief in an invisible god. Mark Edmundson, in "Defender of the Faith?" in *The New York Times Magazine* of September 9, 2007, explains that "Freud argues that taking God into the mind enriches the individual immeasurably. The ability to believe in an internal, invisible God vastly improves people's capacity for abstraction." Edmundson is author of *The Death of Sigmund Freud: The Legacy of His Last Days* (2007).

Emile Durkheim

Born near Strasbourg, France, Emile Durkheim (1858–1917) was the son and grandson of rabbis, but he chose a secular path in all his activities. However, he was not an active atheist, like Freud. After completing a demanding regimen to earn academic credentials, he began to teach, first at secondary schools near Paris, then at the University of Bordeaux, and finally at the University of Paris (the Sorbonne). He is considered to be a founder of the discipline of sociology. Throughout his career, he was concerned with the scientific analysis of society, believing that a population was more than simply a conglomeration of individuals and that its communitarian aspects were worthy of investigation with scientific methods.

Durkheim is noted for his book *The Elementary Forms of Religious Life* (1912). In this text, he reviews, as others did before him, studies of totemism among Australian aborigines. He asserts that the religion of these people is the simplest possible, and he demonstrates that Australian totemism has all the features that would be expected to be found in any advanced religion. Then he applies the studies to generalize about religion and its relationship to a society or culture in which it appears. It was Durkheim's belief that "there are no false religions."

His provided the following definition: "a religion is a unified system of beliefs and practices relative to sacred things, that is to say, things set apart and surrounded by prohibitions—beliefs and practices that unite its adherents in a single moral community called a church" (46).

Note that there is no reference to gods or the supernatural, only to the "sacred," which is distinguished elsewhere in the book from the "profane." Religion, as defined by Durkheim, does not require gods; Buddhists have none, but they have their Four Noble Truths and other statements, as well as accompanying sacred texts. The sacred is not necessarily all good; Satan is sacred but bad. The profane is not necessarily bad; it is simply mundane and refers to the private interests of individuals, as opposed to the highest values of the community. Durkheim's view here bears some similarity to that of W. Robertson Smith.

Durkheim's overall philosophy is that religion is eminently social and represents the collective hopes of society. Note the difference with Freud's orientation, which approached religion from the psychology of the individual. Durkheim states that humans envision a perfect or ideal world where justice and truth are sovereign and where evil in all its forms is abolished, and then comments, "These aspirations have their roots in us: they come from the very depths of our being... They are already religious in themselves. The ideal society, then, presupposes religion rather than explains it" (315).

Additionally, he sees secular celebrations to be similar to religious ceremonies. He asks, rhetorically: "What essential difference is there between an assembly of Christians commemorating the principal moments in the life of Christ, or Jews celebrating either the exodus from Egypt or the giving of the Ten Commandments, and a meeting of citizens commemorating the institution of a new moral charter or some great event in national life?" (322).

This issue will be revisited in Chapter 6.

Bronislaw Malinowski

Quoted above with his view on death, Bronislaw Malinowski was born in Poland and earned a doctorate there in the physical sciences. He later studied ethnology in Germany and at the London School of Economics (LSE). He did fieldwork (ethnological research) in the South Pacific during World War I, and his book *Argonauts of the Western Pacific* (1922) was recognized as a masterpiece in the field. Malinowski, who eventually taught at the LSE and became a British citizen, was eloquent in his adopted language. The following comparison of magic and religion is included in the postmortem collection *Magic, Science and Religion, and Other Essays:*

> We have defined, within the domain of the sacred, magic as a practical art consisting of acts which are only means to a definite end expected to follow later on... The practical art of magic has its limited, circumscribed technique: spell, rite, and the condition of the performer form always its trite trinity. Religion, with its complex aspects and purposes, has no such simple technique... Religion establishes, fixes, and enhances all valuable mental attitudes, such as reverence for tradition, harmony with the environment, courage and confidence in the struggle with difficulties and at the prospect of death. (88, 89)

An example of the continued use of magic in modern times is reported in *Religion Explained*. Pascal Boyer's data concern the Cuna people of Panama.

Mircea Eliade

As a profound thinker and prolific author on the history of religion, Mircea Eliade (1907–86) can be agreed with or disagreed with, but he cannot be ignored without leaving an unacceptable void. One could be almost certain without checking that he would not be referenced by the New Atheists (he is not). Eliade was born in Romania and obtained his initial education there. He spent several years in India, studying the basics of Indian philosophy. He obtained a PhD in 1933 with a dissertation on the practice of yoga.

Returning to Romania, he worked as a journalist and contributed to literary magazines. He was briefly arrested in 1938 for his association with a far-right political group, but that movement achieved power as World War II began. It collaborated with the Nazis and, during the war, Eliade's association with it aided him in his selection by the government to serve with Romania's foreign service, first in London and then in Lisbon. After the war, as the Communists obtained power, he moved to France instead of returning home. He taught there, and became active in intellectual circles. In 1950, he started to attend the series of conferences known as "Eranos," at an estate on Lago Maggiore in Switzerland. The meetings began to be held in 1933 at the suggestion of the German theologian Rudolph Otto (1869–1937), and apparently continue to be held annually. The conference serves as an intellectual discussion group dedicated to the study of psychology, religion, philosophy, and spirituality. These meetings included, among many others, Carl Jung (1875–1961), the psychiatrist and one-time associate of Freud, and Gershom Scholem (1897–1982), the expert in Jewish mysticism. Eliade continued to meet privately with Jung and to discuss his ideas with him.

Eliade moved to the United States in 1956, having been asked to give a series of lectures at the University of Chicago. He replaced his sponsor on the faculty upon the sponsor's death and, in 1964, he was named the Sewell Avery Distinguished Service Professor of the History of Religions. Mircea Eliade is the first in this list of theorists of religion who was born in the twentieth century and lived through World War II. It has been written about him that his own religion, the Romanian form of Eastern Orthodoxy, colors his views. That appears to be a reasonable conclusion.

One of his most important books is *Patterns in Comparative Religion* (1949), originally written in French. He begins by noting that religion can be examined with sociology, psychology, economics, or some other body of knowledge, but those methods would not provide a complete picture unless they also included concern for the "sacred." His identification of three special bodies of knowledge suggests that he was thinking of the interpretations of religion provided respectively by sociologist Max Weber (1864–1920), psychiatrist Sigmund Freud, and political philosopher Karl Marx (1818–83). For the latter, everything was a question of economics, and, in the writings of each of the three, the concept of the "sacred" was not salient.

In *Patterns*, Eliade examined religious phenomena that, he said, involve "hierophanies," that is, "anything which manifests the sacred" (xiv). There are an enormous variety of such appearances— for example, myths, rites, venerated objects, symbols, consecrated persons, animals, plants, certain places, and more. A hierophany is always a historical event, that is, it is an actual occurrence. Note that hierophany is a larger category than theophany. The latter is, specifically, the appearance of a god.

Every interior chapter of Eliade's book examines a separate category of hierophanies. These include the sky and sky gods; the sun and sun worship; the moon and its mystique; waters and water symbolism; the Earth, woman, and fertility; vegetation and symbols of regeneration; sacred time; morphology and function of myths; and others. His elaboration of hierophanies in cosmic phenomena considerably expands on the brief discussion given above in the section "Religion and the Universe." Of particular importance is his view of the moon's role. He writes, "The moon . . . is a body which waxes, wanes and disappears; a body whose existence is subject to the universal law of becoming, of birth and death . . . For three nights, the starry sky is without a moon. But this 'death' is followed by a rebirth, the 'new moon.' . . . This perpetual return to its beginnings, and this ever-recurring cycle, make the moon *the* heavenly body above all others concerned with the rhythms of life" (154).

This concept of repetitional birth, death, and rebirth is fundamental to Eliade's view of religion. Additionally, Eliade refers several times to a "companion volume" in which his ideas will be further elaborated. The name of the second book is not given, but perhaps it is *The Myth of the Eternal Return* (1949), which was also first published in French in the same year as *Patterns*. In Eliade's writings, "repetition" is a synonym for "return."

In *Myth*, Eliade distinguishes the beliefs of "archaic" people from those of "modern" humans. The beliefs of archaic people are, primarily, those polytheistic systems of the Middle East and Mediterranean regions existing before Judaism. For these ancient people, linear history does not exist. Instead, time is circular, returning constantly to the creation of the world "at the beginning of time," put in the form of myths. "Creation realizes the passage . . . from chaos to cosmos." Yearly celebrations mark the anniversaries of mythological events. According to Eliade, "reality is a function of the imitation of a celestial archetype." Thus normal profane existence is not real unless it involves actions that repeat the stories about gods or heroes; these are the archetypes.

Judaism and Christianity (as well as Islam, not mentioned by Eliade) have a linear view of time instead of a circular one. These religions view particular events as existing solely at their actual moments, and not repeating a mythical beginning. However, the end of this linear time is seen, when a final judgment by God will occur. The final section of this book concerns the different methods used by premodern and modern people to confront "the terror of history." This term apparently means the succession of horrendous events that result in suffering and that continue ad infinitum. Eliade writes that premodern people could accept suffering because it was regarded as having a "meta-historical meaning." However, modern humans have been infused with the idea of continual progress, indicating that history is meaningful and will continue in an upward direction. If disastrous events continue, the idea of continual progress may be untenable. Eliade sees an eventual reaction: "The horizon of archetypes and repetition cannot be transcended with impunity unless we accept a philosophy of freedom that does not exclude God" (160).

Another book by Eliade, *The Sacred and the Profane* (1959), described as a "general introduction to the history of religions," presents his ideas in a simpler way. Here, he is concerned only with "religious man" and his opposite, "nonreligious man." He describes the latter as follows: "Desacralization pervades the entire experience of the nonreligious man of modern societies" (13). "Modern nonreligious man . . . regards himself solely as the subject and agent of history, and he refuses all appeal to transcendence . . . *Man makes himself*, and he only makes himself completely in proportion as he desacralizes himself and the world . . . He will not be truly free until he has killed the last god" (203).

Eliade describes religious man as always believing "that there is an absolute reality, *the sacred*, which transcends this world but manifests itself in this world, thereby sanctifying it and making it real. He further believes that life has a sacred origin and that human existence realizes all of its potentialities in proportion as it is religious—that is, participates in reality" (202).

Religion as a Cultural System

The last theorist to be discussed, Clifford Geertz (1926–2006), is considered separately in this section because his interpretation of religion, as presented in *The Interpretation of Cultures* (1973), is particularly relevant to the concept considered here. If religion is a cultural system, as Geertz states, then the elimination of religion, as desired by the New Atheists, is more than just disbelief in miracles; it is the abolition of an entire method of thinking about the world for each group that practices its own religion.

Geertz was born and died in the United States. Native to San Francisco, he obtained his undergraduate degree from Antioch College in 1950 and his PhD in anthropology from Harvard in 1956. He did fieldwork in Indonesia, specifically in Java and Bali, and also in Morocco. In the former country, he examined in detail the religion of Bali, involving an indigenous set of beliefs with overtones of Hinduism and paganism. With his experience in Morocco, he was able to distinguish significant cultural differences between that country and Java, despite the fact that the people of both areas are primarily Muslim. His outstanding research was a major reason for his appointment in 1970 as professor of social science at the Institute for Advanced Study in Princeton, New Jersey; he retired in 2000.

The word "culture" has been used above and extensively in the previous chapters. There are a large number of definitions of culture, as the term is used here. E. B. Tylor's definition, reported by Daniel L. Pals, is as follows: "Any organized community or culture must be understood as a whole—as a complex system made up of knowledge and beliefs, of art and morals, tools and technology, language, laws, customs, legends, myths and other components" (22).

In 1952, two anthropologists, Alfred Kroeber (1876–1960) and Clyde Kluckhohn (1905–60), compiled a list of 164 definitions of culture in a paper titled *Culture: A Critical Review of Concepts and Definitions*. One of their definitions is that "Culture is an integrated pattern of human knowledge, belief, and behavior that depends upon the capacity for symbolic thought and social learning."

A third definition, said to be from the University of Manitoba, is that "Culture is defined as the system of shared beliefs, values, customs, behaviors and artifacts that the members of a society use to cope with their world and with one another, and that [is] transmitted from generation to generation through learning."

Note that all three of these definitions include "belief" as an element of culture. Geertz has his own definition, presented in "Religion as a Cultural System," a chapter included in the book previously cited. He writes, "[Culture] denotes an historically transmitted pattern of meanings embodied in symbols, a system of inherited conceptions expressed in symbolic forms by means of which men communicate, perpetuate, and develop their knowledge about and attitudes toward life" (89).

Geertz then expands on this definition by explaining "sacred symbols," which are applicable to religion. He writes, "Sacred symbols function to synthesize a people's ethos . . . and their worldview" (89), in which it appears that "a people" are all the members of a particular culture and that their ethos and worldview are what are received as "meanings." He provides the following definitions applicable to these "people" in another chapter from the same book, titled "Ethos, World View, and the Analysis of Sacred Symbols": "A people's ethos is the tone, character, and quality of their life, its moral and aesthetic style, and mood . . . Their world view is their picture of the way things in sheer actuality are . . . their most comprehensive ideas of order" (127).

Geertz then asserts that religion, "in belief and practice," renders the worldview emotionally convincing and the ethos intellectually reasonable because it describes a way of life consistent with the worldview. Thus, religion and culture are closely intertwined.

He also recognizes, with great insight, the importance of religion in enabling humans to deal with suffering. He writes, "As a religious problem, the problem of suffering is not how to avoid suffering, but how to suffer, how to make of physical pain, personal loss, worldly defeat, or the helpless contemplation of others' agony something bearable, supportable—something, as we say, sufferable" (104).

Bart D. Ehrman, cited in Chapter 1, has drawn a different conclusion about the impact of human suffering. Originally educated at fundamentalist schools, he has rejected Christianity and has become agnostic because of this very issue. In his recent book, *God's Problem* (2008), he asks, "If there is an all-powerful and loving God in the world, why is there so much excruciating pain and unspeakable suffering?" (1). He responds for himself: "The problem of suffering . . . was the reason I lost my faith" (1).

The Continuation of Religion

Many persons, some of high intelligence or significant professional accomplishment, continue to classify themselves as members of a specific religion, despite crimes that may have been committed in its name. These individuals may attend worship services, even if they do not fully believe in their religion's theology because it clashes with scientific findings or historical experiences. Richard

Dawkins names two such Englishmen, one Christian (scientist Martin Rees) and one Jewish (physician Robert Winston), with seeming puzzlement. His confusion is understandable if he thinks of religion only as a belief in the supernatural. There are many reasons for retaining membership in a religion, and if agreement with the theology is not one of them, there are others, including the simplistic "that's the way I was raised," as well as those stated by the two individuals named, and also the reason "it provides a social life with friendly and compatible people."

According to Dawkins, Rees said that he attends church "as an unbelieving Anglican . . . out of loyalty to the tribe"; Winston stated that he found that "Judaism provided a good discipline to help him structure his life and lead a good one." A fifth alternate motive could be a continued association in a sanctified setting with other individuals with whom one has a shared history; and still another might be the continued involvement in a culture deemed too valuable to let die, because it has enriched humanity with much art or literature, or a praiseworthy presentation of ethical ideas, or a special philosophy of life worthy of examination and consideration. A seventh reason might be defiance of others who would destroy it. An eighth might be a stubborn refusal to be cowed by a majority religion whose robotlike myrmidons have the arrogance to insult and threaten the minority adherent with the totally unsubstantiated assertion that torment after death awaits every person who fails to join their belief-system.

As has been just shown, religion is an important aspect of culture. Failure to continue the existence of unique cultures defined in large measure by their religions might leave us with only a bland, uniform world without diversity. It is diversity of thought, on various topics including religion, and the ability to make those thoughts heard in the public marketplace, that ensures the continuation of a democratic society. *Worldwide universal atheism would be no better than a worldwide, single, universal religion. The implementation of either would lead to the kind of society envisioned by Stalin or by those who set the Inquisition in power.*

Sam Harris, similar to Dawkins, doesn't appreciate that the continued association with a religion might be due to causes other than strict belief in the efficacy of the supernatural. He states that "It appears that even the Holocaust did not lead most Jews to doubt the existence of an omnipotent and benevolent God. If having half of your people systematically delivered to the furnace does not count as evidence against the notion that an all-powerful God is looking out for your interests, it seems reasonable to assume that nothing could" (*End of Faith*, 66, 67).

Yes, even after being delivered to the barracks of the death camps, Jews so confined continued to observe their religious rituals as best as they could. One reason was probably that, having been stripped of all their dignity and humanity for simply being Jewish, they were as defiant as possible by observing the rituals of their religion. They found a way to go on with life, a sacred duty, by creating a continued association in a setting that they made holy together with other individuals with whom they had a shared history.

A relevant anecdote is reported by Hugo Gryn (1930–96), who became a noted and well-respected rabbi in England. The story is included in his book *Chasing Shadows* (2000), coauthored with his daughter Naomi Gryn. He grew up in eastern Europe and was deported by the Nazis to Auschwitz with his parents and siblings, but soon only he and his father remained alive. As Hanukkah approached in December 1944, the Jewish prisoners in their barracks decided to fashion, as best they could from debris, the special type of menorah (candelabra) used in this festival. It was agreed to save the week's ration of margarine for fuel. On the first night of Hanukkah, most of the barracks gathered round, including Roman Catholic Poles, Protestant Norwegians, and a German count implicated in an attempt on Hitler's life. Unfortunately, no one realized that the melted margarine would not burn. Gryn bemoaned the waste of precious calories. Whereupon, his father told him, "Don't be so angry. You know that this festival celebrates the victory of the spirit over tyranny and might. You and I have had to go once for over a week without proper food and another time almost three days without water, but you cannot live for three minutes without hope" (237). This use of Judaism was not new. Chapter 4 reports many instances when it needed to be used in that manner. (Gryn's father did not survive; he became ill on the death march that preceded liberation, and he died soon after.)

Furthermore, many people throughout the world still believe in miracles, regardless of the facts brought to light by scientists and others who understand what has been discovered and reported. Religions, whether or not they depend on miracles, will continue to exist for the indefinite future, if not in Great Britain—the native country of both Dawkins and Hitchens—then in many other parts of the world. Millions of Muslims make the Hajj at Islam's holiest site each year, and millions of Hindus wash themselves in the Ganges in a religion-related ritual. The remarkable variety and depth of contemporary religious practices in India is related by William Dalrymple in *Nine Lives* (2009). Other multitudes continue to make pilgrimages to Lourdes and to Santiago de Compostela, and to visit the holy sites of Jerusalem. The practical question is not how to eliminate religion—an impossibility—but how to minimize the likelihood of wars and violent conflict brought on by differences in religious belief, or, more correctly in modern times, by differences in cultures that include religion as an important aspect.

RELIGION AND CHILDREN

Richard Dawkins wants us to believe that all children should be religion-free until they reach some (unstated) age. He writes, "I think we should all wince when we hear a small child being labeled at belonging to some particular religion or another. Small children are too young to decide their views on the origins of the cosmos, of life and of morals. The very sound of the phrase 'Christian child' or 'Muslim child' should grate like fingernails on a blackboard" (338). Here again we see the failure to understand religion as an important aspect of culture. In the West, Christianity is the majority culture, and someone enmeshed within it may not appreciate the fact that it is just one particular culture out of many. In this era of increasing mixing of cultures through immigration, easy international travel, and instant worldwide communication, a more discerning view is necessary if one's propositions are to have any significant impact.

Of course, young children can't discourse on the meaning of life or the origin of the universe. (Many adults can't, either.) Still, there is much more to religion as a part of culture than only these philosophical issues. Loving parents will make their children an integral part of the household, and the children will begin to understand the culture and religion of their families. Additionally, children living with parents will hear adults talk about issues of the day that are important to them from points of view indicative of their beliefs, history, and heritage. They may hear about cooperation or conflict with members of other ethnicities. Children are likely to absorb much of what they hear.

The following is probably known by many readers, but not apparently by Dawkins. In many Christian denominations, infants are brought into the community with the rite of baptism. The ceremony for Jewish boys is the rite of circumcision on the eighth day of life, and for Jewish girls, the naming ceremony. By contrast, for Muslims, the community ceremony related to birth includes a head-shaving done on the seventh day of life; the hair's weight in gold or silver is given to charity. Muslim boys are circumcised early in life; it may occur at the head-shaving ceremony. Thus, many newborns become Christian children, Jewish children, or Muslim children almost immediately.

Life's milestones besides birth, that is, coming of age, marriage, and death, are often recognized with rituals that include participation by an entire community. Thus, these significant events are given a cultural as well as a religious flavor. There are other such community-wide events, for example, the holy day of the week, as well as yearly celebrations and solemn occasions. In addition, some religions have special prayers for meals, and special foods that are either encouraged to be eaten at certain times or deliberately forbidden. Children of the household are certainly aware of these practices.

There are holy languages used in prayers, regardless of the vernacular commonly employed in daily life; for Jews it is Hebrew, while for Muslims it is Arabic. (For Roman Catholics, it used to be Latin, but no longer.) There are also artifacts commonly associated with religions and that may be present in homes; for Christians, they include a cross and possibly a picture of Jesus or Mary; Jews and Muslims forbid representations of God or the prophets. Artifacts in Muslim homes may include a *musalla* (a prayer rug) and calligraphic decorations that may display sayings of the Prophet; in Jewish homes, they may include a *mezuzah* (a small rectangular box fastened to doorposts and containing a prayer), the seder plate used at Passover, and the *hanukkiah* (the nine-branched menorah used at Hanukkah). Children note these objects and see them being used. They may participate in some rituals.

At meals, children may hear grace said beforehand or immediately after. Jewish children will hear the prayers in Hebrew; Muslim children will hear them in Arabic. Observant Muslims and Jews employ food restrictions; both religions forbid eating any part of a pig, or the use of pig fat (lard). Observant Muslims drink no alcohol; certain Christian denominations have a similar requirement. For Muslims, the word for religious-food purity is "halal"; the word for Jews is "kosher." (Muslims wanting to buy foods that are halal may buy kosher foods because the latter assuredly include no pig products.) Jews maintaining a kosher home only eat seafood with fins and scales; thus, they do not eat shellfish, octopus, squid (calamari), or eel. Additionally, they separate by a time interval the ingestion of meat dishes and dairy dishes (fish may be eaten with either). Children in a household are likely to learn about these restrictions.

The holy day of the week is Friday for Muslims, Saturday for Jews, and Sunday for Christians. Each group may attend religious services on its respective holy day and on other days as well. At Muslim and Orthodox Jewish services, the sexes are separate; not so in Christian or non–Orthodox Jewish worship. The sacred languages of Muslims and Jews will be used at their respective services. Children may attend such services with their parents. Additionally, the Jewish day begins at sundown the previous evening. Thus, on Friday evening at sundown, in a Jewish home, the female head of the household will light Sabbath candles, and the daughters will assist.

Important yearly Christian holidays include Christmas and Easter. Important Jewish holidays include Passover, Sukkot (also known as Tabernacles), and Yom Kippur (Day of Atonement). On Yom Kippur, observant Jews fast the entire day. During the eight days of Passover, Jews eat no leavened bread. On the first evening of this holiday (and for some, the second also), they have a holy meal called a seder. In the associated ritual, there is a specific point at which a child participates. For Muslims, Ramadan is a solemn month. Due to the strictly lunar nature of the Muslim calendar, the first day of Ramadan starts earlier each successive year by about 11 days. From sunrise to sunset, during Ramadan, Muslims fast. This is more difficult for Muslims when Ramadan falls in the summer and the days are longer and hotter. An important Muslim festival is Eid ul-Fitr. The name translates to "festival at the end of the fast." It begins on the first day of the month following Ramadan. Families celebrate and go to the mosque together. Muslims send cards to each other to celebrate this special time. Children receive presents, similar to those received by Jewish children at Hanukkah and Christian children at Christmas. Another important Muslim festival is Eid ul-Adha. The name means "festival of sacrifice." It celebrates Abraham's willingness to sacrifice his son who, in the Muslim tradition, is Ishmael, not Isaac. This festival occurs about 70 days after Eid ul-Fitr.

As Christian children understand the basics of Christmas and Easter, Jewish children understand Passover and Yom Kippur, and Muslim children understand Ramadan and Eid ul-Fitr. All are involved in these holidays with their parents, other relatives, and members of the community. They may attend, also, weddings and funerals carried out in the traditional manner of their culture. (Muslims bury their dead within 24 hours; Jews similarly, unless the sabbath intervenes. Both Muslims and Jews have strictures against elaborate funerals and burials. Christians have no such requirements.)

As they grow up, children will be taught the moral principles of their respective religions. Every religion teaches charity for the poor and, in the twenty-first century, nearly all teach that human life is sacred, regardless of belief. Hopefully, they will be taught respect for others not of their faith, but this not necessarily the case. It is a valid concern of the New Atheists that hatred of nonbelievers and outsiders is being taught by some persons claiming a religious basis for that idea. This is no alternative to parental influence on children, unless the New Atheists can arrange for all children to be separated from their parents and raised by the state. The US government attempted that for a while with American Indian children in order to eliminate their indigenous cultures and religions; it was a contemptible process and deeply regrettable.

Even if children drop their affiliations later in life, their early association with their respective cultures will stay with them. In general, that is a good thing, unless hatred of outsiders has been taught, lies have been told about scientific findings, or the children have been sexually or otherwise seriously abused by persons in authority. Civilization is immensely enriched by these multiple traditions, but grievously hurt by mutual hatreds and suspicions. May the special practices and beliefs of each religion that do not hurt its adherents or others, or harm the environment, continue as long as people find them a positive contribution to their lives.

Those Awful Verses in the Hebrew Bible

After reading the New Atheist books, a reasonable conclusion is that these authors think that *only atheists* live in the twenty-first century. *Only atheists* accept the findings of science about the supremacy of the laws of nature, the history of the universe, and the evolution of humanity. (Daniel Dennett calls these knowing people "brights.") All other people are lumped into a category of persons of lesser understanding, regardless of whether they simply have loyalty to culture, or have limited belief and a low level of acceptance of the theologies of their respective religions. These others are stuck, according to these authors, in some century of the Dark Ages where witches fly, ghosts haunt, clergy are all-knowing, formulaic incantations and rituals prevent evil and ensure purity, the sun revolves around the Earth, and the holy books are the literal truth to be followed to the letter. Such people may be living today, possibly as the fundamentalists of every religion, but many others are far more knowledgeable about the world, and also, more understanding of the contradictions inherent in the human condition. Many of the latter engage in religious activities.

Death Penalty for Noncapital Offenses

The New Atheists and others cite passages of the Hebrew Bible that could be said to be barbarous, looking back from the twenty-first century to the time when they were first written, around 2,800 to 2,200 years ago. No question, these passages were written by persons having no sense of a government based on the consistent rule of settled law, as we understand it today. Decisions about the penalties for particular crimes in this ancient era certainly were not adopted by a democratically elected legislature. A person accused of crime did not likely face a "jury of one's peers," common today in US courts. Additionally, based on the fiats prescribing death sentences, individual circumstances were not being taken into account, so that there was no gradation of punishment according to the severity of the offense.

Several of these passages occur in Leviticus 20, in which death is the punishment prescribed for a man who curses his mother or father, commits adultery, has intercourse with his father's wife or his daughter-in-law or with another man or a beast. Death is also the penalty for a man or woman "that divineth by a ghost or a familiar spirit." Additionally, in Deuteronomy 13, death is the prescribed penalty for a "dreamer of dreams" or a relative or close friend who calls upon a person to serve other gods. Deuteronomy 21:18 ought to be the favorite example of atheists because, in that verse, death by stoning by "all the men of his city" is the penalty for a "stubborn and rebellious son who will not hearken to the voice of his father or the voice of his mother."

These passages would be worthy of concern if there were actually people today who were carrying them out under public law, or even surreptitiously. Muslims believe that the Hebrew Bible and the New Testament have a certain holiness, but the requirements therein have been superseded by their Koran. They would not carry out penalties solely prescribed by the Hebrew Bible. If some Islamic countries remain in thrall to fundamentalist practices, which appears to be the case in Iran, Saudi Arabia, and possibly others, the sources are indigenous.

The view of Christianity toward the Hebrew Bible is similar to that of Islam. The earlier book remains holy but, according to

Christian theology, certain specific requirements have been superseded by the New Testament. Christians, since the Enlightenment, would not be expected to act today on these penalties as written. This was not true in the Middle Ages in Europe, or in the seventeenth century in the Massachusetts Bay Colony. The Puritans who settled in the latter place established a theocracy. According to John Micklethwait and Adrian Wooldridge, authors of *God Is Back* (2009), "they worked hard to organize their lives according to scripture. The death penalty awaited not just murderers but also witches, heretics, adulterers and sodomites" (56). Literal application of biblical requirements in Massachusetts ended as Puritan power was reduced, partly the result of an adverse reaction to the Salem witch trials of 1692. "Puritanical" remains a useful adjective.

Jews still treat the Hebrew Bible as holy writ not superseded by any other text. If any group is to carry out its requirements today, Jews might. No evidence is provided by the New Atheists, however, that any Jew in modern times has had a relative killed because he proposed service to a different god or had his son stoned to death for being "stubborn and rebellious." Since intermarriage is not uncommon in the Jewish community in Christian-majority countries, there would be many dead prospective in-laws if this requirement was actually being treated literally. Furthermore, it is a modern Jewish interpretation that there never has been a son so stubborn and so rebellious that he deserved being stoned to death. Certainly, if these acts had occurred, there surely would have been plenty of hungry reporters, media outlets looking for sensational news, and anti-Semites to have brought the facts forward and made certain that they were well-publicized.

Ever since Judea was taken over by the Romans in 63 BCE, excepting in Israel since 1948, Jews have not lived in any country in which, by themselves, they could determine public secular law and carry out the death penalty. Since the seventh century Common Era, the laws in almost every country in which they have lived were determined by persons who were either Christian or Muslim. Thus, the biblical passages that have been cited as particularly objectionable could not have been implemented in law by Jews. Furthermore, it is a principle of Judaism that the laws of the countries in which Jews reside must be obeyed. Even in Israel today, the passages cited are not public law, because there is no death penalty in that country for offenses committed since the establishment of the state. Very different penalties, if any at all, are now assigned in Israel or in Christian-majority countries to the actions referenced in the passages. Interestingly, before the era of separation of the state from the religious establishment, attempts to convert Jews to the majority religion would have been lauded by the state, while attempts to convert from the majority religion to Judaism might have resulted in death. This is the opposite of what the author intended in Deuteronomy 13, written when Jews were a majority in their own country.

Meanings Are Not Immutable

Early in Chapter 1, it was stated that interpretations of biblical passages, called *midrashim*, have been written for over two thousand years and continue to be written to explain meanings of text. Very many verses in the Hebrew Bible have been subject to such interpretations. An interesting example is the biblical book called *Song of Songs*. Many Bible scholars have been scandalized by the overt story of a young woman's sexual awakening and her search for her boyfriend. Rabbinic interpreters and Christian exegetes alike have invented the most fantastic allegories to convert the story to asexual solemnity. As it is fundamental to Judaism that each generation must interpret scripture to fit its own circumstances, it is possible that in current times, the plain text of *Song of Songs* can be accepted for what it is. Sexual feelings are naturally human and are not sinful unless acted on inappropriately, at least in Judaism.

An Eye for an Eye

Another passage of the Hebrew Bible often cited as barbarous is from Exodus 21:23–25: "But if any harm follow, then thou shalt give life for life, eye for eye, tooth for tooth, hand for hand, foot for foot, burning for burning, wound for wound, stripe for stripe."

Sometime after the return from Babylonian exile, the concept embodied in this text was clarified by Jewish scholars. It was decided that no example of an object was identical to any other example, so that one could not exactly replace the other. As a result of this interpretation, this passage does not literally imply that if a life, or foot, or hand is lost, compensation is required by the identical loss to the perpetrator. The wording means that any compensation must be equivalent to the value of the injury and *not more than that*. Compensation, if the injury was an accident and not intentional, may be in the form of money. When the passage was written, use of money by common people may not have been widespread; if so, compensation might have been with possessions such as sheep or produce. If the injury was due to criminal conduct as defined by law, the result might be jail for the offender, assuming that the distinction between "civil" and "criminal" proceedings was understood and implemented, and assuming that the concept of state involvement and its jails actually existed when the passage was applied. In application, that could mean, for example, that if a crime does not take a life, then the death penalty is improper, since that punishment would significantly outweigh the crime. Thus the Christian interpretations in the Middle Ages as well as in Salem in the seventeenth century were their own; they were not taken from the Jewish view.

The Binding of Isaac—The Issue of Child Sacrifice

Another controversial text is the account of the binding of Isaac in Genesis 22. This story is that God first tells Abraham to offer his son Isaac as a burnt-offering. When Abraham prepares to comply and is ready to slay his son and light the fire, God, through an angel, cancels the demand because Abraham has shown that he is "God-fearing." Hitchens called the story "frightful" (206). Dawkins writes that the story is "infamous" (242). To theologians who explain that the tale is mythical to teach a moral lesson, Dawkins asks rhetorically, "What kind of morals could be derived from this appalling story?" (243). He can't imagine a rational answer.

At least one *midrash* highlights a condition in the ancient Near East referred to by Greek and Roman sources: the practice of child sacrifice to the gods by the Phoenicians. The Hebrew Bible mentions the practice in several instances, every one with a negative implication. Richard Dawkins cites the sacrifice of Jephthah's daughter in Judges 11:39 (243), but he fails to mention the very next verse, in which "the daughters of Israel went yearly to lament the daughter of Jephthah . . . four days in a year." Clearly, Jephthah's action, which occurred as a result of an oath that he had made, set no example to be followed. A *midrash* on this particular story could be that no person has the right to pledge someone else's property, certainly none as fundamental as a daughter's life.

In Micah 6:7–8, a supplicant asks whether the firstborn shall be given "for my transgression; the fruit of my body for the sin of my soul?" The response is clear: "It hath been told thee . . . what the Lord doth require of thee: only to do justly, and to love mercy, and to walk humbly with thy God." The meaning is certain: child sacrifice is not appropriate.

Psalm 106:37–40, similarly, reports that some Israelites had "shed innocent blood, even the blood of their sons and of their daughters whom they sacrificed unto the idols of Canaan." As a result, "the land was polluted with blood . . . they were defiled with their works . . . therefore was the wrath of the Lord kindled against His people."

One interpretation of Genesis 22 is that human sacrifice is unnecessary to demonstrate faith or to appease God. The sacrifice of infants to a god is child abuse to the maximum, and thus the story opposes child abuse. This is the opposite of the assertion of Dawkins and Hitchens.

Interpretations Are Fundamental in Judaism

The above discussion about the concept of interpretation in Judaism, including the examples given, should demonstrate that Sam Harris's statement that "Judaism is . . . ridiculous in its literalism" (94) is totally incorrect. The very opposite is true. If Judaism is anything, it is not literal, as has just been explained at length. Harris's statement may actually show, on the other hand, that a book concerning religion can be successful in sales and evaluations even if the author fails to demonstrate knowledge of the elementary facts of an important religion that is discussed.

CHAPTER 4

RELIGION AND THE STATE

A TYRANNOUS ALLIANCE

THE CONTINUATION OF RELIGIOUS INTOLERANCE, CARRIED OUT internationally and expressed violently, was a major reason for the authorship of the New Atheist books. Some historians see the problem in a larger context as a "clash of civilizations." This term was first used by Bernard Lewis (b. 1916), scholar of Islamic history, in an article in the September 1990 issue of *The Atlantic Monthly* (47–58) titled "The Roots of Muslim Rage." Historian Samuel P. Huntington (b. 1927) expanded on the idea with a 1993 article in the magazine *Foreign Affairs* and then with a book titled *The Clash of Civilizations and the Remaking of World Order* (1996). In this context, "civilization" is "culture" writ large, and the identification of religion as an important aspect of culture is consistent with this outlook.

The heinous activities of religious activists carried out against those who are nonadherents of their particular message may be divided into three types. The first type is historical: discrimination and violence carried out in earlier eras by empires in the course of conquest. The second type is the same type of activity carried out currently by a government against its own citizens who belong to a minority sect or religion. Both types are considered in this chapter. The third form of hostility is contemporary cross-border intolerance: that is, acts of violence, hatred, or denigration of other sects or religions, being carried out now by individuals or groups acting on their own or by governments acting across their borders. This latter type is discussed in Chapter 5.

Equal-Opportunity Persecutors

By the end of the fourth century CE, the Roman empire had become officially Christian. With political and military power as well as a defined creed, Christianity was able to implement a totalitarian policy. That is, no variant sect or wholly different religion had equal standing within its territory, and all polytheistic religions were proscribed. Centuries later, new political conditions enabled independent branches of Christianity to arise in different parts of Europe and the Middle East. Even then, almost every Christian-ruled nation made some Christian denomination its official religion.

According to its tradition, Islam originated in what is now Saudi Arabia in the early seventh century. It gained strength with the defeat of opposing local forces. Then Islamic armies began a march of conquest. Within one hundred years, Islam had spread widely, carried by military force through the Middle East, then west to the Atlantic coast of northern Africa and to Spain and Sicily. It advanced east beyond Iran to the Indus River valley (now in Pakistan) and northeast past the Caspian Sea. Muslim supremacy was established in central Asia with centers at Bukhara and Samarkand (both now in Uzbekistan).

With the establishment of nations that were officially Islamic, that religion was able to implement religious totalitarianism, similar to the Christian model. This orientation was based on interpretations of the Koran. It has statements proscribing paganism but indicating tolerance of other monotheistic faiths. However, the text has been interpreted as only permitting the existence of other religions, not their full equality with Islam. The schism that created the Sunni and Shi'a branches of Islam did not affect this basic understanding.

Within Christendom, Judaism had an ambiguous status. Its continued existence was a disputatious issue among Christian theologians. The Jews had no military power, and their possible ill-treatment depended on the whims of Christian princes, prelates, and occasional mobs incited by rumors or by preaching. Within the territories of Islam, both Christianity and Judaism had secondary status. Christianity was powerful in nearby nations, but Judaism was impotent. The treatment of Jews within the realms of the two religious behemoths forms an important aspect of intolerance in the past 13 centuries.

Both religions, when they have had military and political power, have been equal-opportunity persecutors. Other religions besides Judaism, as well as nonconforming sects of the primary faiths, have been the object of state-sponsored discrimination. In *The Jews of Islam* (1984), Bernard Lewis states the following as he looks back from the present era: "For Christians and Muslims alike, tolerance is a new virtue, intolerance a new crime. For the better part of the history of both communities, tolerance was not valued nor was intolerance condemned" (3).

Examples given below of persecution in Christendom are historical, as the influence of religious doctrine over political power in Christian-majority countries has waned as secular government has spread. Examples of Muslim intolerance are current as well as historical, as the power of religion over state action continues to be significant in many Muslim-majority nations.

Limitation of space prevents discussion of many examples of state-sponsored discrimination, such as the annihilation of the Cathars in France by Roman Catholic power in the thirteenth and fourteenth centuries and the Catholic/Protestant hostility that took place in Europe during and as a result of the Reformation. Similarly, persecution in Muslim countries against Hindus, past and present, is not covered. Muslim invaders ruled much of India, a Hindu-majority nation, from the thirteenth until the eighteenth century. A sect not discussed is the Ahmadiyya religious movement. It is under attack today in Pakistan and several other Muslim nations. Classified as an apostasy from Islam, it is either illegal or vehemently opposed by Islamic political parties or clergy. Also not discussed is the persecution of Jews in Hugo Chavez's Venezuela from 2007 to 2009. This was orchestrated to demonstrate the bona fides of that caudillo to Mahmood Ahmadinejad of Iran (see bibliographic reference by Roger Noriega).

The Disastrous Impact of Christian Anti-Judaism

The Romans Occupy Judea

A significant political occurrence that presaged the beginning of Christianity was the occupation of Judea in 63 BCE by Roman legions under Pompey the Great. Romans with their troops would be the primary power in the country for the next several hundred years. The failure of the Jews to dislodge them and to regain independence, despite revolutionary efforts, provided the conditions in which political turmoil and human misery thrived. Widely held apocalyptic theories of the time provided fertile ground for the germination of a new religion.

Pompey was in nearby Syria with his legions in 63 BCE. The excuse for his invasion was that he was invited to intervene in a Judean civil war by partisans supporting monarch John Hyrcanus II against his brother Aristobulus II. They were of the Hasmonean lineage. Pompey's forces laid siege to Jerusalem and it fell in three months. This time, the Temple was not destroyed nor was anything taken from it. Pompey allowed Hyrcanus II to retain the high priesthood, but not the kingship. Instead, he named, as governor, Antipater the Idumaean, a military leader of Judea and supporter of Hyrcanus II. The Idumaeans (Edomites of the Hebrew Bible) had been converted to Judaism in about 135 BCE. It is not clear whether their conversion was coerced or occurred voluntarily for economic advantage. If coerced, it was one of very few examples of Jewish totalitarianism in the ancient world. (Another example is the Biblically reported ethnic cleansing of 31 cities in Canaan by the Hebrews under Joshua; there is no verification of this nationalistic puffery. Other than Hazor, there is no proof of any Canaanite city, such as Jericho, being destroyed in the thirteenth century BCE, when Joshua and the Israelites supposedly entered the area.)

There was no separation of church and state at the time of Pompey—not in Judea, not in Rome, not anywhere. After Augustus (63 BCE–14 CE) became the first emperor in Rome in 27 BCE, he was also named *pontifex maximus* (chief priest), a title held by Roman emperors for the next five centuries. The name has been applied to popes. Later emperors wanted to be worshipped as deities and desired statues of themselves to be placed in temples. Efforts to mount symbols of Rome in the Temple in Jerusalem incensed the nonassimilated Jews of Judea and resulted in riots.

HEROD THE GREAT

The Roman occupation of Judea resulted in the demise of Hasmonean rule. Their ancestors, the Maccabees, had led the revolt in 167 BCE that eventually freed Judea from the rule of the Greco-Syrian monarchy. The last Hasmonean king, the son of Aristobulus II, was overthrown in 37 BCE by Herod, later called "the Great." Herod, son of Antipater the Idumaean, had been named "king of the Jews" in 40 BCE by the Roman senate. He achieved the kingship in three years with the help of Roman legions. Neither Herod's mother nor his father was Judean, and so he was mistrusted by his subjects.

As king, Herod was known for the extensive remodeling and expansion of the Temple in Jerusalem; also, he constructed the fortresses of Masada and Herodium and the city of Caesarea as a port on the Mediterranean. He murdered one of his wives, a Hasmonean princess, and three of his sons, as well as those whom he considered insurrectionists. The latter included a certain Hezekiah of Galilee and a large number of his followers; these deaths were protested by the Sanhedrin, the Jewish court. Later, he had burned to death two leaders of the crowds who tore down Roman insignia placed over the Temple gate. He died in 4 BCE.

FROM THE DEATH OF HEROD THROUGH THE GREAT REVOLT

The death of Herod resulted in violent outbreaks among forces of several pretenders to the throne and, to quote James Carroll, author of *Constantine's Sword: The Church and the Jews* (2001), "among the followers of messianic movements who sought to seize an opening against Rome" (83).

The Romans cruelly suppressed these revolts, raping, killing, and destroying. Cities held by rebels, including Sepphoris in Galilee, as well as Jerusalem, were retaken and many rebels and those suspected of rebellion were executed. The number was put at two thousand, by Roman-Jewish historian Flavius Josephus (37–100 CE). Since the method of Roman execution was crucifixion, that means that about two thousand crosses were erected, each holding a Jew who would slowly and painfully die of suffocation as his muscles failed. This scene contrasts, as Carroll notes, with the "three lonely crosses on a hill, as in the tidy Christian imagination" (83).

In the year 6 CE, the Romans combined Judea with Samaria and Idumaea. The area came under direct Roman control as the province of Judaea, with Coponius as the first prefect (not procurator). The capital was now at Caesarea, and the area was administratively ruled as a subprovince of Syria. The new governor of Syria, Publius Sulpicius Quirinius, ordered a census and assessment of Judaea for taxation purposes. This activity was greatly resented by the Jews; it triggered a revolt. The rebels stated that "this taxation was no better than an introduction to slavery," according to Josephus. The Romans eventually tracked down their leader, Judah of Galilee, and killed him.

Pontius Pilate was appointed prefect in the year 26 CE and served until 36. Paula Fredriksen, author of *From Jesus to Christ* (2nd edition, 2000), quotes the description of Pilate by Philo (20 BCE–50 CE), the Jewish philosopher of Alexandria, who lived at the same time. Fredriksen writes: "Philo describes him as a man of 'inflexible, stubborn and cruel disposition' whose administration was marked by his 'venality, thefts, assaults, abusive behavior, and his frequent murders of untried prisoners' among whom [was] probably Jesus of Nazareth" (79). Philo's description of Pilate, as reported by Fredriksen, should be contrasted with that of the New Testament, in which responsibility for the death of Jesus is deflected to the Jews.

In 37 CE, Caligula became the third emperor of Rome, succeeding Tiberias. A close friend of Caligula was Herod Agrippa, a grandson of Herod the Great. Agrippa had been schooled in Rome and had been befriended by Tiberias. In 39, Caligula named him tetrarch of Galilee. When Caligula was assassinated in 41, Agrippa assisted Claudius to achieve his accession as the next emperor. As a reward, Agrippa was given dominion over both Judea and Samaria, in addition to Galilee. He could now call himself king of an area as large as that ruled by his grandfather.

Relations between the Jews and Rome may have improved when Herod Agrippa became king. No Roman prefect was appointed. However, Agrippa died suddenly in 44, probably of natural causes; relations deteriorated. The Romans appointed a series of procurators, and a Jewish political party, the Zealots, sought independence without compromise. They drew their inspiration from Judah of Galilee, the leading opponent of the tax assessment of 6 CE. Associated with them was a group called the Sicarii (knife-wielders), who threatened assassination of the collaborators of the Romans and may have acted accordingly. At first, the seekers of independence were a minority, but with rapacious Roman procurators such as Lucceius Albinus (62–64 CE) and Gessius Florus (64–66 CE), the desire for revolt grew.

Historian Solomon Zeitlin (1886–1976), author of *The Rise and Fall of the Judean State* (*2nd ed., 1969*), has recorded the outrages perpetrated by Albinus and Florus. About Albinus, Zeitlin states, "His main object was to get money from whatever source, private or public. He also welcomed bribery in return for his favors" (227). Zeitlin quotes Josephus in stating that in comparison with Florus, the Judeans considered Albinus righteous. After a perceived insult, Florus ordered his troops to sack a market in Jerusalem, and they killed 3,600 men, women, and children. The Jewish leadership decreed that no more temple sacrifices would be offered for the Roman emperor nor would tribute be paid to Rome. In effect, in the year 65, a revolt had begun. Judean soldiers wiped out the small Roman garrison stationed in Jerusalem. Another force sent by the Roman governor of Syria was similarly destroyed. Many Jews thus began to believe that they could defeat Rome, and the Zealot ranks swelled. Again, the Roman legions came, but this time they consisted of some sixty thousand heavily armed professional troops under Vespasian. The Romans attacked Galilee first, the most radicalized region; an estimated hundred thousand Jews were killed or sold into slavery. Among the places conquered was the Jewish city of Gamla, located in what is now called the Golan Heights. (Its ruins have been excavated in modern times.) After that, the Romans reconquered all areas but Jerusalem and the fortress of Masada near the Dead Sea.

Inside besieged Jerusalem, the Jews were engaged in a civil war, with various factions murdering each other. All the more-moderate Jewish leaders who headed the government in 66 CE were dead by 68, killed by fellow Jews. There was a lull in the Roman efforts in 68 when Emperor Nero died. He had reigned since 54, when Claudius died. Vespasian returned to Rome to press his claim as Nero's successor. Vespasian became emperor in 69 and the war continued under Titus, Vespasian's son and heir. Additionally, the stockpiles of food, created by the defenders in expectation of a Roman siege, were deliberately destroyed by one of the factions in the hope that this would persuade the uncommitted to join in the defense of the city. Starvation resulted as the siege progressed.

In 70 CE, the walls were breached by the Romans and the city fell. The Romans totally destroyed the Temple, and they stole its treasures. The Arch of Titus, in Rome, records in marble the procession (called a Triumph) in which the major trophy, the Temple's golden menorah, was carried through the streets of the imperial city. Masada held out until 73. Titus had an access ramp constructed for his troops to reach its high entrance. (Its deteriorated remains are still there to be seen.) According to Josephus, the defenders committed suicide rather than fall into Roman hands and become slaves. It is estimated that more than one-half million Jews died in the Great Revolt.

The Concept of a Messiah in Judaism; Its Alteration in Christianity

The word *mashiach* (messiah) occurs 39 times in the Hebrew Bible. It refers to a person anointed with oil when assuming a high office. Thus it was applied to the king of Judah or Israel, or to the high priest, all human beings. The concept of the messianic delivery of Israel or of the Jews was understood to have occurred in the Exodus from Egypt, in which the people were led by Moses (a human); in the defeat of the Philistines by David, the warrior king (a human); and in the end of the exile in Babylon, which was facilitated by Cyrus the Great of Persia (a human). Cyrus had defeated the

Babylonians and allowed the Jews to return to Judea. The most recent example for the Jews under the heel of the Roman occupation was the regaining of independence from the Greco-Syrian monarch Antiochus IV. In that war, the people were led by Judah Maccabee (a human). Later, in 133 to 135 CE, the leader of the final revolt against the Romans, Simon bar Kokhba (a human), would be declared a messiah while there was still a chance of his success.

The Messiah in the Hebrew Bible is always a human being, never a god. He is, however, divinely inspired, leading God's forces to victory in a final battle in which the forces oppressing the Jews are defeated. In Daniel 7:13–14, the idea of the "Son of Man" is presented. These verses of the Hebrew Bible were written during the time of the revolt under the Maccabees. The "Son of Man" is recognized by God in this text and is given a "kingdom which shall not be destroyed." There is no intimation that this individual is the same as God.

The concept that the Messiah would suffer and die to atone for others' sins is not a Jewish view. Paula Fredriksen, in *From Jesus to Christ*, comments on the messiah as follows: "Like the David esteemed by tradition, the messiah will be someone in whom are combined the traits of courage, piety, military prowess, justice, wisdom, and knowledge of the Torah . . . But . . . we find in the Judaism of this period no idea that the messiah is to die to make atonement for sin" (86).

That idea of sin-atonement by Jesus appears in the New Testament, for example in Matthew 1:21. With clear distinctions between Jewish and Christian theologies, it is hardly surprising that most Jews refused to accept the new message when given a voluntary choice.

Another early Christian concept was that the End of Days was quickly approaching. This apocalyptic belief in the soon-to-come End of Days is made clear in 1 Thessalonians 4:15–17, in a letter by Paul, said to be the oldest surviving piece of Christian literature: "For the Lord himself . . . will descend from heaven, and the dead in Christ will rise first. Then we who are alive, who are left, at the very same time will be caught up in the clouds together with them to meet the Lord in the air."

Another New Testament text indicating the approaching End of Days is from Matthew 16:17–28. This text uses the idea of the "Son of Man," found not only in Daniel but in a nonbiblical document called the Book of Enoch, said by scholars to have been written about 1 CE: "Truly I tell you, there are some standing here who will not taste death before they see the Son of Man coming into his kingdom."

Soon, it would become clear that the End of Days had not arrived. Greed, lust, hatred, anger, murder, and war continued all over the Earth as before, as if nothing significant had happened to change the ways that humans treat each other. Thus it was necessary to assert that Jesus would come again, lest hope be wiped out among the Christian faithful. Jews continued to wait for a messiah appropriate to their faith.

The Anti-Judaism of the New Testament

Among the four Gospels included in the New Testament, it is generally agreed by scholars that Mark was written first, probably just after the Temple was destroyed in 70 CE. Matthew and Luke were written somewhat later, probably around 80 or 85. John was the last Gospel written, possibly in 95 or later. The writers were probably not Judeans or Galileans but, more likely, resided in Asia Minor or possibly Alexandria.

The Gospels evidence no compassion for the Jews in the ancestral homeland caught up in the catastrophic war against the Romans. The Zealots, and the attempts to throw off the Roman yoke, are never mentioned. The stories have a very narrow focus, specifically about the life of Jesus, his sayings, his healing activities, his relationships with his Apostles, the role of the Jews in Jesus's death, and his views on two of the several Jewish groups of the time, the Pharisees and the Sadducees. These parties had different theological and political orientations. "Pharisee" would become a pejorative among Christians, despite the fact that actual teachings of this group became the precursor of normative Judaism for the next eighteen hundred years. Missing is an overall picture of the political situation in Judea at that time. Indeed, one could learn very little about the contemporary history of Judea from the Gospels, and some of what little there is would be incorrect.

The situation in Judea/Galilee in the first century CE bears some similarity to other hated occupations, in particular the Nazi occupation of much of Europe during World War II. In the 1940s, there were willing collaborators such as Pierre Laval in France and Vidkun Quisling in Norway. In the first century, the Hellenized upper classes cooperated with the Romans. There were armed resistance groups at both times, as well as many other persons who didn't participate on either side. Much art and other precious items were stolen by the Nazis, just as extortion was used by procurator Albinus to enrich himself. The occupiers in both cases reacted harshly against active resisters. If there was more than one resistance entity, they may have had opposite political orientations and fought among themselves; that was the case in Yugoslavia (Chetniks vs. Partisans) in the 1940s as well as in Judea/Galilee, nineteen hundred years earlier. In France, under Nazi occupation, there were at least nine separate resistance networks, each with its own political or social orientation. In Poland, there were separate Jewish and Christian resistance groups.

In World War II, the occupation lasted only about five years, because the "arsenal of democracy," the United States, along with Great Britain and other allies, served as the messiah to free defeated populations in western and northern Europe as well as in Italy and Greece. It is ironic that General Dwight Eisenhower (1890–1969) titled his memoir of leading the Allied armed forces *Crusade in Europe* (1948). Although a fine military manager and a decent human being, Eisenhower was no academic. Having finished saving what remained of Western European Jewry from Nazism, he named his book, thoughtlessly, after the campaigns that had murdered Jewry in the same area some 850 years earlier. In Judea/Galilee, no messianic hero came to remove the oppressive, occupying force. A totally different type of messiah was envisioned in the first century by those who would be called Christians: a supernatural messiah who suffered and died as a human for the benefit of all humanity. Jews would pay dearly in coming centuries by not accepting the new set of myths to replace their own.

The fact that many anti-Jewish statements appear in various books of the New Testament is generally acknowledged by scholars, as well as by many others. For example, James Carroll, a committed Roman Catholic and a former priest, titles Part Two of his book named above as "New Testament Origins of Jew Hatred." Another book with this theme is *Jesus, Judaism, and Christian Anti-Judaism: Reading the New Testament After the Holocaust* (2002), a compendium of six articles, edited by two of the authors, Paula Fredriksen and Adele Reinhartz. Their purpose is this treatise is to dispassionately review the various books of the New Testament and examine the purportedly anti-Jewish statements. Reinhartz and two additional contributors are quoted below.

The general conclusion of the articles appears to be that many of the Gospels' statements must be seen in historical context. Original supporters of the idea that Jesus was the messiah were Jews who wanted all their coreligionists to adopt this conclusion. Thus there was an internal Jewish debate filled with vituperation, yet it was only among Jews. It has not been uncommon, at any period in history, for Jews to argue among themselves about the best or proper way to be Jewish.

When the approach to Jews failed in large measure, advocates of Jesus as messiah turned to Gentiles. Many Gentiles in the Greco-Roman world had Jewish friends, or had participated in Jewish rites and festivals, or had observed Jews at prayer without actually converting. These people were candidates for the new understanding and, with the elimination of the food-taboos and the requirement that males be circumcised, the new view prospered and became a separate religion: Christianity. The more removed the new Christians became from the culture of Judea/Galilee, the more they saw themselves as differentiated from Judaism and free to criticize it from the outside. The Gospels reflect this difference, and the last-composed Gospel, that of John, reflects it in the strongest way. In this Gospel, Jesus says to a group of Jews, "You are from your father the devil" (John 8:44). Adele Reinhartz, a dean at Wilfred Laurier University in Waterloo, Ontario, notes about this verse,

"This association of the Jews and the devil has had a long and tragic afterlife in Western art, literature, and theology" (99).

E. P. Sanders, a professor of religion at Duke University, and author of several relevant books, employs the texts of the Hebrew Bible and the New Testament in his article to demonstrate that certain longtime criticisms of Judaism are untrue. He concludes, "It is not true that Judaism was legalistic. It is not true that Judaism was a religion of wrath and vengeance, which rejected love and mercy. It is not true that Jesus opposed the essentials of Judaism. His arguments . . . measure not rejection, but commitment" (55).

Amy-Jill Levine, chaired professor of New Testament Studies in the Vanderbilt University Divinity School, includes the following in her article: "The verse that has caused more Jewish suffering than any other in the Christian Testament is the . . . cry attributed to 'the people as a whole:' 'His blood be on us and on our children!' (Matthew 27:25) . . . Christian Europe witnessed centuries of pogroms promulgated by church members, inflamed by sermons about the Jews' 'blood guilt' who rushed to Jewish homes (often in ghettos established by Christian governments) to avenge their Lord. While the violence has mostly subsided, the charge remains. I have been accused of being a 'Christ-killer'; so have my children" (91). She continues, "the scene is unlikely to have any historical basis," and she goes on to explain why.

Not pointed out by Levine is that the outburst in Matthew 27:25 attributed to the Jewish crowd is in direct contradiction to a key principle of Judaism, as enunciated in Deuteronomy 24:16: "The fathers shall not be put to death for the children, neither shall the children be put to death for the fathers; every man shall be put to death for his own sin."

The concept in that verse, that parents are not responsible for the independent actions of their fully competent adult children, is consistent with modern jurisprudence. Nevertheless, each religion has its own internal logic, constrained by its theology. For its own interpretation of Matthew 27:25, a religion that claimed to be ethical adopted the incredibly unethical view that children of later generations were still responsible for what their ancestors might have done, even 80 generations earlier. It took the enormous slaughter of the Holocaust for leaders of the Church to recognize the necessity of officially ending this monstrous doctrine.

Christianity Becomes Rome's State Religion

One result of the destruction of the Temple in 70 CE was that emperor Vespasian imposed a special tax, the *fiscus Judaicus*, on all Jews living anywhere in the empire. The tax was ostensibly for the upkeep of a pagan shrine, a humiliation for Jews who previously supported their own Temple with an equivalent amount. The tax was probably continued into the fourth century. As Christians began to think of themselves as a separate religion, they asked for an exemption. It is likely that emperor Nerva granted their wish in 96, at the same time that he abolished the practice, begun by his predecessor Domitian in about 84, of requiring persons accused of "living like Jews" to prove they were not Jews in order not to pay the tax. Exemption from the tax was another reason, besides elimination of the food taboos and circumcision, for a person to opt out of Judaism. In the United States today, all religious institutions receive tax benefits, if they qualify as nonprofit entities that do not intervene in partisan political campaigns.

However, as Christianity increased in popularity, it drew the hostility of Romans who still observed the longstanding pagan rites. Roman religion was practiced with the belief that it was necessary to respect and worship the gods properly to prevent all kinds of bad occurrences. Christians were called impious and ungodly. The Roman historians Tacitus and Suetonius, both of whom were active adults in the year 100 CE, called Christianity a "superstition," that is, it was foreign and different. There were persecutions of Christians by pagan emperors, from the reign of Nero in 64 CE through the reign of Maximinus in 312. The reason was, primarily, that Christians refused to sacrifice to the old Roman gods. Tacitus reported that, during the reign of Nero, some Christians were thrown to the lions or burned to death. In 177 CE, in the city of Lugdunum (now Lyon, France), there was general violence against Christians and 48 were killed. The conversion of anyone to either Judaism or Christianity was forbidden by Septimus Severus in 202.

In 250 CE, Decius required all citizens to sacrifice to the emperor while a Roman official watched, so that a necessary certificate could be obtained. A general persecution was instituted by Diocletian in 303: churches were torn down or burned, church leaders were imprisoned, and church property was seized. Diocletian also began the system of having two Roman emperors, one for each region—East and West.

A change in religious orientation occurred when Constantine appeared on the scene. His victory in 312 CE over rival claimant Maxentius resulted in his elevation to emperor of the western region. Constantine was friendly toward Christianity (his mother had adopted the faith) and he ended persecutions of it in his region. Modern estimates put the number of Christians killed throughout the 260 years of persecutions at approximately three thousand, yet with many others tortured, imprisoned, or exiled. The relatively small number killed is due to the fact that leaders—bishops and lesser clergy—were singled out. The massacre at Lugdunum was probably the only pogrom of believers at any time. In fact, scholars believe that far more Christians were persecuted by the Roman Empire after 312 than before, because their beliefs were "heretical."

Constantine and Licinius, the latter an emperor of the eastern region and a pagan, together signed the Edict of Milan in 313. That document granted tolerance throughout the empire to all religions—whether Christianity, Judaism, or "any other cult." However, the full tolerance implied by the Edict of Milan did not last long. In the same year, Constantine wrote to a deputy in Africa calling on him to persecute the Donatists, a Christian sect with different ideas than those held by persons close to the emperor (there was not yet an official set of Christian beliefs). In 315, Constantine issued an edict forbidding Jews the right to proselytize. This order indicated that Jews were achieving some success in attracting converts in the Diaspora, such as in Asia Minor and Egypt, despite the catastrophic second defeat in the homeland in 135. In 324, Constantine became sole ruler of the empire by finally defeating Licinius after several battles. Thus there was no longer any rival religion to oppose the power of Christianity.

Constantine, although not baptized until he was close to death, made himself head of the Church. He supported the religion financially, constructed a number of basilicas, returned property confiscated by Diocletian, and granted exemptions from taxes to Christian clergy. Pagan temples were no longer supported and their wealth gradually dissipated. Constantine called all the bishops of the empire to a conclave in 325 in the city of Nicaea. Christian theology was defined there in what would be called the Nicene Creed. The purpose was to identify an official Christian belief, in order to eliminate dissenting groups. In particular, the Creed disagreed with the views of a particular sect called Arianism, and thus its adoption permitted persecution. Additionally, the conference defined Easter so that it would not occur exactly at the beginning of the Jewish Passover.

Following the death of Constantine in 337, his several sons vied for power. Eventually, a nephew, Julian, became emperor in 361; he attempted to return the empire to paganism. However, he died in battle in 364, and there was never again another pagan emperor. Theodosius became emperor of the eastern region in 379 and, a few years later, became the last emperor of both the East and West regions. A decree of Theodosius from 379, discovered in modern times, permitted the destruction of certain synagogues in Illyria and Thrace (areas north of Greece). In 380, together with the emperor of the western region, he decreed that Nicene Christianity was to be the only legitimate religion of the empire; heresy became a capital crime. Judaism was permitted because it was monotheistic, but pagan worship was officially banned.

Views of the Jews by Early Church Leaders

In the year 388, a mob of Christians, led by their bishop, burned down the synagogue in Callinicus (now Raqqah, in Syria), a town on the Euphrates River. The destruction came to the attention of Emperor Theodosius, and he ordered the synagogue rebuilt. However, the demolition had also come to the notice of Ambrose (340–97), Bishop of Milan. He wrote to Theodosius that a synagogue is "a haunt of infidels . . . under the damnation of God

Himself." Theodosius was willing to eliminate the rebuilding, but insisted that the sacred articles of worship must be replaced. Ambrose personally confronted the emperor at a Mass in the cathedral in Milan. He stated that the destruction had been a righteous act, and that the worship service then in progress would not continue unless the emperor agreed to restore nothing. Theodosius assented and the service went on. Ambrose was canonized as a saint.

John Chrysostom (mentioned in Chapter 1) eventually became Archbishop of Constantinople. He was known for his eloquent preaching; his name means "golden-mouthed." Earlier, while serving in Antioch, he spoke against Jews and Judaizing Christians in a series of eight sermons that have come down to us. In none of these sermons does Chrysostom actually call for physical attacks on Jews, although the inference is clearly there. In one sermon, he points out that when animals are fattened, they become difficult and hard to manage; then they are ready for slaughter. "This is the very thing that the Jews have experienced," he stated (Carroll, 213). In 415, there were actual attacks on Jews in Antioch and its synagogue was destroyed. Chrysostom is venerated as a saint in major branches of Christianity.

Augustine of Hippo (354–430 CE) was a most learned man, known for his books, *Confessions* and *City of God*, and also for his views on original sin and on what constitutes a just war. He was not born a Christian but was converted and baptized by Ambrose in Milan. His origin was the Roman province of Africa, and he eventually returned there. He became bishop of Hippo (now Annaba in Algeria) in 395. He approved of the harsh policies of the Christian emperors against heretics.

Augustine's view on the Jews was in opposition to much theological opinion of the time. According to him, they should not be killed, as others proposed, but should be permitted to live. "Do not slay them," Augustine quotes from Psalm 59, totally turning around the original intent of this text. (This psalm's introduction makes clear that its subject is David, pleading with God not to slay the men of Saul looking for him.) As with other Christian interpretations of the Hebrew Bible, the original context does not matter. It is assumed by the Christian interpreter that, regardless of the particular situation and time period in which the original was written, the function of the Hebrew Bible is to serve Christian purposes.

Augustine's writings demonstrate a strong belief that the Jews killed Jesus, and that their scattering throughout the Roman empire was a fulfillment of prophecy. His desire for the Jews was "bend down their backs always." Thus they should remain alive, but not be permitted to thrive. Augustine is similarly venerated as a saint in many Christian denominations.

Implementations of Christian Anti-Judaism

It is unnecessary to be exhaustive in listing all the anti-Jewish regulations and violent actions in the Christian world from the fifth century through the twentieth. There are far too many to list them all. In many cases, the violent actions were based on incitements that Jews killed Jesus, or that Jews killed a particular child to use his blood in a ceremony (the blood-libel). The various regulations and actions against Jews over this 16-century period may be categorized as follows:

- Unconditional killings by mobs or by order of Christian authorities
- Unconditional expulsions from specific countries, provinces or cities
- Requirements to convert or be expelled
- Requirements to convert or die
- Taking children forcibly from their parents to be raised as Christians; an example, the Mortara case in Italy in 1858, discussed by Dawkins (311–15), occurred in the Papal States, where the Pope had absolute power
- Regulations requiring residence in specific ghettos, with curfews
- Regulations limiting occupations, property ownership, or citizenship
- Regulations changed in order to confiscate legitimate property or monetary resources
- Regulations limiting the right to testify in court against a Christian

- Regulations limiting the right of Jews to employ Christian servants
- Regulations requiring identification through specific dress
- Organized destruction of synagogues or holy books
- Requirements that Jews not show themselves on the streets during the week of Easter

Multiple occurrences of each of these acts can be identified.

Some of the most significant mass killings include the following, listed by year:

- 414 CE, the Jewish community of Alexandria is destroyed in a large-scale pogrom
- 629, troops of the Byzantine empire enter Jerusalem, murder Jews living there
- 1096, groups involved in the First Crusade murder many Jews in Rhineland cities when they capture Jerusalem, they murder Jews and Muslims who live there
- 1190, Jews in Norwich and York, England, are massacred
- 1212, 1366, 1391, Jews in Christian Spain are massacred
- 1236, some three thousand Jews are murdered by crusading bands in regions of France
- 1298, during a civil war, mobs under German nobleman Rindfleisch massacre thousands of Jews in what is now southern Germany and Austria;
- 1348, Jews in many European countries are blamed for the Black Death with the accusation that they poisoned wells; about 200 communities are destroyed
- 1492, in Mecklenburg, Germany, 27 Jews are burnt at the stake
- 1556, in Ancona, Italy, Jews who were baptized in Spain to avoid persecution and then fled and resumed the Jewish religion are burnt at the stake
- 1648–51, Ukrainian Cossacks under Bohdan Chmielnicki massacre thousands of Jews and Polish nobles; many Jewish communities are destroyed
- 1881–84, pogroms sweep Russia, resulting in mass emigration, mostly to the United States

- 1903, in a pogrom in Kishinev (now Chisinau, Moldova), 49 Jews are murdered
- 1938–45, about 5.5 to 6 million Jews are killed by deliberate efforts mounted by the Nazi government of Germany, with roundups aided by collaborators in some conquered countries
- 1946, in a pogrom in Kielce, Poland, 37 Jews are murdered and 80 wounded

A Final Word

James Carroll has commented with great insight about Augustine's ambivalent view that Jews should survive but never thrive. Carroll has written, "For a thousand years, the compulsively repeated pattern of that ambivalence would show in bishops and popes protecting Jews—but from Christian mobs that wanted to kill Jews because of what bishops and popes had taught about Jews" (219).

Christianity Complicit in the Destruction of Distant Cultures—The Case of the Maya

In the fifteenth and sixteenth centuries, Christian nations of Europe, in particular Portugal and Spain, began the age of exploration and conquest. One of the pope's priorities at that time was conversion of pagans into Christians, even if that occurred by conquest followed by a choice of conversion or death. The pope gave specific permission for non-Christians to be enslaved by Christian conquerors. Clearly, Christianity's desire for more adherents ignored the methods by which they might be obtained. Thus Christianity must accept responsibility both for its facilitation of destruction of indigenous cultures of Africa and the Americas and for the delivery of many of those continents' inhabitants to slavery or to toiling for the benefit of new European masters. In fairness, Islamic theology did not oppose slavery, either, and it will be seen that non-Muslim monotheists under Islamic law would be treated as second-class citizens. Both religions have much to be ashamed of, in particular, for blessing their governments for the undertaking of actions which, by today's standards, would be called crimes perpetrated in God's name.

Of particular poignancy is the conquest of the Yucatan peninsula, now in Mexico and Belize, which, along with the neighboring country of Guatemala and a small area of western Honduras, is the homeland of the indigenous people called the Maya. By the time of the Spanish arrival in the sixteenth century, the Maya were well beyond their most advanced period. They were the only people of the New World to have a written language. King-lists and their dates are found incised into many vertical surfaces, such as walls or *stelae* (stone pillars). The Maya wrote many books that revealed their astronomical knowledge and religious myths. Books were in the form of connected panels made of deerskin that could be folded compactly, in the style of an accordion.

Most Maya lived in organized towns, each of which had a central plaza and stepped, pyramidal temples. The temples at Tikal, built in the eighth century, were the tallest structures in all the Americas until steel-frame buildings began to be constructed in the late nineteenth century. At Palenque, craftsmen carved the marvelous cover of the coffin of ruler Pacal, who was buried in a crypt inside a stepped pyramid. At Uxmal, their architects built an unusual pyramid with rounded sides. At Chichen Itza, the Temple of Kukulkan (El Castillo) is constructed for a particular display on the spring and autumn equinoxes, at the rising and setting of the sun. At those times, the corner of the structure casts a shadow such that the sun highlights the sculpture of Kukulkan, their mythical plumed serpent, along the west side of the north staircase. At Bonampak, Maya artisans drew magnificent murals. All of these, fortunately, remain for our education about the remarkable capabilities of these early exemplars of human progress. The Maya were also fine astronomers and had a very interesting calendar. Many of their myths were related to the planet Venus, whose motions in the sky they had studied extensively.

It is true that the Maya engaged in human sacrifice, which resulted in denigration of their religion by the Spanish invaders who, in their own country, murdered nonconformists by binding them to stakes, building fires under them, and letting them roast to death. Perhaps it was only the *method* of killing (slicing open the chest and removing the beating heart) that was objectionable to European murderers. Europeans and their American cousins have spent much effort since the late eighteenth century researching and devising efficient methods of killing individuals sentenced to death. There was, first, the guillotine of the French Revolution, then the electric chair, then the mass-murdering gas chambers at Auschwitz-Birkenau, then individual gas chambers for the condemned following trial, and recently, the lethal injection. Modern methods aim to achieve death without the spilling of blood. Neatness is, after all, next to godliness.

Following the discoveries of Columbus for Ferdinand and Isabella, "the Catholic Monarchs," Spain sent settlers to the islands of Cuba, Hispaniola, Jamaica, and Puerto Rico. According to Charles Gibson, author of *Spain in America* (1966), "Spaniards established themselves in the Caribbean islands as ranchers and slave owners, the masters of native Indians and imported Negro populations" (24).

The Spanish were content with these colonies alone until 1519, when the attempt began to bring the mainland population under their control. Hernan Cortes and his small band of adventurers were successful in conquering the Aztecs of what is now Mexico. This tribe had subjugated other tribes in the vicinity, which was their temporary glory and ultimate downfall. The *conquistadores* were able to defeat the Aztecs for several reasons:

- They had muskets and horses, neither of which had been seen by the indigenous people that they met.
- The Indian spears could not kill at a distance; the Spanish muskets and crossbows could do that.
- The Spaniards cleverly enlisted the aid of native peoples who had been subjugated by the Aztecs to provide the necessary manpower to equal the Aztec forces. The Aztecs were not peaceful; they were warriors who conquered others and then were conquered themselves.
- The Spaniards built boats and attacked by crossing the lake that protected Tenochtitlan, the city of the Aztecs (now Mexico City). It was a tactic unexpected by the defenders.

The Yucatan peninsula is at the southeastern border of Mexico. (That nation runs more east and west than is commonly understood.) To its east is the Caribbean Sea, and to the peninsula's north and west is the Gulf of Mexico. The largest city, Merida, is due south of New Orleans, across the width of the gulf. In 1527, Francisco de Montejo, who had served in previous Spanish expeditions, began the conquest of the Yucatan, having obtained a Crown charter the previous year. With his soldiers, a surgeon, two pharmacists, and three priests, he explored the area and determined that it held no gold, silver, or precious stones. The territory could support only certain types of crops, and its land was a limestone shelf containing no rivers. Fresh water was obtained primarily at *cenotes*, wells at points where there were holes through the hard crust. Some of these *cenotes* were holy to the Maya, and they prayed there and submitted offerings to various gods.

The Maya sporadically fought the invaders, and despite their fear of the Spanish horses, muskets, and great mastiff dogs trained for war, they gave a good account of themselves. One Maya disadvantage was that they were not unified, although all of them spoke the same language. Each city was separate, although there were alliances and family ties among them, as well as hatreds. In 1535, the Spanish departed, realizing that they would not make their fortunes there. However, they returned in 1540 with a different aim, that of settlement. Inga Clendinnen, author of *Ambivalent Conquests: Maya and Spaniard in Yucatan, 1517–1570* (2nd edition, 2003), relates the Spaniards' thinking on how they might live successfully from the labor of the local Indians: "The [native women's] intricately embroidered cotton garments now spoke to more chastened men of a raw material, local technical skill, and the chance of a commercial product tuned to European needs. Honey, wax, indigo, cacao, all suggested the possibility of a modest but useful trade. Above all . . . the enslavement of the native population was the most promising road to profit" (29).

The Spaniards laid out four cities, including Merida, still a provincial capital. The Maya organized attacks on the Spaniards coincident with the building of the first two cities, but were beaten back. The Maya then resorted to a "scorched earth" policy. They fouled their own wells, tore up their corn plants, and fled to the jungles. They planned to deny the Spaniards the benefits of conquest. The invaders responded with viciousness: they destroyed villages still intact "and massacred or enslaved their inhabitants," according to Clendinnen. In one particular area, "the Spaniards pursued deliberate policies of terror." In late 1546, the Maya again coordinated a large attack on the eastern side of the peninsula. Some Spanish families were seized and slaughtered. Very soon, the Spaniards developed a plan for counterattack. They authorized the Maya of the western side of the land to enslave any of the revolters that they could capture. This was consistent with Maya views of warfare. By the spring of 1547, the revolt had been squelched. Many Maya were now slaves, and several priests of the Maya religion were burnt at the stake.

In pursuit of settlement, Montejo parceled out native towns to each of his worthy followers, in a system called *encomienda*. This process established plantations, such as might have been found in the American South before the Civil War. Each *encomendero*, or plantation owner, had the right to exact tribute and labor from the natives living within his assigned area. The natives were "his" to assign responsibilities to meet his requirements, but his duty was also to protect them and ensure their welfare.

The conversion of the Maya to Christianity was assigned to the Franciscan order by the Spanish Crown. Diego de Landa (1524–79) was an important figure in this effort. Sent to Yucatan as a friar, he became Provincial of the Franciscan order in Yucatan and Guatemala, and then Bishop of the Archdiocese of Yucatan. His fervent actions, filled with violence against practitioners of the indigenous religion, remain a major aspect of his reputation. While much of our knowledge of the Maya comes from his own book, *Account of Things in Yucatan* (ca. 1566), he burned as many Maya books as he could find. Clendinnen quotes him on this subject: "These people also make use of certain characters or letters, with which they wrote in their books their ancient matters and their sciences . . . We found a large number of these books . . . and as they contained nothing in which there was not to be seen superstition and lies of the devil, we burned them all, which they regretted to an amazing degree and which caused them great affliction" (70).

In 1562, the discovery of a cave in the town of Mani containing Maya idols and human skulls was the primary source of an orgy of whippings of thousands of Indians by the Franciscans led by Landa. To the Maya, caves may be holy as entries to the underworld. The Maya explained that ceremonies in the cave were to bring rain, cause crops to grow, and guarantee success in hunting deer. Landa established an Inquisition in which the following occurred, according to Clendinnen: "More than 4,500 Indians were put to the torture . . . and an official enquiry later established that 118 had died . . . as a direct result of the interrogations. At least thirteen people were known to have committed suicide to escape the torture" (76).

It has been argued that the result of Landa's fervor to exterminate the Maya religion had the opposite effect. This is perhaps partially true, since certain Maya beliefs and practices have been mixed into Christianity as it is practiced in the Yucatan.

JEWS AND CHRISTIANS UNDER MUSLIM RULE

Origin of Islam

Muhammad (570–632 CE), the founder of Islam, was born in Mecca, now in Saudi Arabia. It must be noted here that revisionist historians dispute the traditional story of Muhammad and Islam's founding. The initial development of Islam, according to them, is discussed by author Nicholas Wade in *The Faith Instinct* (2009) in his Chapter 7, "The Tree of Religion."

In the traditional history, Muhammad began to preach his revelations in 612, which he said were from God (*Allah* in Arabic) through the angel Gabriel. His message was controversial in pagan Mecca, and he seemed to be in danger there. Fortunately for his future, he was approached by men from Yathrib, a city 200 miles to the north, soon to be called Medina, short for *Medinat al-Nabi* (the City of the Prophet). They had heard of his reputation for integrity, and they asked him to come to Yathrib to settle disputes among various factions. An agreement was made under which

Muhammad, as well as his family and supporters, emigrated in 622 and were given protection in the new city. This relocation, called the Hegira in English (Hijra in transliterated Arabic), marks the start of the Islamic calendar. (According to the revisionist history, 622 was originally important because it was the year of a definitive defeat of the Persian Sassanian empire by the Byzantines. The defeat of the Sassanians freed the Arabs from their yoke. The Byzantines decided not to retain Arab territory, totally freeing them from foreign domination. Later, Islam adopted that year as its founding date.)

With the arrival of Muhammad, the number of his supporters began to grow, and they were known as Muslims (people who have submitted to God). Muhammad wrote a constitution for Medina that solved the problems for which he had been called to the city. This formal document placed all the various groups into one community called the *umma*. There were Jews in Yathrib, as well as many pagans. The constitution stated that "The Jews have their religion and the Muslims theirs." In effect, Jews were to be accepted, provided they did not actively oppose the *umma*. Only monotheisms were permitted, and pagans were required to convert. From 624 to 627, battles raged between Medinans led by Muhammad and the Meccans. Muhammad and the Muslims of Medina emerged victorious.

There were three Jewish tribes in Medina that supported the Meccans in the conflict (and therefore opposed the *umma*). Two were given the option of conversion or expulsion, and the third was supposedly given the option of conversion or death. The first two were expelled in 625 and the third, consisting of some six hundred to nine hundred people, was possibly eliminated in 627. According to one tradition, the third tribe, the Banu Qurayza, refused the option of conversion and chose death. The men were killed and the women and children sold into slavery. Other scholarly opinion is that this murderous outcome did not happen unless there no option had been given. It seems unlikely that men would willingly die while allowing their wives and children to become slaves. What is certainly true is that, some time later, Muslim leaders decided that no non-Muslims would be allowed to live in the holy region of the Hijaz, the area along the Red Sea coast including both Mecca and Medina. All Jews and Christians were expelled.

Thus as with Christianity, a serious conflict arose between Jews and the founding members of a new religion that became powerful and could be said to have descended from the older faith, or at least have taken some concepts from it. However, unlike Christianity, Islam did not turn this violence into a theological imperative dictating an unquenchable Jew-hatred. Following the initial conquests, when Islam found many non-Muslims under its jurisdiction, all persons were divided into two categories: believers and unbelievers. Judaism, Christianity, and Zoroastrianism (the ancient Persian religion) were identified as religions of unbelievers. However, these religions could be tolerated because they were monotheisms. There was no hierarchy among them; they were equally inferior to Islam.

The Dhimma—Second-Class Citizenship

Under Islamic law, the relationship between the state and unbelievers was regulated by a pact—in Arabic, *dhimma*. The unbelievers are called *dhimmis* in English-language texts. The content of the pact had its origin in the Koran and was not subject to negotiation. In accordance with it, the *dhimmis* were protected by the state, provided that they recognized their second-class status with respect to Muslims, and paid a yearly tax called a *jizya*. *Dhimmis* could accept the pact or be killed or expelled.

Establishment of the *dhimma* was consistent with the Islamic idea of justice. The concept that one class of persons, however identified, was superior to others would remain unchallenged for another millennium in the West as well as in the East. Then, a new political philosophy arose in the West, resulting in the revolutionary announcement of 1776 that "all men are created equal." Back in the seventh century and for another thousand years, severe consequences could affect *dhimmis* if they violated the pact, and it was considered justice that Muslims were not to violate the pact, either. Various Muslim rulers interpreted the pact in different ways.

Public indications of their inferior condition were required of *dhimmis*. At various times and places, these restrictions were minimal; in other cases, they were harsh. Typically, male *dhimmis* were required to go unarmed in a society where Muslim men were armed; they could not ride horses but could ride donkeys. *Dhimmis* could not wear certain types of clothing, hats, and shoes worn by Muslims. They had to wear, also, emblems identifying their religion on their clothing. They were not permitted to actively pursue petty attackers—typically children or teens—who would throw stones or mud at them. Bernard Lewis cites reports of visitors to Muslim lands in recent times who observed such attacks, including a physical attack on a handicapped woman, to which no response was made. *Dhimmis* could not build new places of worship, only restore old ones. Restored churches or synagogues could not be higher than mosques. Public displays of the religion of unbelievers (such as holiday celebrations or funeral processions) were not permitted. Under the Ottoman Empire, *dhimmis* could not give their babies certain names, such as David and Joseph, spelled in a particular way. The spelling was required to be somewhat different than that allowed for Muslim children.

Apostasy out of Islam was punishable by death, for Muslims or for *dhimmis* who had converted previously. If a Jew who had converted to Islam wanted to revert, it would be safer for him to go to a Christian country to do so, but to one where Judaism was permitted. Apostasy from Christianity was, similarly, a capital offense in some Christian countries, including those Spain and Portugal. In those countries, Jews who had converted to Christianity, usually forcibly or under duress, often fled to Islamic countries to resume being Jewish. Others left for the Netherlands, when asylum in that country became possible (e.g., the family whose descendants would include philosopher Baruch Spinoza).

In addition to the distinction between Muslims and *dhimmis*, there was, in Islamic society, a social distinction between men and women much stronger than in modern Western culture. (An example of this is seen today when the Taliban, a Muslim fundamentalist force, attempts to close schools for girls.) Free Muslim women were required to veil their faces in public. Enslaved or *dhimmi* women, in some cases, were not permitted to veil in order both to distinguish them and to make the point that they were socially inferior and lacked the virtue of free Muslim women. Thus *dhimmi* women were more likely to be harassed. Muslim men could marry *dhimmi* women, but *dhimmi* men could not marry Muslim women. *Dhimmis* could not own Muslim slaves, and a *dhimmi* slave owned by another *dhimmi* could obtain his freedom by converting to Islam. The court testimony of a *dhimmi*, if allowed at all, was not given much credence. Payments granted by a court to a *dhimmi* victim for wrongs done by a Muslim were likely to be less than if the same wrong was done by a *dhimmi* to a Muslim victim.

Insults against Islam by *dhimmis* were treated as significant crimes. Writings by Muslims on this subject considered the proper punishments for various levels of this offense. Penalties might be flogging or death, depending on the severity and repetitiveness of the evil speech or writing. Thus there is a strong religious source in the signs "Death to those who insult Islam" carried by Muslims in protest against the caricatures of Muhammad printed in a Danish newspaper in 2005. The *fatwa* (religious decree) issued against author Salman Rushdie in 1989 by Iranian Ayatollah Khomeini had a similar theological origin.

Under Shi'a Islam, which became the official religion of Iran, the issue of the impurity of *dhimmis* was and continues to be important. Centuries ago, impurity began to include the concept of uncleanliness. Application of inherent *dhimmi* uncleanliness required that Jews not go outside while it was raining. Theology inculcated a general fear among the Muslim populace that the rain would wash off dirt from Jews and pollute Muslims with whom they came in contact. Roya Hakakian, an Iranian Jewish refugee and author of *Journey from the Land of No* (2005), relates how her father was not allowed to go to school when it rained, and how this problem was resolved for him, individually. Bernard Lewis reports in *Jews of Islam* that a book by Ayatollah Khomeini published in the early twentieth century states that unbelievers are unclean, just like ten other items, including feces, pig, and dog (34). "The entire body of the unbeliever is unclean," wrote Khomeini, who became the Supreme Leader of the Iranian theocracy in 1979. With this background, the complaint by other Jewish refugees from Iran, that Muslims refused to shake hands with them, becomes more understandable.

INVADING ARMIES, CHANGING RELIGIONS, MOVING POPULATIONS

In the Middle East and North Africa

When the Roman empire became enforceably Christian in the late fourth century, believers in pagan religions found themselves abandoned by authorities. Indeed, public rituals of pagan religions became criminal acts, and these religions died out. Asia Minor, the Middle East, and north Africa, which had been mostly pagan, became Christian. When Islamic forces, primarily Arabs, conquered the Middle East and north Africa in the seventh and early eighth centuries, the Christians faced a somewhat similar dilemma to that which they had imposed on the pagans three hundred years earlier.

Many Christians converted to Islam; they had no personal experiences of being second-class, and did not wish to be *dhimmis* and pay a tax. (The conquest of Christian lands by the Arabs and Berbers and, later, other lands in the Balkans by the Ottoman Turks, followed by the conversion of much of the population to Islam, is ignored by Al Qaeda in its constant reiteration of Christian aggression in the Crusades.) Slowly, in the Middle East and north Africa, Christianity became a minority, with small pockets of believers in the territories known in the present day as Iraq, Syria, Lebanon, Palestine, Israel, Jordan, and Egypt. (The temporary reconquests by the Crusades may have added to that population.) Christianity disappeared from north Africa west of Egypt. Jews lived in all these regions, also. They had experienced persecution under Christianity and, while some converted to Islam, it was simply an exchange of masters for those who kept the faith.

In Iberia

In 718 CE, Muslim armies, having crossed the Strait of Gibraltar from north Africa, completed their conquest of most of the Iberian peninsula (now Spain and Portugal). The native population in the area was primarily Christian at that time. The occupying force was smaller than the native population, and a considerable Christian presence remained. In addition, there were Jews in Iberia when the Muslims invaded. Of course, members of both religions became *dhimmis* under Muslim rule, but the Jews welcomed the Muslims because they had been severely persecuted by the Christian Visigoths whom the Muslims had defeated. That persecution had involved forced conversions as well as required baptism of any children born of mixed marriages.

During the first three centuries of Muslim rule (718–1031 CE), the Jews were well-treated if the *jizya* was paid. Additionally, there was an influx of Jews from other lands where their treatment was harsh. It was a time in which there was an interchange of ideas among members of the three monotheisms, leading to a flowering of knowledge in several fields, and respectable publications in medicine, philosophy, and poetry. Translations of literary works from Greek, Arabic, and Hebrew into each of the other languages, and from all of them into Latin, provided the basis of the Renaissance, several centuries in the future. A major city in which this occurred was Cordoba. After the end of the Caliphate of Cordoba in 1031, even though Muslim control remained, the position of the Jews became less assured. In 1066, there was a massacre of some four thousand Jews in Granada, including Joseph ibn Naghrela, who had served as the vizier to the local Muslim monarch.

Christian-controlled territory had not totally disappeared in Iberia during the Muslim conquest; it had continued in the north of the peninsula. The *reconquista* began in the eleventh century; Toledo was retaken in 1085. Soldiers of the Almoravides, a Muslim dynasty then in control in what is now Morocco, arrived in 1090 to assist the Muslim cause. At first, the Almoravides persecuted the Jews in Muslim Iberia, and there were enforced conversions. However, their rule became more relaxed and, for a time, several Jews served as diplomats and physicians to the Almoravid leadership. Later, that dynasty was displaced by the Almohads, who controlled most of Muslim Spain by 1172. The Almohads were severely fundamentalist. Properties of *dhimmis* were confiscated, forced conversions occurred, and some *dhimmi* men were killed and their wives and children were sold as slaves. Most Christians departed for areas controlled by members of their faith.

Similarly, Jews emigrated to the Christian areas of Spain in the late twelfth century because their treatment there was then better than in Muslim areas. Nevertheless, mass murders took place, such as in Christian Toledo in 1212. Cordoba fell to the Christians in 1236 and Seville in 1248. Only Granada remained in Muslim hands in the late thirteenth century. Many Muslims in areas reconquered by the Christians emigrated back to north Africa. In the fourteenth century, conditions worsened for the Jews in Christian Iberia. Significant massacres occurred in 1366 and 1391, in many cities of the peninsula. Acceptance of baptism saved many from death. The fifteenth century was a continuation of the fourteenth in its violence and persecutions. Granada fell to the Christians in 1492. In that year, all Jews who had not converted to Christianity were expelled from Spain; Muslims were expelled soon after, and Arabic became a forbidden language. Jews were expelled from Portugal in 1496.

In the Ottoman Empire

The center of the Ottomman empire was Anatolia, the name given to the area that is now central Turkey. Longtime residents of this region, while mostly Muslim, are not Arabs nor are they Arabic-speakers. They are descendants of tribes that emigrated west from central Asia; their language is related to languages spoken in that part of the world. The empire began in the late thirteenth century, arising in a Muslim emirate in western Anatolia. This state was ruled by Osman I, whose name has been corrupted to form "Ottoman." Osman extended his control to the borders of the Christian Byzantine empire by 1300. The latter empire was past its prime and was ripe for conquest. By the middle of the fifteenth century, the Ottomans had captured the important city of Thessaloniki (also known as Salonika, now in Greece) as well as other locations in the southern Balkan peninsula. The Byzantine empire was essentially reduced to its capital city, Constantinople. That city fell to the Ottomans in 1453. Its name was eventually changed to Istanbul.

With the severe persecution of Jews in Spain and Portugal, and their respective expulsions in 1492 and 1496, many Jews emigrated to the Ottoman empire. Even after 1496, many Jews came, including those who had feigned conversion and departed later in fear of the Inquisition. (That holy body was constantly on the lookout for secret Jews to torture and kill.) Jews came from Germany and France, as well as from Spain. Immigrant Jews were desired by the Ottoman sultan. One reason was that he wished to provide a counterweight to the Christians in his empire. The Christians were treated suspiciously because of the existence of Christian countries nearby that were the major Ottoman enemies. The Jews would certainly have no loyalty to those nations.

An unusual aspect of the Ottoman empire was that the leadership could enforce transfer of groups of residents from one city to another without their prior agreement. This process affected settled groups with particular skills, as well as immigrants. Places in which new settlers were wanted were often those recently captured from Christian control. Salonika, Cyprus, and Rhodes are examples. Many Jews were directed to Salonika. At one point, some Jews in Safed (now in Israel) were told to resettle in Cyprus. This order was later cancelled; Turkish peasants from central Anatolia, who were ranchers, were actually sent there.

The Ottomans showed some tolerance in dealing with the *dhimmis* under their control. They developed and put into place a legal system called the *millet*. Under this scheme, each ethnic or religious minority was allowed to manage its own affairs with significant independence from central control. Minorities included Armenians, Greeks, Jews, Egyptian Christians, and others. A disadvantage of the system for the Ottoman government was that these minorities failed to develop loyalty to the state. In the nineteenth century, the *millet* system served as a conspiracy center for nationalists who wanted independence or at least more autonomy for their particular minority.

Ottoman forces conquered the Balkans, including most of Hungary, by 1526. They laid siege to Vienna, but were driven back. Most of what is now Romania and Moldova became tributary about twenty years later. About the same time, Ottoman control also extended west from Egypt through an area that is now Libya, Tunisia, and Algeria. The middle of the seventeenth century was the height of Ottoman expansion; after that, the empire declined. Vienna was besieged again in 1683, but again the Christians held. The downward spiral of the empire continued into the eighteenth and nineteenth centuries. Serbia revolted, beginning in 1804, and was confirmed to be independent in 1830. Greeks revolted and achieved independence of part of what is now Greece in 1829; they obtained more territory later, for example, Salonika in 1912. Wallachia (now in Romania), Moldova, and Montenegro achieved independence in the late nineteenth century. Algeria and Tunisia came under control of the French, and Egypt under the control of the British.

With the return to Christian dominance, laws of Muslim supremacy through the *dhimma* were cancelled. Within the Ottoman empire, the *dhimma* was abolished by a *ferman* (edict) of 1856 and further ensured by a new national constitution in 1876. These reforms were partially the result of pressure on the Ottoman government by the "Great Powers," Great Britain, France, and Russia. These countries wanted Christian subjects of the Ottomans to be treated equally with Muslims.

After the end of World War I in 1918, the Ottoman empire collapsed (as did monarchial rule in Russia, Germany, and Austria-Hungary). After several years of strife, a new government of the former empire, called the Republic of Turkey, was formed in 1923. A purely secular state was instituted, headed by Mustafa Kemal Ataturk (1881–1938). Attempts by groups with an Islamic orientation to return the government to *sharia* (Islamic law) remains a continuing threat.

Ottoman Persecution of the Armenians

A relevant situation within the Ottoman empire was the severe Armenian persecutions of 1894–96 and 1915–17. Some scholars classify the later persecution as genocide, although the Turks protest that it was not carried out as official Ottoman policy. Armenia, an early national adopter of the new Christian religion in the fourth century, came under Ottoman rule in the fifteenth and sixteenth centuries. While some Armenians lived in cities, and a few had risen to high positions in the Ottoman government, most lived in the countryside. In rural areas, Armenians were persecuted by the local Muslim community. They were subject to exploitive taxation, kidnappings, and enforced conversion to Islam.

The position of Armenian residents of the Ottoman empire worsened as a result of the Russo-Turkish War of 1877–78. Their home territory in the Caucasus region was close to the Russian border. Armenians were looked at as traitors, supporters of the Christian enemy. In 1890, Ottoman Sultan Abdul Hamid II created a paramilitary unit known as the *Hamidiye* that was instructed to "deal with the Armenians as they wished." Some massacres resulted immediately. In 1895, a large group of Armenians assembled in Constantinople to petition the government for reforms, but the rally was broken up by the police. Soon after, there were nationwide attacks on Armenians. This situation, known as the Hamidian massacres, resulted in the deaths of about two hundred thousand Armenians.

World War I, which began in 1914, again saw the Russian Tsarist empire and the Ottoman empire on opposite sides. The former was allied with Britain and France, and the latter with Germany and the Austro-Hungarian empire. Again, Armenians under Ottoman rule were accused of being in league with the Russians. There appeared to be a nationwide effort to eliminate the Armenians. Among the methods used were (1) forcing Armenians onto boats that were sunk in the Black Sea, (2) attacking Armenian villages, during which residents were herded into buildings and burned to death, (3) instigating forced marches of thousands of Armenians into the Syrian desert, where they died of starvation or heat prostration, and (4) shipping Armenians crammed into railroad cars to extermination camps. Estimates of the number of Armenians killed varied, but six hundred thousand appears to be a minimum. Other estimates suggest one million were murdered. Adolf Hitler is said to have admired the Turkish methods. He is reported to have said that no one would remember the pogroms against the Armenians, and he used some of the procedures against the Jews and Gypsies.

Exodus of the Jews from Arab Countries and Iran

The emigration of most of the Jews from Arab countries and Iran began in the late nineteenth century. Most of the emigration occurred from 1948 to 1972. The 1948 population of Jews in these countries was about 950,000 (according to the World Organization of Jews from Arab Countries, WOJAC) while the 2004 estimated population was less than 8,000. In Iran (not an Arab country), the 1948 Jewish population was estimated at 120,000 while a 2008 population estimate was 21,000. Much Iranian emigration occurred in 1979 and soon after. Destinations for Jewish *émigrés* from Arab countries and Iran have been primarily Israel (about 85 percent), France (about 7 percent), United States (about 5 percent), as well as Canada, Brazil, Argentina, and Spain. A discussion of the causes of this Jewish hegira follows.

The decline of the Ottoman empire, beginning in the late seventeenth century, was symptomatic of a general alteration in the relative strengths of the Christian states of Europe versus the Muslim states of western Asia and north Africa. The later the date, the more the economies and standards of living of Europe improved over those outside that continent. The relative standards of living of the Jews in Muslim lands declined, along with the Muslim and Christian populations, but even more so. The difference was due to the increasing importance of the economic interactions between the two major blocs. While Jews who had relocated from Christian countries had an initial advantage in pursuing international commerce, that advantage ended after several generations. Many Ottoman Christians began to have better European connections. Furthermore, European Christians preferred to do business with Ottoman Christians. Where the Europeans had influence or importance, appointments of Ottoman Christians rather than Jews to positions of negotiation and financial interaction were preferred. (There were no laws of fair employment practices in those days.)

Hostility to Jews appeared to increase in Muslim lands from the late eighteenth century onward. Christians had protectors from powerful European countries; Jews had none. Massacres of Jews occurred in several cities of Morocco in 1790, 1859, and 1880; in Algeria in 1805; in Safed in Ottoman Palestine in 1834; in Meshed, Iran, in 1839; in Sfax, Tunisia, in 1864; and in Barfurush, Iran, in 1867. Survivors of the Meshed massacre was forced to convert. Iranian Jews were severely persecuted until a change in the ruling dynasty in 1925.

In the nineteenth century, the ancient charge that Jews used the blood of Christians for rituals surfaced in the Arab areas of the Ottoman empire. Bernard Lewis stresses the source of this vicious calumny: "From the 1860s onward, there was an ominous growth of European-style anti-Semitism among the Christian communities of the [Ottoman] empire" (170). "European consuls and traders . . . were . . . active in the spread of certain classical themes of anti-Semitism—for example, in the introduction of the blood libel, and in conjuring up fantasies of Jewish plots to gain world domination" (185).

Sources report 30 major accusations of the blood libel in 16 cities of the Ottoman empire, from 1840 to 1902. The most prominent was the first one, the Damascus blood libel of 1840, widely reported internationally. In this case, a Franciscan friar had disappeared, and the French consul in Damascus, Syria, promoted the theory that the Jews had killed him and used his blood in a ritual. Despite the fact that there was no physical or even circumstantial evidence whatsoever, 13 members of the Jewish community, several of them prominent, were arrested and tortured. An international outcry and a personal visit by prominent Europeans to the ruler of Syria (who resided in Egypt) resulted in the freeing of nine who remained alive.

The end of World War I, which witnessed the collapse of the Ottoman empire, had put Britain in colonial possession of Iraq, Palestine, and what is now Jordan. The British also retained their suzerainty in Egypt. France obtained colonial control of Syria and Lebanon, and retained its previous control of Tunisia, Algeria, and Morocco. Hostility to Jews increased further in these countries. Perhaps it resulted partially from the increase in anti-Semitism in Europe in the late nineteenth century and its continuing increase in the twentieth. For example, the anti-Semitic fiction *Protocols of the Elders of Zion*, published in St. Petersburg in 1903, was republished in Arabic in Cairo in 1927. In 1929 in Hebron in British-mandated Palestine, a massacre by Muslims of 67 Jews occurred, in revenge for insults to Islam that were rumored but untrue. In 1934, in Constantine, Algeria, a pogrom was carried out against the Jews by a Muslim mob, although some courageous Muslims did what they could to protect their Jewish neighbors.

In 1933, Adolf Hitler was elected Chancellor of Germany and by 1935 he had achieved total power as Fuhrer. Soon, he made an alliance with Mussolini's Italy. World War II began in September 1939 when Hitler invaded Poland; Britain and France, supporters of Poland, responded with a declaration of war. Nationalistic hopes were raised in the Arab countries that were colonial possessions of Britain and France. Furthermore, Hitler's murderous anti-Semitism raised the fears of Jews in Arab countries to new heights, as they believed that local Muslims would envision Jews as favoring their British and French overlords.

With the defeat of France in 1940, the pusillanimous and servile Vichy government that signed the armistice implemented anti-Jewish regulations in France's north African colonies: Morocco, Algeria, and Tunisia. In Algeria, citizenship of Jews was cancelled and their property confiscated. However, Muslims were told in their mosques not to participate in the stealing of Jewish property. Jews who joined the anti-Nazi underground but were found out were sent to labor camps or executed. In Morocco, the courageous Sultan Muhammad V protected Jews from Vichy predations. (Recall that the setting for the famous movie *Casablanca* is Morocco during the Vichy period.)

In Libya, which was under Italian suzerainty, the Nazi occupation, beginning in 1941, resulted in depredations against Jews. Adult Jewish men were sent to forced labor camps where thousands died of hunger and epidemics. The Libyan occupation was part of Hitler's plan to capture the Suez Canal and the oil wealth of the Middle East.

Tunisia was occupied by Nazi-led troops in November 1942 when the Americans and British landed their forces in Morocco and Algeria. At that very time, British General Montgomery was defeating German General Rommel and his *Afrikakorps* at El Alamein in Egypt. The Germans began their westward retreat through Libya to Tunisia. Until the Nazi defeat and surrender of many troops in Tunisia in May 1943, Jews were treated as their coreligionists were in Nazi-occupied Europe. Jewish property was seized, some Jews were shot in their homes, and about five thousand Jews were sent to forced labor camps where more died. A Nazi roundup of Jews on December 9, 1942, has been recently commemorated in Paris.

In Iraq, under nominal British control, a pro-Nazi coup d'etat in 1941 was staged with the connivance of the Grand Mufti of Jerusalem, Amin al-Husayni (1893–1974), then living in Baghdad. With the support of this new government, there was a two-day premeditated *farhud* (pogrom) beginning on June 1, in which about six hundred Jews were killed. Over five hundred Jewish-owned businesses were looted and about one hundred Jewish-owned homes were destroyed. However, the coup leaders were soon turned out by British forces, who returned the monarchy to power. The Grand Mufti fled to Berlin, where he arranged for the raising of a Muslim military regiment from the Balkans to support Hitler's forces. After World War II, he was permitted to depart to Cairo, where he died a natural death. Other attacks against Jewish communities between 1941 and 1948 occurred in Aden, Egypt, Syria, and Yemen. Bernard Lewis has discussed this period, writing that "hundreds of Jews were killed or injured, while far greater numbers found their homes destroyed, leaving them homeless and destitute. All these events preceded the establishment of Israel" (190).

With the vote of the United Nations in 1947 to partition the British mandate of Palestine into two states, along with the establishment of Israel in 1948 in accordance with the UN decision, the position of Jews in Arab countries became even more precarious. WOJAC has reported that a resolution adopted by the Arab League in 1949 ordered Arab governments to facilitate the expulsion of Jews living in their countries. It is asserted also by WOJAC that Jewish property abandoned in Arab countries would be valued at more than $300 billion at 2007 prices.

Reasons for the departure of Jews include those relating to all countries as well as specific ones relevant to each country. The general reasons were (1) increased nationalism and Islamic intolerance, conditions that generated a widely held view that Jews were a foreign element that needed to be eliminated, and (2) the establishment of Israel and its victories in the wars of 1948, 1956, and 1967 against Arab armies. Reasons specific to each nation included, in Iran, the establishment of a Muslim theocracy in 1979 and, in several other countries, the denial or withdrawal of citizenship and limitations on employment. In other countries, there were specific attacks and bombings directed against the Jewish community as a whole, and arrests and hangings aimed at specific members of the community in order to frighten the rest. In Iraq, following the *farhud* of 1941, Jews were targeted for violence, persecution, boycotts, confiscations, and near-complete expulsion in 1951. Privately chartered aircraft facilitated the community's departure to Israel at that time. In Yemen, after Israeli independence, there was a similar airlift. In several countries, permission for departure was conditioned on the reversion of all property to the state, or an equivalent that amounted to the same thing in the end.

The number of Jews remaining in Muslim-majority countries, as of 2007, was approximately 77,000. Most of these were in Iran, Uzbekistan, Turkey (all three non-Arab countries), and Morocco.

CURRENT PERSECUTION OF CHRISTIANS IN EGYPT

The Christians of Egypt are known as Copts. About 90 percent are members of the Coptic Orthodox Church, but 10 percent are members of various Christian denominations, for example, the Roman Catholic Church. Christian church families or groupings found in Egypt, within which are denominations, include Oriental Orthodox, Eastern Orthodox, Eastern Catholic, and Protestant. The Coptic Orthodox Church is a denomination of Oriental Orthodox. With regard to the number of Copts in Egypt, one source says that the Coptic population is "less than ten percent" while another states that the 6 percent of the population that is not Sunni Muslim is either "Coptic or other." Other sources claim a Coptic population of up to 15 million, but eight million is more likely. The total population of Egypt is about eighty million.

Muslims conquered Egypt in the seventh century. Since then, their Muslim rulers have alternated between toleration and persecution of the Copts. The worst period of history for Copts was the Mameluke era of 1250 to 1517. While the *dhimma* was abolished in 1856 because Egypt was part of the Ottoman empire, full equality is not yet a fact. A resurgence of anti-Coptic feeling has occurred over the past several decades. Since 1972, several Coptic churches have been burned, and Islamist groups frequently denounce Copts in pamphlets and prayer meetings. There were three days of interreligious riots in Cairo in 1981 that left at least 17 people dead and more than one hundred injured. Sporadic violence of a similar type has continued to the present. On September 2, 2010, American and Canadian Copts peacefully demonstrated at the White House to protest a visit of Egyptian President Hosni Mubarak. The organizers claimed that "Mubarak brought Coptic persecution to the level experienced under the Mamelukes."

In early May 2011, after Mubarak's fall, Christians in the Imbaba district of Cairo reported that they were assaulted by Muslims who also looted and burned two churches. It was reported that 12 Copts were killed. A Coptic bishop was quoted as saying, "These things are planned. We have no law or security . . . One rumor burns the whole area." It is believed, with justification, that the attacks are being organized and carried out by Salafi Muslims whose political arm is the Muslim Brotherhood. They want Egypt to be ruled under *sharia*, Islamic law. See Chapter 5 for a discussion of Salafi Islam.

The website of the US Copts Association lists 19 demands that, if satisfied, would bring to the Copt population equality with Muslims in Egypt. Among the conditions claimed to exist now in Egypt are the following:

- There is no freedom to change one's religion. Christians are welcome to become Muslim, but Muslims who attempt to convert to Christianity "are usually subjected to imprisonment and torture."
- Permission to repair churches, even to repair a leaky toilet, requires the signature of the president of the country; mosques have no such restrictions.
- Religious affiliation is required to be listed on national ID cards and on job applications.
- There is a 5 percent quota on Coptic enrollments in police and military academies, "and this percentage is not even met by actual enrollment."
- Government-controlled media are conducting a campaign of hate against Christians, labeling them as infidels, "thus creating a climate of intolerance."
- There is discrimination against Copts in job appointments and promotions, particularly in public sector positions and in the educational establishment.
- There is discrimination in criminal justice proceedings. Muslim perpetrators of crimes against Copts receive lighter sentences than those meted out to Coptic perpetrators of similar crimes against Muslims.
- There have been cases of forced conversion of Christian girls who are kidnapped and raped by Muslim extremists. "There are reports of police protection given to the abductors."

Current Persecution of the Baha'i Faith in Iran

The Baha'i Faith began in Iran with an individual originally named Mirza Husayn 'Ali Nuri (1817–92). He took the title of Baha'u'llah, meaning Glory of God, in the course of his life. He declared that he was the "Promised One" of all religious traditions. That is, he claimed that all religions envisioned the coming of a new divine messenger or messiah-like person, and that he was that person for all religions. Religions cited include Judaism, Christianity, Shi'a Islam, Sunni Islam, Zoroastrianism, and Babism. The latter is the precursor of the Baha'i Faith, having been founded by Siyyid 'Ali-Muhammad of Iran (1819–50), who called himself "the Bab," meaning "the Gate." Later, Baha'u'llah would be associated with messiah-like figures from Hinduism (the final avatar of Vishnu) and Buddhism (the future Maitreya Buddha).

Thus the Baha'i Faith attempts to combine related aspects of leading religions. Its core principles are the unity of God (monotheism), the unity of religion, and the unity of humankind. To quote a short description from the official website (http://www.bahai.org), Baha'is maintain that "Throughout history, God has revealed Himself through a series of divine Messengers, whose teachings guide and educate us and provide the basis for a the advancement of human society . . . Baha'u'llah, the latest of these Messengers, brought new spiritual and social teachings for our time."

From the very beginning of their faith, Baha'is were persecuted in Iran; the Iranian clergy concluded that the new religion was an apostasy of Islam. For them, Muhammad was the final messenger of God; there could be no other. In traditional Islam, apostasy is a capital crime. In fact, the Bab was executed and many of his followers were murdered. While Christianity, Zoroastrianism, and Judaism are considered lawful religions in Iran, the Baha'i Faith has no standing whatsoever. Baha'u'llah was imprisoned in Tehran in 1853. Soon, he was expelled to Baghdad in the Ottoman empire. During that period, he declared his claim to a divine mission and gained the allegiance of most of the followers of the Bab. Believers started to call themselves Baha'is. In 1868, he was banished by the Ottoman Sultan to a penal colony in what is now Akko, Israel. Some years later, he was permitted to live in a home near Akko, even though still a prisoner. He died in 1892 and is buried at that house. Baha'is have erected their headquarters building, the Universal House of Justice, in Haifa, Israel, not far from Akko. The Shrine (and tomb) of the Bab is also in Haifa.

The Baha'i Faith is persecuted in Muslim-majority countries in which Islam is the official religion and apostasy is a crime. These countries include Iran and Egypt. There are 350,000 Baha'is in Iran, but their major population center is India, where there are 2.2 million adherents. There are about 150,000 Baha'is in the United States and some 6.5 million believers worldwide.

The most severe persecution has been in Iran because of the fierce fundamentalism of its Shi'a clergy and their significant and longstanding influence over public policy in that country. Starting in the late nineteenth century, they declared Baha'is to be enemies of God. Mob attacks and public executions resulted. In the twentieth century, Baha'i institutions as well as individuals were targeted. According to the Wikipedia entry on "Baha'i Faith," in the city of Yazd in 1903, more than one hundred Baha'is were killed. Baha'i schools were closed in the 1930s and 1940s. Baha'i marriages were not recognized, and Baha'i texts were censored.

An anti-Baha'i campaign, approved by the Iranian government, began in 1955, with messages on national radio stations and in official newspapers. Baha'is were portrayed as economic threats and supporters of Israel and the West. Following the Islamic Revolution in 1979, over two hundred Baha'is were executed through 1998. These have included members of two Baha'i National Spiritual Assemblies. The homes of Baha'is are regularly ransacked; members of the faith have been banned from attending universities or holding government jobs. Several hundred believers have received prison terms for participating in study circles, or for other trumped-up reasons. Reports indicate an increase in persecution since Mahmoud Ahmadinejad became Iran's president.

In May 2008, seven leading Baha'is were arrested and have been continually held since then. The defendants' lawyers had difficulty in getting to see them, and even in gaining access to the courtroom in which they were tried. The seven were convicted in August 2010 and sentenced to 20-year terms. The charges included "propaganda activities against the Islamic order" and spreading "corruption on earth." On August 26, 2010, US Secretary of State Hillary Clinton expressed "deep concern" over religious persecution in Iran, specifically addressing the recent convictions of the seven Baha'i leaders. "The United States is committed to defending religious freedom around the world," she stated, "and we have not forgotten the Baha'i community in Iran." In early 2010, Iranian authorities arrested ten more Baha'i leaders.

Countering Current Persecutions

Only international pressure can influence national governments to stop oppressing religious minorities. As the United States presses autocratic countries toward democracy, it ought to include separation of church and state in its objectives.

CHAPTER 5

CONTEMPORARY INTERRELIGIOUS CONFLICTS

TERRORISM BY ISLAMIST GROUPS

ABOUT ONE HUNDRED TERRORIST ATTACKS HAVE BEEN carried out from 1993 through 2011 by nongovernmental groups claiming an Islamic basis. (This discussion excludes attacks on the armed forces of the United States in Iraq and NATO in Afghanistan.) The primary instigator has been Al Qaeda, its affiliates in North Africa and the Arabian peninsula, and other groups, such as Lashkar-e-Taiba, a Pakistani group; Army of Islam in Gaza; and Abu Sayyaf, active in the southern Philippines. Most of the attacks have occurred in countries that are almost totally Muslim. Attacks in these countries have specifically targeted different groups on various occasions and may be categorized as follows:

1. Assaults against other Muslims who were members or supporters of the local national government
2. Attacks specifically targeting adherents of a different sect or ethnic group of Islam
3. Attacks targeting local citizens who were Christian; Pakistan's Minister for Minority Affairs was assassinated in March 2011
4. Attacks directed against local citizens who were Jewish; these have occurred in Morocco, Tunisia, and Turkey
5. Assaults against citizens of Christian-majority nations who were visiting or working in these countries; victims have included tourists, journalists, employees of private companies, military personnel, diplomats, and other government workers

Christian-majority countries in which Islamist terrorist attacks have occurred include Argentina, Kenya, Netherlands, Philippines, Spain, United Kingdom, and United States. The apparent intention of the attackers in many of these incidents is to kill as many people as possible, targeting non-Muslims deliberately but not restraining themselves if Muslims might die also. The attack in Argentina targeted the Jewish Community Center in Buenos Aires. The latest data from the international crime-fighting organization INTERPOL suggest that the attack may have been carried out by Iranians. The several assaults have varied in their effect, from the one person shot dead in the Netherlands (movie-maker Theo van Gogh) to the nearly three thousand killed in the United States on September 11, 2001.

In the 9/11 attack carried out by Al Qaeda, persons of many different religions (including Muslims) working in the twin-towered World Trade Center were murdered. A vicious lie was publicized by the Lebanese terrorist group Hezbollah, repeated by a small, radical black group in the United States, that Jews were responsible for the attack and that Jewish workers were notified not to come to work that day. (This fantasy has been adopted by anti-Semitic conspiracy theorists; see below under "Worldwide Anti-Semitism.") The 19 hijackers of the four planes were Arabs, mainly with Saudi passports, and about 10 percent of those killed at the World Trade Center were Jewish, consistent with the percent of Jewish population in commuting distance of that place of work. US intelligence agencies began to search for Osama bin Laden, the leader of Al Qaeda. On May 1, 2011, US Special Forces, under the direct order of President Barack Obama, attacked a compound in Abbottabad, Pakistan, where Osama bin Laden and some members of his family were living. Bin Laden was killed and his body was taken with the returning US forces. After his body was identified with certainty, it was dumped into the Indian Ocean.

In the United States, besides the audacious 9/11 attacks planned overseas and carried out by nonresidents, there have been a number of murders that appear to have been perpetrated by American-resident Muslims. These include the July 2006 attack on the Jewish Community Center in Seattle, the February 2007 mall attack near

Salt Lake City that killed five persons, the June 2009 attack on the military recruiting center in Little Rock, and the November 2009 killing of 13 military personnel at Fort Hood, Texas.

Several intended attacks have been foiled by passengers on airplanes and by government intelligence efforts in the United Kingdom, the United States, and other nations. In December 2010, an intended attack in Copenhagen on the Danish newspaper that published the controversial cartoons in September 2005 was foiled in a cooperative effort by Danish and Swedish authorities. The Swedish effort was concentrated in Malmo, close to Denmark across the narrow strait leading to the Baltic Sea. Malmo has been, also, the scene of attacks on Jews by local Muslim immigrants. It has been reported that Jews, who form a very small percentage of the Swedish population, no longer feel safe in Malmo.

Hindu-majority India was the victim of a major attack on November 26–29, 2008, in which the terrorists landed on the shore at Mumbai, having come by sea from Pakistan. The purpose of the 2008 attack, organized by Lashkar-e-Taiba and not by the Pakistani government, was possibly to provoke a war between India and Pakistan. There is credible evidence that certain agents of the Pakistani intelligence agency (ISI) assisted the development of data on targets to attack. Assaults were mounted against two major hotels, the city's main railroad station, a hospital, a café, and other facilities. About 164 people were murdered. The home of the only nonnative rabbi in the city was deliberately targeted; he and his wife were killed. Their son was saved, due to heroic actions of their nanny, a local resident. Several assaults on the same city by Muslim terrorists had occurred previously, including one in 1993 that killed 257 people. A more recent attack on July 13, 2011, was carried out with three carefully placed bombs that exploded in crowded locations, killing 17 people. The perpetrators are unknown.

Jewish-majority Israel was beset with murderous suicide attacks until it built its border fence and, since then, has been and continues to be subject to attacks by Hamas from Gaza and Hezbollah from Lebanon, both clients of Iran. In March 2011, a bomb blast in Jerusalem killed one and wounded many others. In August 2011, armed men from Gaza attacked civilians near Eilat in southern Israel. Attempting to retaliate, Israeli forces mistakenly killed several Egyptian soldiers. Increased political difficulties with Egypt have resulted.

THEOLOGICAL UNDERPINNING: SALAFI ISLAM

In 1776, Thomas Jefferson wrote, in the Declaration of Independence, that "We hold these Truths to be self-evident, that all Men are created equal, that they are endowed by their Creator with certain inalienable Rights, that among these are Life, Liberty, and the Pursuit of Happiness."

At roughly the same time, a religious man living in what is now Saudi Arabia was teaching and writing with a very different orientation and from a very different background. He was Muhammad ibn Abd al-Wahhab (1703–92). As an influential religious scholar in his home town, he decreed that an adulteress should be stoned to death, but he was forced to flee by an opposing chief. He settled in a nearby town with the approval of its ruler, Muhammad ibn Saud. A pact was made between the two in which the teachings of the cleric were to be implemented in all land under the control of ibn Saud and his descendants. By 1922, ibn Saud's family had taken control of all of Saudi Arabia, and the country's name still includes the family name. As a result, what is known in the West as Wahhabism, an extreme form of Sunni Islam, is the official religion of that country. The two families of ibn Saud and ibn Abd al-Wahhab remain close; members of the latter have served recently in the government and with the national religious establishment, which is closely tied to the government.

A major point of the theology developed by ibn Abd al-Wahhab is that Islam must return to the form of the faith practiced by the first three generations of Muslims, meaning that practiced in the seventh century. This form of Islam is called Salafiyya, or Salafi Islam. The Arabic word *salaf* means "forefather," and the first three Muslim generations are referred to as the *Salaf as-Saaleh*, meaning pious forefathers. The beliefs of this branch of Islam are uncompromising. Its doctrine states that nearly all interpretations of the Koran written after the first three generations are "innovations," known in Arabic as *bid'ah,* and are null and void. A tenet is that apostasy from Islam requires a death sentence for the apostate. Furthermore, according to Salafi doctrine, Christians are polytheists; polytheism is a sin called *shirk,* and Allah will not listen to the prayers of polytheists. This view is the same, with different religions, as that put forth a few years back by a former president of the Southern Baptist Convention, who stated that "God does not listen to the prayers of a Jew."

Recent money from Saudi Arabia has expanded the Wahhabi presence in many countries. In Pakistan, the hostility of Wahhabism toward the Sufi strain of Islam is documented by William Dalrymple in *Nine Lives* (130–41). Wahhabis have actively opposed Sufi use of music and dance in rituals and in their permission for women to attend rites. Sufi shrines have been blown up by the Taliban, who have adopted an ideology similar to Wahhabism.

Freedom House, an American nonprofit located in Washington, D.C., published a report in 2005 titled *Saudi Publications on Hate Ideology Invade American Mosques.* The report details specific passages in documents obtained at mosques in the United States that are filled with hateful characterizations of both non-Muslims and non-Salafi Muslims. The concern is that Muslims living in the United States are receiving print materials as well as religious instruction that are filled with shockingly intolerant descriptions of Christians, Jews, and others, which could result in religious conflict as well as home-grown terrorism. According to a report by the British Broadcasting Corporation in late 2010, the same sort of hate material, primarily directed at Jews, exists at mosques and *madrassas* in the United Kingdom.

The importance of Salafi Islam as a political force was furthered in Egypt in 1928 with the establishment of the Muslim Brotherhood. A founder was Hassan al-Banna (1906–49). He was appalled by the many signs of foreign military and economic domination, for example, the Suez Canal Company, run by the British. With al-Banna's organizing skills, the movement became large and influential. The Egyptian government disbanded it in 1948, putting many members in jail, following indications that it was planning a coup. A Brotherhood member assassinated the prime minister soon after, and al-Banna himself was assassinated by unknown gunmen in early 1949. The latter murder was carried out, possibly, on orders of the government or by extremists who disagreed with his opposition to assassination as a political tool.

An important Egyptian theoretician of the movement was Sayyid Qutb (1906–66). A prolific author, he visited the United States in the period 1948 to 1950 on a scholarship, and was horrified by his understanding of the nation as one filled with materialism, lack of faith, un-Islamic individual freedoms, and "animal-like" mixing of the sexes. He particularly disliked the freedom of women, and abhorred their ability to initiate divorce or contest divorce initiated by their spouses, not possible under Islamic law (*sharia*). He never married. In 1952, after he returned to Egypt, the monarchy was overthrown by young military officers. The Brotherhood initially supported the coup, but became opposed with the failure of the secular military to institute *sharia* as the law of the nation. Qutb saw everything un-Islamic as evil and corrupt. His writings were seen by the Egyptian government as dangerous and, after a show trial, he was executed by hanging.

Osama bin Laden was born in Riyadh, Saudi Arabia, in 1957 and was raised as a devout Salafi Muslim. His father was a wealthy businessman with close ties to the Saudi royal family. Bin Laden was active in the war against the Soviet invasion of Afghanistan, using his inherited wealth to finance the resistance. When Iraq, under Saddam Hussein, invaded Kuwait in 1990, the government of neighboring Saudi Arabia felt threatened. The Saudis invited American troops into its territory, and the war to remove the Iraqis from Kuwait was organized from there. Bin Laden broke with the Saudi government on this issue, saying that non-Muslim troops in its territory profaned holy soil. He migrated to Sudan, continued to oppose the Saudi government, and, within a few years, saw his native country cancel his citizenship.

In Sudan, bin Laden became associated with a terrorist organization called Egyptian Islamic Jihad (EIJ). Ayman al-Zawahiri, born 1951 in Egypt, became its leader in 1991. Trained as a physician (as was Che Guevara), he had been arrested by the Egyptian government following the assassination of Anwar Sadat in 1981. He served three years in prison for dealing in weapons. In 1995, EIJ attempted to assassinate Egyptian President Hosni Mubarak, but the attempt failed. The organization was expelled from Sudan and, in 1996, bin Laden left for Afghanistan. Al-Zawahiri, who became his second-in-command, left with him. They were in Afghanistan or in Pakistan through April 2011. The Mubarak government became more suspicious and tyrannical following the assassination attempt. Its increased suppression of civil rights was partly responsible for its overthrow by mass public protests in February 2011.

In 1998, bin Laden and al-Zawahiri coissued a *fatwa* (religious decree) that declared that the killing of North Americans and their allies was an "individual duty for every Muslim" in order to "liberate the al-Aqsa Mosque [in Jerusalem] and the holy mosque [in Mecca, Saudi Arabia] from their grip." The *fatwa* was issued in the name of the World Islamic Front for Jihad against Jews and Crusaders. The implications are clear: all individuals (including women and children) are at risk if they are Jews of any nationality or if they are Christians ("Crusaders") who live in any NATO-member country. Another statement of bin Laden established, for his followers, the four primary enemies of Islam: heretics, Shia Muslims, America, and Israel. (Shia Islam is the official and majority religion of theocratic Iran; Shiites are a majority also in Iraq.) Al-Zawahiri has been named the new leader of Al Qaeda following the death of bin Laden.

It is worthy of note that Mecca, Saudi Arabia, is cited for required "liberation," as, obviously, Mecca is within a totally Muslim country. A theory behind this, according to Salafi Islam, is that the world is divided into two areas: *Dar al-Islam* (the territory of Islam) and *Dar al-harb* (the territory of war). *Jihad* (struggle) must be waged against the latter, where the *jihad* is not just persuasion, but includes armed action. Furthermore, *Dar al-harb* is itself divided into two parts: the far enemy and the near enemy. This concept was promoted by Muhammad abd-al-Salam Faraj (1954–82), an Egyptian terrorist and theorist. The far enemies are the "Jews and Crusaders" while the near enemies are those Muslim countries, such as Egypt and Turkey, in which *sharia* law is not the national law. Inclusion of Saudi Arabia in the latter category, even if its law is close to *sharia*, simply recognizes the necessary dependence of Saudi Arabia on the West as its very important crude oil customer and its cooperator in efforts against dangerous neighbors and terrorists, such as Iran and Al Qaeda.

Christian Prejudice and Violence against Muslims

Three major sources of anti-Muslim rhetoric and actions exist both in the United States and in Europe. First, there is the inherent xenophobia of a native population that finds people with a different culture settling nearby. These new residents may have a darker skin or hair color; they practice a different religion with a different holy language; they want to build a different type of structure for worship, and they may have variant beliefs about the relationships between men and women or parents and children. They may wear somewhat different clothing, such as head scarfs. It is apparently difficult if not impossible for some resident individuals of the more settled culture to identify the peaceful majority of the newcomers from the violent minority.

A second source is the belief by evangelical and some other Christians that their religion is the only true one and that Islam is not only false but dangerously so. Islam is seen as particularly threatening since it is worldwide and is the official religion in many nations. It has more than one billion adherents. This understanding, translated into missionary zeal, may generate hate against an increasing Muslim presence along with actions to eliminate this cause of perceived spiritual pollution. The Anti-Defamation League (ADL) has reported that Pat Robertson, the well-known evangelical preacher, stated "We have to recognize that Islam is not a religion. It is a worldwide political movement bent on domination of the world." Actually, Al Qaeda and its associated organizations are a very small fraction of Islam.

A third source has been the violence that is perpetrated by terrorists claiming an Islamic basis, and thus is a concern based on reality. In Europe, the transit system bombings that caused significant losses of life in London and Madrid have had an effect on Christian attitudes. The same is true in the United States after the 9/11 attacks. Fear has been furthered with the additional murders by Muslim perpetrators at various locations as well as dissemination of information on arrests of several persons planning to carry out violence who were, fortunately, discovered beforehand.

The Norway Massacre

On July 22, 2011, there were two explosions in the office buildings of the Norwegian government in its capital city, Oslo, that killed eight persons. Later that day, a gunman arrived at a summer camp for teenagers established by Norway's ruling Labor Party. Wearing a policeman's uniform to gain entry, he systematically murdered almost seventy people. Police captured the gunman at the camp, and he admitted to setting the bombs in Oslo. He was not a Muslim terrorist, as initially suspected. The person arrested was Anders Behring Breivik, a Norwegian of typical local ancestry. He admitted to being the murderer, and claimed to have acted from a Christian perspective. None of the people he murdered were Muslim; they were all Christian or of Christian heritage. In a manifesto posted on the Internet, he strongly opposes Muslim immigration to Norway, a view not held by the Labor Party. He believes that, unless stopped, there will be "a certain Islamic takeover of Europe to completely annihilate European Christendom." The manifesto claimed that Breivik was the founder of a modern Knights Templar organization, and that there were other cells including similar-minded persons. Whether these cells really exist is questionable. The ultimate determination of Breivik's mental state at the time of the crimes, that is, sane or insane, will determine his future type of incarceration.

Anti-Muslim sentiment is rife in Europe but, in general, it has been lawful and not murderous. In Sweden, according to an article in *The New York Times* of July 24, 2011, a man was arrested in Malmo in 2010 for a series of shootings of immigrants, including one fatality. That rampage was apparently the sole work of the arrestee. Security services in Europe and the United States have been so focused on Islamic militancy that Christian extremism has been ignored. The Norwegian police were totally unprepared to quickly respond to the summer camp massacre.

Actions in the United States

One result of the 9/11 attacks was a spate of individual assaults by Americans against mosques, individual Muslims, or persons perceived to be Muslims either because of their "foreign" names or appearance, or because they were wearing clothing believed to be of Muslim culture. Due to the perpetrators' ignorance, at least one Sikh wearing a turban was mistakenly attacked. A second outcome has been the establishment of several anti-Muslim organizations in the United States and western Europe. In the latter, an organization called Stop Islamization of Europe has been formed, and it has an equivalent in the United States, Stop Islamization of America (SIOA). Another organization with a similar agenda in the United States is ACT! For America. SOIA was a leader in the effort to try to stop the approval for construction of a Muslim community center near the site of the 9/11 attack in lower Manhattan, New York City. Local residents in other parts of the country have similarly attempted to prevent mosque constructions, even though the planned buildings met all the zoning and other statutory requirements.

The pastor of a small church in Gainesville, Florida, called for an "International Burn a Koran Day" on September 11, 2010. The pastor was dissuaded by a phone call from a high official of the US government. The plan had, through its dissemination over the Internet, offended Muslims in Iraq and Afghanistan. General David Petraeus, then head of all US forces in Afghanistan, was concerned that the public burning of copies of the Koran would put American lives in jeopardy. The burning was cancelled, but that was temporary. On March 20, 2011, the pastor and several associates subjected the Koran to a mock trial and burned it. American news media refused to carry the story but Afghan President Hamid Karzai revealed it on March 31. The next day, a mob in the city of Mazar-i-Sharif, Afghanistan, attacked a UN Assistance Mission in retaliation. At least thirty people were killed, including seven UN workers.

Irrational Fear of Sharia

A fear expressed by anti-Muslim activists is that *sharia* will be forced on an unwilling American population. As an example of this concern, some people in Oklahoma instituted a ballot initiative to ban *sharia* from being considered in state courts. The measure was approved by 70 percent of voters in the general election of November 2010. In Tennessee, similarly, a bill was submitted to the state legislature to ban *sharia*. It was worded to limit civil rights for those who even discuss *sharia*. Newt Gingrich, former speaker of the US House of Representatives, expressed the fear, in a speech in 2010, that an American judge might attempt to apply *sharia*. It appears that the First Amendment to the US Constitution is unknown to these people.

Christian Anti-Abortion Violence

While most "pro-life" Christians are law-abiding and nonviolent, there are a few who have attempted to kill or maim abortion-providing physicians and their staff members and to assault and vandalize their facilities. In the United States, since 1993, the National Abortion Federation, a providers' organization, reports that the persons killed in these attacks include four doctors, two clinic employees, one security guard, and one patient escort. Additionally, since 1977 in the United States and Canada, there have been 17 attempted murders, 153 cases of assault or battery, three kidnappings, and 383 death threats against abortion providers. The most recent high-profile murder occurred in Wichita, Kansas, on May 31, 2009. Dr. George Tiller was killed with a handgun at close range. Tiller was known to perform late-term abortions and was killed in the church he attended, while serving as an usher. The perpetrator was caught, tried, convicted of first-degree murder, and sentenced to imprisonment without parole for 50 years.

Crimes against abortion clinic properties since 1977 (as differentiated from crimes against persons) have included 41 bombings, 173 arson attacks, and 100 attacks with "stink bombs." There have been, also, many incidents of bomb threats, vandalism, and trespassing. Other countries in which such attacks have occurred include Australia and New Zealand. In 1994, the US Congress enacted the Freedom of Access to Clinic Entrances Act to prevent blockades, and to strengthen laws against violent threats, assault, and vandalism. Democrat Bill Clinton was president at the time, and signed the law.

Overzealous Christian Proselytization

Some years ago, Gary Lamston, mentioned in Chapter 1, was sitting in his office at work in a large, bureaucratic organization when another employee (let's call him Donald) walked in uninvited and sat down in the spare chair. Donald, an engineer, proceeded to tell Gary that it was important that he convert to Donald's brand of Christianity lest Gary go to hell when he dies. Gary politely told him "no, thanks" and the conversation ended soon after. Gary later found out that Donald had also approached another colleague, a Roman Catholic, with a similar story. Gary was puzzled about this, since Roman Catholics also believe in Jesus, but apparently not exactly in the manner approved by Donald's sect.

Not too long before his wife, Susan, passed away, Gary was walking in the local mall when he was accosted by a young woman with an eastern Asian countenance. The woman bluntly asked him to tell her what religion he professed. In most cases, Gary would be afraid of this type of approach, fearing a physical attack, but since it was in a well-lit public place with many people nearby, he responded. He was naively curious about what the woman wanted. "Jewish," he said. "Well, then," said the woman, "if you don't believe in Jesus, you will go to hell when you die." After that verbal assault, the woman stated that she was a member of the local Korean Baptist Church, as if that was enough of an explanation. So it wasn't a physical attack against his life, it was only a verbal attack against the content and meaning of his life. Again, Gary demurred politely and walked away.

Soon after Susan died, obituaries for her were published in metropolitan newspapers. A few days later, Gary received two handwritten letters addressed to him at his residence. They were from ladies who were totally unknown to him and did not live in his local community. They were members of separate Seventh Day Adventist churches and they had a similar message. If Gary was lonely or sad, he could receive solace by contacting them. Since the obituaries made clear that Susan and Gary had a large family to fall back on and that Susan was Jewish, the approach made little sense. It was the prospect of conversion that had driven the letters' authors. Gary felt violated. His private grief had been invaded with the object of personal gain by outsiders. He made no response and his anger eventually subsided, to be filed away with prior hurts that remained in the back of his mind.

It is not known whether Gary's experiences with evangelists are similar or dissimilar, compared with attention that other non-Christians have received. What is clear is that some Christian denominations actively pursue converts with little regard for the sensitivities of those whom they target. When the perspective converts are members of an established religion, the approach must include, either explicitly or implicitly, a denigration of that faith. Evangelists claim for Christianity some special content and access to the Spiritual World not possessed by the mark's current religion. Thus, this effort is hostile, regardless of the disclaimers of those who sponsor the evangelization.

In 1974, 2,400 Christian leaders from many nations attended the Lausanne Congress (in Switzerland) convened by a committee headed by Dr. Billy Graham (b. 1918). They formed the Lausanne Committee for World Evangelization (LCWE) and wrote a document describing their purposes, called the Lausanne Covenant. The text includes the following: "every person, regardless of race, religion, colour, culture, class, sex or age, has an intrinsic dignity because of which he or she should be respected and served, not exploited ... We affirm that evangelism and socio-political involvement are both part of our Christian duty."

It is a tribute to the enormous capacity of humans for self-deception that the contradiction between respect for every person's "intrinsic dignity" on one hand, and a "Christian duty" for evangelism on the other, is not understood by the writers of that document.

In 1989, the same group met in Manila, Philippines, and issued a new manifesto. This document asserts, with clear certainty, the correctness of Christian theology, and also states, unequivocally, that: "We affirm that other religions and ideologies are not alternative paths to God."

It appears that evangelicals, without being openly hateful, are so filled with their arrogant correctness—that is, the sin of pride—that they sponsor efforts to tell adherents of other religions that they are wrong and must convert before they die, or else. The sin of greed also permeates these people, but it is not money that they covet, but souls. They have an insatiable lust to acquire converts. If questioned about this attitude, they respond that they "love" nonbelievers, but this is love turned backward: the word "evol" is not quite "evil," but close to it. The challenge of our time is to ensure that these single-minded ideologues, as well as the Muslim fanatics discussed above, can live tolerantly on the same Earth with the rest of us.

Deceptive Evangelization

The Manila Manifesto also stated that "We . . . reject the thesis that Jews have their own covenant which renders faith in Jesus unnecessary."

The manifesto included, with strangely twisted logic, the statement that not bringing its message of salvation through Christ to the Jews would be "anti-Semitism." This approach to Jews affirms the activity of the LCWE, and makes no objection to Christian groups whose techniques of evangelization are deceptive. The latter include organizations called Jews for Jesus and Messianic Vision, among others. Members of these groups have the same beliefs about Jesus as Christians, yet they continue to claim that they are "Jews." A person who believes that God became incarnate is not a Jew. These groups parody Jewish rites with changed wording to demonstrate their Christian beliefs, an offensive practice to genuine Jews. The group called Jews for Jesus is a member of numerous Christian groups, including the aforementioned Lausanne Consultation, as well as the World Evangelical Alliance and the evangelical alliances of Canada, Great Britain, France and South Africa.

Messianic Vision claims that "we have acquired the names and addresses of two million Jewish people in the United States. It is our intent to mail Sid Roth's God-directed Jewish evangelical book *They Thought for Themselves: The Story of Ten Amazing Jews* to the two million Jewish households." (Susan and Gary Lamston received the mailed book.) The deceptive title implies that the subjects of the book are Jews. The fact is that they believe in Jesus as a Christian would.

In 1993, the Jewish Community Relations Council of New York published a report of the Task Force on Missionaries and Cults. The report, endorsed by all the major Jewish denominations, called these "messianic" groups "Hebrew-Christians" and characterized them as follows: "Hebrew-Christianity claims to be a form of Judaism, it is not . . . It deceptively uses the sacred symbols of Jewish observance . . . as a cover to convert Jews to Christianity, a belief system antithetical to Judaism."

Israel's Descent into a "Morally Repugnant" Occupation

The issue covered here is not discrimination by Israel against its Arab citizens, although certainly there is some of that. The subjects of this presentation are the Palestinians who live in the West Bank. That is the area west of the Jordan River and east of the 1949 truce line that, since the 1967 Six-Day War, no longer separates opposing forces. The area is under Israeli military occupation; Palestinian West Bank residents are not citizens of Israel. The author of the quote in the heading above is Nicholas Kristof in his op-ed article titled "The Two Sides of a Barbed-Wire Fence" in *The New York Times* of June 30, 2010.

Before the death of Yasser Arafat (1929–2004), longtime chairman of the Palestine Liberation Organization, Israel's control of the West Bank was morally defensible on the basis of national security. Israel had been invaded by armies from Egypt, Syria, Jordan, Lebanon, and Iraq, after its founding in 1948. The intent of the invaders was to destroy the country. The new nation successfully defended itself. An armistice was signed in 1949, but the threat of war continued. Thus, national security has been a very realistic concern.

The 1967 hostilities began when Egyptian dictator Gamal Abdul Nasser (1918–70) created a state of war by closing the Strait of Tiran to Israeli shipping. This narrow waterway is at the mouth of the Gulf of Aqaba, an arm of the Red Sea. The Israeli port of Eilat stands at the head of the gulf. As a result of that war, Israel captured the Old City of Jerusalem and the West Bank from the Jordanians, the Gaza Strip from the Egyptians, and the Golan Heights from the Syrians. During occupation of the Gaza Strip and West Bank by Arab armies, 1948 to 1967, the local residents were never offered self-government or integration into the countries of the occupiers. The Syrians had removed their own residents from the Golan Heights so that its army would have unimpeded movement in planned attacks against Israel. After the Six-Day War, Israelis began to build settlements in the captured territories; settlers are full citizens of Israel. An excuse for the settlements was provided by the Arab nations themselves, who resolved at a meeting, soon after the war, that there would be "no peace with Israel, no recognition of Israel, and no negotiation with it" (the infamous "three noes"). In 1973, the Arab nations tried again to fight Israel with surprise attacks that began on the Jewish holy day of Yom Kippur. The result was a stalemate, with no changes in borders.

A peace treaty between Israel and Egypt was signed in 1979, defining their official border. The principals in that negotiation were Menachem Begin (1913–92), prime minister of Israel, and Anwar Sadat (1918–81), president of Egypt. Sadat was assassinated by Islamic extremists for his courageous act. A peace treaty between Israel and Jordan was signed in 1994, establishing a firm boundary along the Jordan River, through the Dead Sea, and down to the Gulf of Aqaba between the ports of Eilat in Israel and Aqaba in Jordan. The airport at the port cities is jointly used by not-unfriendly neighbors. Religious and ethnic differences have not prevented cooperation.

Attempts to achieve peace in the 1990s between Israel and Palestinians resulted in the Oslo Accord of 1993. Principal negotiators were Israeli Prime Minister Yitzhak Rabin (1922–95) and Yasser

Arafat. The photo, on September 13, 1993, of those two shaking hands in Washington, D.C., with US president Bill Clinton (b. 1946) just behind their extended arms, is justly famous and often reproduced. The accords established three types of areas in the West Bank, as well as a Palestinian Authority (PA) to have limited authority in two of the three areas. In certain limited urban areas (such as in Jericho), the PA exercises both civilian and security authority. In the second type of area, it only has civilian authority, and, in the third area, it has no authority at all. A democratic method of selecting the officials of the PA was put into place, and Yasser Arafat became its president. Further negotiations, planned under the accord, have not been successful and have been broken off.

On February 25, 1994, in a terrorist act, an Israeli carrying an automatic weapon entered a room in Hebron on the West Bank being used as a Muslim prayer-hall and began shooting. He killed 29 people and wounded 125 before being killed himself by guards. He was Baruch Goldstein, a physician born in New York in 1956 but living in Kiryat Arba, a Jewish settlement near Hebron. Palestinians rioted after the incident and more people were killed or wounded. Israeli Prime Minister Rabin described the attack as a "loathsome, criminal act of murder" and most Israelis agreed with him. On November 4, 1995, Prime Minister Rabin was himself assassinated by a Jewish extremist who opposed the peace process.

In a January 24, 2011, article in *The New Yorker*, Hendrick Hertzberg commented on the 1995 murder, stating that "for months, certain ultra-Orthodox rabbis and scholars had been suggesting that, because . . . Rabin was willing to consider territorial concessions in negotiations with the Palestinians, it would be permissible, even obligatory to kill him" (19). The magazine additionally noted that there was a large rally by right-wingers a month before the assassination while Israel's Knesset (parliament) was meeting to ratify those accords. The protesters carried posters showing pictures of Rabin with cross-hairs over his face and chanted "*Rabin boged!*" (Rabin is a traitor) and "Death to Rabin!"

The Orthodox Jews in Israel are primarily right-wing, buttressing their ritual observance with uncompromising rhetoric about

God-given land. With Israel's system of multiparty parliamentary democracy, the Orthodox parties form a swing bloc that is often part of the ruling coalition. As a result, Israel remains a partial theocracy; there is no civil marriage or civil divorce; each religion has its own separate religious rules. Jewish couples without the purest of ancestry meeting Orthodox rabbinic requirements often fly to nearby Cyprus to get married; non-Orthodox rabbis have no power to marry their congregants. Similarly, Jewish women who want a divorce must face an Orthodox rabbinic court in which agreement or nonagreement to a divorce is the sole prerogative of the husband. Ancient patriarchal rules are still in force. Apologists who claim that Israel is the Middle East's only democracy make sure not to mention this theocratic aspect of the state.

The desire of the world's leaders for peace in the region was demonstrated at Rabin's funeral, with the attendance of about eighty heads of state, including King Hussein of Jordan, President Hosni Mubarak of Egypt, and President Clinton of the United States, as well as high governmental officials such as Russian Prime Minister Viktor Chernomyrdin and UN Secretary-General Boutros Boutros-Ghali.

In July 2000, President Clinton invited Arafat and Prime Minister Ehud Barak (b. 1942) of Israel to Camp David, a rural retreat in Maryland, to attempt to achieve a peace agreement between the two sides. The negotiation failed; much expert opinion puts the blame on Arafat for not accepting a reasonable offer. A result that Arafat wanted but could not attain was the "right of return." This would mean that all the persons who left Israel due to the 1948 conflict, as well as their subsequent descendants born in exile, would be permitted to enter Israel to settle. It is usual for displaced persons to be resettled in their new countries, but the Jordanians, Syrians, and Lebanese have never permitted that. The displaced Palestinians remain in refugee camps, more than sixty years later. According to one report, when Arafat realized that he would not achieve all his demands, he called for the start of the Second *Intifada* (literally "shaking off"). There is evidence that this violent program was planned before the start of the Camp David talks. The series of attacks on Israelis began in September 2000. During this period, about five thousand Palestinians and one thousand Israelis died from violent interactions. Arafat died in Paris in November 2004 of natural causes; the Second *Intifada* ended soon after.

In 2005, Israel unilaterally evacuated its settlers from the Gaza Strip. Entreaties from Arab moderates that the withdrawal be carried out as the result of negotiations with them were rejected by Israeli Prime Minister Ariel Sharon. Thus, the claim was made by Hamas, the terrorist group now in control of Gaza, that its attacks on the settlers forced the evacuation, and this claim appeared credible. Hamas was thereby strengthened at the expense of the moderates. Since the withdrawal, Israel has maintained a sea and land blockade of the Gaza Strip. Egypt had similarly closed its border, but has lifted it since the revolution that toppled Hosni Mubarak. A UN panel reported on September 2, 2011, that Israel's interdiction of the blockade-testing flotilla from Turkey to Gaza in 2010 was lawful, although its use of force was "excessive." Israel has refused Turkey's demand for an apology for the killing of several people on the largest ship as they resisted the unnecessary, counterproductive takeover by Israeli commandos. Turkey has expelled the Israeli ambassador, but Israel appears willing to absorb the additional hostility, thereby demonstrating to itself the self-fulfilling prophecy that "the world is against us." In *The New York Times* of September 18, 2011, Pulitzer Prize–winning author Thomas L. Friedman wrote that this government is "the most diplomatically inept and strategically incompetent . . . in Israel's history" (Sunday Review, 13).

Expensive hydroponic equipment used in special agricultural production by the former Israeli settlers was left in the Gaza Strip for Arab use, but the equipment was destroyed by Arab militants. Open hostility toward Israel has been continually demonstrated by Hamas and by Hezbollah, the terrorist Shi'ite group in Lebanon. Lebanon is so fractured that its weak government cannot control Hezbollah. Both groups are clients of Iran, whose theocratic Shi'ite government has called for Israel's destruction. The reactions of Israel to the continuing rocket fire from the Gaza Strip and to incursions of Hezbollah forces into Israel must be classified as self-defense and necessary for the safety of its population.

The rampage of Baruch Goldstein and the murder of Yitzhak Rabin are symptomatic of a larger problem. In 2009, a study titled *Jewish Terrorism in Israel* was authored by Ami Pedahzur and Arie Perliger, Israeli academics. Each author received his PhD from the University of Haifa, Israel, and both served as fellows at the university's National Security Study Center. A chronology of 192 terrorist events by Jews is included in the book (175–92), beginning with the murder of mediator Count Bernadotte of Sweden on September 17, 1948, and ending with the murder of an Arab taxi driver by a Jewish extremist on May 14, 2007. A typical entry is the following, from November 11, 2000: "Settlers fired at a Palestinian in the area of Kfar Malek in the Ramallah district. The Palestinian, from the refugee camp Askar . . . died as a result of the shooting" (189).

Terrorist actions by Israelis have continued. One occurred on December 4, 2008, after some two hundred Jewish settlers in Hebron in the West Bank had been forcibly removed by Israeli troops from a building that they illegally occupied. The settlers launched a riot, not only in Hebron but also across the West Bank, injuring at least 17 Palestinian civilians, including five by gunshot, and destroying massive amounts of property. This action was reported by several news services, including Reuters and the Daily Kos. According to the latter, "the combined reports of dozens of attacks across the West Bank . . . paint a horrific picture of a violent, racist mob completely out of control." Reporters at *Haaretz*, a widely read Israeli newspaper, declared the series of attacks a "pogrom." According to a Reuters report, Israeli Prime Minister Ehud Olmert (b. 1945) said that Israeli police must end "intolerable leniency" toward such violent offenders.

The depth to which those with a terrorist inclination will sink is shown by the 2009 publication of a commentary on Jewish religious law by two rabbis from the West Bank settlement of Yitzhar. According to the online site of Haaretz.com, on March 21, 2010, the views of these rabbis are as follows: "The prohibition 'Thou Shalt Not Murder' applies only 'to a Jew who kills a Jew' . . . Non-Jews are 'uncompassionate by nature' and attacks on them 'curb their evil inclination' while babies and children of Israel's enemies may be killed since 'it is clear that they will grow to harm us.'"

In October 2010 in Beit Fajjar and in June 2011 at Maghayer, both West Bank towns, mosques were torched and sprayed with graffiti. "Israeli authorities suspect Jewish residents . . . from a nearby settlement," according to a statement from the American Jewish Committee, which condemned the attacks. Newer attacks are described in a statement posted online by Haaretz.com on July 10, 2011. The newspaper reports: "Field officers [of the Israel Defense Forces] describe as a daily recurrence incidents, most of which they say are initiated by settlers, of arson and of bodily and property damage to Palestinians. Favorite targets include Palestinian groves and orchards, whose trees are cut, uprooted and poisoned."

In late 2010, attempts to restart peace talks between Israel and the PA faltered. On February 18, 2011, the UN Security Council voted 14–1 to enact a resolution that would call for a return by Israel to the pre-1967 border (the 1949 armistice line) and would invite Palestine to join the United Nations as a member. Only the United States voted "no" among all the Security Council members, permanent and nonpermanent. The US veto was cast on the basis that only negotiations between the two parties can resolve the issue. However, the United States has so far failed to exert its power to force an agreement in a fair-minded fashion. The PA has given up on negotiations and, in September 2011, asked the United Nations for membership as an independent country. Full membership in the world body can only be granted by the Security Council; the United States will oppose it again, with a veto if necessary. It is expected that, in the near future, the UN General Assembly will grant memberlike status to Palestine. That new standing would enable the Palestinians to use the International Criminal Court or International Court of Justice to bring charges against Israel.

The reason the Israeli occupation of the West Bank is not morally defensible now is that there is no longer any serious military threat from that area. Following the death of Arafat, a revolutionary who was unlikely to ever accept peaceful coexistence, the PA is headed now by realistic people interested in economic development and not destruction of Israel. With promised guarantees from the United States of Israeli security associated with a withdrawal, the need of the Palestinians for self-determination in an area freed of foreign occupation is a necessity consistent with international standards of human rights. An impartial review of conditions on the West Bank shows that water resources are being monopolized by the settlers, leaving very little for the native Arabs. The Kristof article previously referenced reported that "[Palestinian] farmers . . . struggle to collect rainwater while a nearby [Israeli] settlement luxuriates in water." The Palestinians are powerless without a government of their own. Documentation of violations of Palestinian rights, such as land and water expropriation, is being carried out by B'Tselem, an Israeli human rights organization. As long as the occupation continues, the attempt by Israel's enemies to "delegitimize" the country has rationality. Supporters of Israel who loudly complain about delegitimization fail to appreciate its connection to the occupation.

The current Israeli government, headed by Binyamin Netanyahu (b. 1949) of the right-wing Likud party, through its continuing construction of settlements in the West Bank, has made clear its intention to retain its totalitarian policy of occupation, regardless of any United Nations vote. Meanwhile, heirs of pre-1948 Jewish terrorist groups (see Pedahzur and Perliger, 10–37), now powerful in the Netanyahu government, want to deny Israeli Arabs equal treatment and talk of expelling Arabs from the West Bank. Also, they want the right to prevent Muslim Israelis from moving into certain neighborhoods in Israel.

An additional example of the Netanyahu government's intransigence is the new insistence that Palestinians must agree in a peace treaty that Israel is a "Jewish" state. This demand has never been made before by Israeli negotiators and it is inconsistent with the name of the nation, which is, in transliteration from the Hebrew, *Medinat Yisra'el*, meaning State of Israel. Since Israel includes Muslims, Christians, Druse, and others, all free to practice their religions, the country was not named the "Jewish State of Israel," as Iran is now named the "Islamic Republic of Iran." The new demand demonstrates the power of totalitarian thinking that permeates the current Israeli government.

A second example is a statute adopted in July 2011 by the Knesset. The law states that initiators of boycotts against Israeli institutions in Israel or "in territories under Israeli control," that is, the West Bank, are subject to civil damage suits by targets of the boycotts. The implication is that demands to boycott products from the West Bank are being voiced by moderate and left-wing Israelis, and they may be having some effect. (Boycott actions have been taken also by some organizations in the United States and Europe.) There is considerable opposition to this new antiboycott law from within Israel. More than thirty Israeli law professors have issued a statement categorically stating that the act is contrary to Israeli citizens' basic rights and does grievous harm to the freedom of political expression and the freedom to protest.

Thoughtful Americans are beginning to become more strident in opposition to the continued occupation of the West Bank. David Remnick, writing the lead article in *The New Yorker* magazine of March 21, 2011, called it "illegal, inhumane, and inconsistent with Jewish values" (19). Some Israelis and Jewish Americans oppose the continuing occupation of the West Bank by speaking through their organizations. These include Americans for Peace Now, the New Israel Fund, Rabbis for Human Rights–North America, the Peres Center for Peace, the Jewish Peace Lobby, and others. They have come together with J Street, a new American pro-Israel, propeace organization that champions a two-state solution for Israel/Palestine. The success of J Street in recent years (it has 38 chapters around the United States) has frightened Netanyahu partisans. Conservative American Jews have worked to deny propeace activists speaking opportunities in Jewish venues. As with all rigid authoritarians, they think of those with differing views as traitorous. (J Street is almost entirely Jewish and has a "Rabbinic Cabinet" consisting of about 650 ordained rabbis.) A committee of the Israeli parliament discussed classifying J Street as "anti-Israel," although four members of the Knesset from the Labor and *Kadima* parties attended the J Street national conference in 2011 and gave strong approval to its agenda.

In May 2011, the Israeli prime minister came to the United States to meet with President Obama and make a presentation to the US Congress, initiated by the Republican majority in the House of Representatives. Prime Minister Netanyahu expressed considerable hostility toward the political position of the president, claiming that the position of the United States had changed, to Israel's detriment. His attitude toward the president of the United States was insolent, and only possible because of sycophantic support of Israel by the Religious Right and a powerful fraction of the Jewish community. Netanyahu mentioned Israel's historic connection to "Judea and Samaria," the Israeli right-wing's code name for the West Bank. The implication is that Israel will not easily give up control of the West Bank unless forced. Fareed Zakaria, an incisive and discerning commentator on international affairs, wrote in *The Washington Post* on May 26, 2011, that, actually, it was Netanyahu's position that had changed. He wrote: "It is Netanyahu who is breaking with the policy of two recent Israeli prime ministers on negotiating borders, in one of a series of diversions and obstacles he had come up with anytime he is pressed . . . [Israel's] physical existence is less in doubt than its democratic existence as it continues to rule millions of Palestinians in serf-like conditions—entitled to neither a vote nor a country" (A23).

Only the active involvement by the US government, with security guarantees to Israel, can end the current standoff. An agreement would improve US standing in the Muslim world and save the Israelis from their own folly. Yet, with its distribution of billions of dollars to Israel each year with no strings, and with its policy decision that only the parties themselves can resolve the impasse, the United States enables the stalemate to continue (through 2011). Only time will tell whether the polite requests of the US government and its allies for negotiations will be successful.

Worldwide Anti-Semitism

Definition of the Term

In Chapter 4, the term "anti-Judaism" was employed, in recognition of its use in the scholarly books cited. The discussion concerned the relationship between Christianity and Judaism long before the term "anti-Semitism" was invented. A person may assert anti-Judaism without being anti-Semitic. One could oppose the theology of Judaism, for example, because it has not accepted Jesus, without hating the Jews who practice that religion. However, it was shown that, even in earliest times, the failure of Jews to accept Jesus resulted in severely negative descriptions of the people themselves. Thus, there was Jew-hatred back then, as well as anti-Judaism.

The term "anti-Semitism" was invented by extension from a name put forth by Wilhelm Marr (1819–1904). Marr founded of the League of Anti-Semites in Germany in the middle of the nineteenth century. His theory was that the "race" of Semites, which included Arabs as well as Jews, was inferior to the "race" of Aryans, to which he claimed membership for himself and other Christian Germans. Despite the total falsity of Marr's concept, "anti-Semitism," now a synonym for Jew-hatred, has entered common usage. Thus, even Arabs can be anti-Semitic.

Attacks by Muslims in Europe

In the twenty-first century, a new type of hostility included attacks on Jews by Muslim immigrants in Europe. Jewish citizens of France, Belgium, Netherlands, and Great Britain have been particular targets, as well as in Malmo, Sweden, already noted. Many of the attacks were connected to the response of Israel to violence directed at it from neighboring Arab-controlled areas. Clearly, these attackers make no distinction between Jews and Israelis.

Hatred by Muslims in Arab Lands, Iran, and Malaysia

Verbal attacks by some important individuals in Muslim countries are also fierce. One example is the preaching of Egyptian Yusuf al-Qaradawi (aired on Al-Jazeera television, January 9, 2009). He is quoted as saying, "Oh Allah, take this oppressive Jewish, Zionist band of people . . . Oh Allah, count their numbers and kill them down to the very last one." In a sermon on April 19, 2002, reported in an online article on "Islam and Anti-Semitism," Abdul Rahman al-Sudais, the leading imam of the Grand Mosque of Mecca, referred to Jews as "the scum of the human race whom Allah cursed and turned into apes and pigs." Mahathir bin Muhammad, who has served as prime minister of Malaysia, has expressed conspiracy-filled ideas against Jews over many years. At a conference of Islamic countries on October 16, 2003, he stated that "The Jews rule the world by proxy. They get others to fight and die for them. They invented socialism, communism, human rights and democracy so that persecuting them would appear to be wrong so they may enjoy equal rights with others."

Holocaust denial, as a tool of attack against Israel, has been used by various persons and media outlets in the Arab world and in Iran. The Huffington Post reported on January 10, 2011, that Mahmoud al-Zahar, a leading Hamas official, said that it is a "lie" that the Jews were victims of the Holocaust. In December 2006, the Iranian regime hosted a meeting named the International Conference on Review of the Holocaust and dedicated to Holocaust denial. There would be no reason, 60 years after World War II, for a country that did not participate in the war, and is located thousands of miles from death camps in Germany and Poland, to hold such a conference unless it had a contemporary agenda.

Hatred and Violence in Russia

In Europe, anti-Jewish actions by Christians in the twenty-first century exist, but are limited. An infamous incident occurred in Russia in 2005. Two letters complaining about Jews were sent to the Prosecutor General of the Russian Federation. The second letter was signed by about five thousand Russians. Both letters, with similar content, called for the banning of Jewish organizations. The letters stated that Jews were extremists, were guilty of ritual murders, and were responsible for perpetrating their own anti-Jewish attacks. Signers included members of the Russian Orthodox clergy. The second missive warned of a "hidden campaign of genocide against the Russian people and their traditional society and values."

The Russian *Duma*, by a 306–58 vote, adopted a declaration saying that the "clear anti-Semitic intent" of the second letter and other appeals for government actions targeting Jews "prompts indignation and sharp condemnation." Russian president Vladimir Putin declared that he was "ashamed" to see signs of anti-Semitism in Russia. It appears that the Russian government will not support open anti-Semitism, a welcome situation.

Hatred in the United States

In the United States, extremist anti-Jewish organizations continue to exist, as they have for the past hundred years and more. These groups are typically also racist; in fact, their focus tends to be anti-black just as much as anti-Jewish, if not more so. With increased Latino and Asian immigration, their hatreds have expanded to include nearly everyone who is not white, straight, conservative, and Christian of northwest European ancestry. In the current century, according to the ADL, the largest neo-Nazi group is the National Socialist Movement, known for its Nazi uniforms and open display of explicit Nazi symbols. It has attracted members from other racist and skinhead groups whose leadership has weakened. They, along with other similar extremist organizations such as Aryan Nation and National Alliance, have been known to celebrate the birthday of Adolf Hitler each year. Some of these groups can be subsumed within the category of the Christian Identity Movement, a concept discussed on the website of Ontario Consultants on Religious Tolerance. This movement is defined there as "a number of small, extremely conservative Fundamentalist Christian denominations which have ... racist, sexist, anti-communist and homophobic beliefs. They view the Jewish people as descendants of Satan." An example of a group that might fit this definition is the Westboro Baptist Church of Kansas, known for picketing the funerals of US soldiers with signs claiming the deaths as God's way of opposing the acceptance of homosexuality in this country. What rational person could believe in a God who would do that? This group has also picketed Jewish facilities with signs stating that "Jews killed Jesus."

The ADL has reported also that conspiracy theories, now being put forward by anti-Semites, claim that Jews and Israelis secretly perpetrated the 9/11 attacks. Much information is available at the ADL website (www.adl.org), including a report titled "Unraveling Anti-Semitic 9/11 Conspiracy Theories."

Anti-Semitism Disguised as Intellectual Analysis

A notable aspect of anti-Semitism is its disguise in supposedly academic research. A practitioner of this type of doublespeak is

Kevin B. MacDonald (b. 1944), a tenured professor of evolutionary psychology at California State University at Long Beach (CSULB). He wrote four books between 1994 and 2004, asserting that Jews have developed a "group evolutionary strategy" that enhances their ability to outcompete non-Jews for resources. The essential point of all of MacDonald's arguments is that the Jews have a grand strategy to improve themselves at the expense of others, even fellow citizens of countries in which they live. Jewish traits, he asserts, are ethnocentrism, intelligence, psychological intensity, and aggressiveness. He apparently claims a biological basis for these traits. Scott Atran (b. 1952), an author whose work is discussed below, identifies MacDonald's "central thesis, namely, that Judaism is a naturally selected, biological and intellectual program for group-level adaptation."

In connection with this claim that the Jews have a "biological program," it is useful to point out that a recent DNA study by universities in Great Britain and Spain has shown that 20 percent of Spaniards living today carry genes of the Jews who were converted to Christianity under great pressure in the fourteenth and fifteenth centuries. Since the reverse, conversion from Christianity to Judaism, was punishable by death, the number of Jews that carry genes provided by Christian Spaniards of the same period must be very small. Due to similar situations in the past one thousand years, the Jewish population living today is primarily a remnant of an original Middle Eastern population that has contributed its genes to surrounding groups, but has received a much smaller admixture to add to its own.

MacDonald's views are essentially a conspiracy theory of action by Jews, similar to the concept presented in the infamous Czarist fiction *Protocols of the Elders of Zion* as well as the ideas of the senior Malaysian official quoted earlier who said that "the Jews rule the world by proxy." There is no real evidence shown by MacDonald of a single-minded, organized Jewish effort. The basic sociological concept of an "organization," particularly one that is not ad hoc or temporary, implies a pyramidal hierarchy of responsibility and control, as well as directives; identified benefits for members of the group who carry out their respective small parts in the grand plan determined by the leadership; evaluations of performance of assigned duties; and punishment for deviance. Among the thousands of examples of such organizations are the Roman Catholic Church, the US Army, the IBM Corporation, Yale University, and many others not necessarily as large. In the United States and other democratic countries that maintain freedom of association for its citizens as well as separation of church and state, a person can easily opt out of a religion. Such an individual may remain unaffiliated or join another religion, just as one can switch employers or retire if eligible. Sweeping assertions about tendencies of all members of a particular religion, such as Judaism or Islam, implies an implausible uniformity only achievable in conspiratorial fantasies.

Jews are divided into several different movements such as Hasidic, Modern Orthodox, Conservative, Reform, Reconstructionist, humanist, and those who identify themselves only as "cultural" Jews. It is a saying among Jews that, wherever there are two Jews, there are three opinions. Jews are so divided in the United States that they had to form a coordinating body named Conference of Presidents of Major American Jewish Organizations. That group tries to set a common policy on public issues for 50 Jewish groups, but doesn't necessarily succeed. For example, the Orthodox tend to support public aid to religious schools, but almost no other Jewish groups are likely to have the same outlook.

Persons who classify themselves as Jews are, like members of a political party, a loosely knit group of like-minded individuals not afraid to state their individual views. Judaism, as a religion without a specific creed (unlike Christianity), would be able to present only a limited set of statements on which all its factions could agree. A political party has a similar problem, some parties more than others. For example, it is likely that almost all members of the Republican Party of the United States would agree that taxes are too high and that government is too large. Reducing the beliefs of the rival Democrats to a similar limited number of statements would be far more difficult. As humorist Will Rogers (1879–1935) quipped, "Democrats never agree on anything; that's why they're Democrats.

If they agreed with each other, they would be Republicans." Rogers also stated that "I am not a member of any organized political party. I am a Democrat." The latter statement resonates with Jews; they cannot agree among themselves on who is a Jew. Additionally, support for Israel is not unanimous: a small sect of Orthodox Jews doesn't believe that Israel should have been established because the Messiah has not yet come. Also, as pointed out above, there is serious disagreement within the US Jewish community about the continued occupation of the West Bank.

One assertion of MacDonald is that "the organized Jewish community" (obviously an oxymoron) has been the single most important and powerful group in favor of unrestricted immigration to the United States. This power, somehow, according to MacDonald, was responsible for the passage of the 1965 Immigration Act that abolished country-of-origin quotas, replacing the stringent requirements of the Immigration Act of 1924. (The earlier legislation is discussed in Chapter 6 in connection with the "eugenics" movement.) Of course, in the United States, national laws must be adopted by both houses of the Congress and, if necessary, by large enough majorities to override a presidential veto, should it occur. At no time in the history of the United States have Jews formed a majority, or even a significant minority, of either house of Congress, nor has there ever been a Jewish president. It is this assertion of Jewish power, without showing any evidence of it, that requires invention out of thin air of a "rule by proxy."

In 2008, the president of CSULB released a statement saying that he considered MacDonald's views "deplorable and reprehensible." Soon after, the university's Academic Senate voted to "firmly and unequivocally disassociate itself from the anti-Semitic and white ethnocentric views" of MacDonald. The History Department said that his work is "professionally irresponsible and morally untenable." The Anthropology Department stated its "grave concern" with MacDonald's use of race, social evolution, and population genetics to "promote intolerance."

MacDonald testified for the plaintiff, English author David Irving (b. 1938), in a libel suit that the latter filed in 1998 against

American author Deborah Lipstadt (b. 1947) and her publisher, Penguin Books. Lipstadt was, at the time, a chaired professor of Modern Jewish and Holocaust Studies at Emory University in Atlanta. Irving claimed that Lipstadt had libeled him in her book *Denying the Holocaust: The Growing Assault on Truth and Memory* (1993). Lipstadt had accused him of deliberately misrepresenting evidence so that it conformed to his ideological viewpoint of Holocaust denial. Irving sued Lipstadt in a court in the United Kingdom after her book had been published there because, in that country, the burden of proof is on the defense. That is, it was up to Lipstadt and Penguin Books to prove that what they wrote and published was true. By contrast, in the United States, it is the plaintiff's responsibility to prove what the defense wrote was false.

Prior to his lawsuit, David Irving had written books about history, for example, *Hitler's War* (1977) and *Churchill's War* (1987). Beginning in the late 1980s, Irving became more active in specifically denying the Holocaust. According to an online biography of "David Irving," he stated in a pamphlet published in London in 1989 that there were no murders at Auschwitz. He called the gas chambers at Auschwitz a "hoax" and said that the existing remains were "mock-ups built by the Poles." In a 1991 speech in Canada, Irving called the Holocaust "a major fraud . . . There were no gas chambers. They were fakes and frauds." In a 1995 speech, Irving claimed that the Holocaust was a myth invented by a "world-wide Jewish cabal" to serve its own ends.

The outcome of the suit against Lipstadt and Penguin Books was that Irving lost. The defendants proved to the satisfaction of the court that what Lipstadt wrote and Penguin published was correct. The trial was before a single judge, Justice Charles Gray. Part of the decision on April 11, 2000, states, "Irving has for his own ideological reasons persistently and deliberately misrepresented and manipulated historical evidence; that for the same reasons he has portrayed Hitler in an unwarrantedly favourable light, principally in relation to his attitude towards and responsibility for the treatment of the Jews; that he is an active Holocaust denier; . . . he is anti-Semitic and racist."

One might hope that the work of Kevin B. MacDonald would not be picked up and cited by others, given its failure to demonstrate the correctness of its conclusions. That hope would be dashed, as shown by some of the content of *In Gods We Trust: The Evolutionary Landscape of Religion* (2002), authored by Scott Atran and published by Oxford University Press. In Chapter 8 of his book, in section 8.11, Atran details MacDonald's views on Jews, and quotes part of MacDonald's testimony in support of "Irving's libel suit against Jewish 'slander.'" He does not mention the subject of the suit, its outcome, and to whom Irving lost. The section includes the following statement, shocking in its ugly hatefulness and presented by Atran without any supporting evidence. The statement appears to be the view of Atran and not MacDonald: "Unlike most other human groups, Jews have developed a highly sophisticated and pernicious two-faced moral system. One face pretends to be humanist and universalist and is intended for show mainly to non-Jews. The other is deeply racist and isolationist and is designed to maintain moral integrity among Jews alone. When others discover this 'truth,' 'reactive' anti-Semitism naturally breaks out . . . Unfortunately, the Jewish cabal does not distinguish between classical anti-Semitic reactions and valid scientific inferences to many of the same anti-Semitic conclusions" (231).

This statement speaks for itself in what it implies about Atran.

Responding to Irrational Hatreds and Violence

To threats of physical violence, responses must be made by self-protection. Intelligence operations are very important in order to stay one step ahead of those persons intent on harming us. The United States has done that domestically, and has carried out proactive operations in cooperation with other nations in Afghanistan, Pakistan, Somalia, and Yemen. There is always a trade-off between personal liberty and national security interests. It is hoped that a felicitous balance will be struck, consistent with the Bill of Rights in the US Constitution.

Verbal or written attacks against groups, even if filled with lies, distortions, and unfair generalizations, are permissible because of the sacred value of free speech in democratic countries. Only an active response in the same medium will suffice. A failure to respond forcefully will allow them to fester and grow. Fortunately, in democratic countries, there are nongovernmental organizations that serve this function.

CHAPTER 6

ACTING ON SACRED VALUES IN A SCIENTIFIC AGE

RESPONDING TO THE NEW ATHEISTS

A SIGNIFICANT IMPETUS FOR THE WRITING OF this book was to provide a vehicle for a rejoinder to the works of the New Atheists, primarily Richard Dawkins, Sam Harris, and Christopher Hitchens. This response is not from a believer's viewpoint; therefore, the dispute is not simply a binary question of belief or no belief. There is agreement on some points of atheist thinking but serious divergence of opinion on others. While it is understood that religion-instituted violence has been significant and unacceptable, the primary proposal presented by the New Atheists, that religion should disappear, is simplistic and has a very low expectation of implementation.

The New Atheists are certain that no God exists, and their view of religion is that it has no value. They characterize the traditional religions primarily by the content of their holy books, written between one and three millennia ago. They claim that these holy books, in particular the Hebrew Bible and the Koran, are filled with examples of violence against nonbelievers, as well as phraseology that they have interpreted to call for more hatred and violence in the present day. The New Atheists and religious fundamentalists have in common the literal reading of holy books.

The writings of the New Atheists demonstrate that they obtained what little knowledge of religion they have from the Protestant-dominant culture found in England and the United States; they show almost total ignorance of Judaism and Islam, as those religions are practiced today by a majority of adherents. They essentially ignore the significant anti-Judaism in the New Testament. That serious omission was corrected with a detailed discussion in Chapter 4. The continued existence of hatred and denigration of nonbelievers in the present day lends itself to the constructive proposals made below, substituting for the demand that religion be abolished.

The New Atheists characterize religion by only a belief in the supernatural and fail to appreciate other reasons for adherence, such as those that indicate conflicted or hidden agendas for membership. Several additional reasons were given in Chapter 3 in the section "The Continuation of Religion." Furthermore, the connection of religion to culture is not understood by these writers, and they have absolutely no clue that religion might serve as emotional support for non-Christian minorities in a Christian milieu.

Humans are not totally logical like robots; religious belief is not subject to arguments solely based on reason. The contradictory aspects of human life must be understood and appreciated. For example, we can plan an infinite future for organizations and arrangements that we support, but at the same time, we recognize that death will soon personally overtake us. Significant and life-altering choices that we make are sometimes the result of compromises, with small differences of apparent advantage on one side forcing a major decision. The unidirectional character of time prevents us from going back and replacing what has been done by something else that might have resulted in a better outcome. Such nuances of human life are simply ignored in the elementary explications of these narrowly focused activists. Dawkins's idea that all children can be raised in a religion-free environment is a "delusion," to use his favorite word.

Additionally, the New Atheists are contemptuous of religious "moderation," by which they apparently mean religion that does not advocate violence against nonbelievers. Their view is that religious moderation is a slippery slope that inexorably leads to extremes. Dawkins has presented anecdotes that support this understanding, using specific instances that have occurred. These instances are so unique that they are front-page material. Then he converts his anecdotes into an unsubstantiated conclusion that is totally unwarranted: "moderation in faith fosters fanaticism" (301). Harris, in his own book, has presented essentially the same view.

The story related in Chapter 1 about the life, death, and burial of Susan Lamston provided an example of people of different religions acting together amicably. Susan did not believe in God, yet she was a member of a religious congregation and knew the appropriate prayers for the various holy days. In rites concerned with her death, the prayers of persons of a different religion were accepted by her family because their meaning was universal regardless of the idiom in which they were expressed. While her story was just one anecdote, it could have been multiplied millions of times. People of different faiths living and working together, at least in the United States, is so normal that it draws no special notice.

Finally, the New Atheists follow their fire and brimstone attacks with pussycat platitudes as prescriptions for the serious world problems that they have described as being the fault of religions. The following is found in Dawkins's final chapter: "If the demise of God will leave a gap, different people will fill it in different ways. My way includes a good dose of science, the honest and systematic endeavor to find out the truth about the real world" (361). Harris sermonizes, adopting an idea and a phrase from a book he appears to despise: "No personal God need be worshiped for us to live in awe at the beauty and immensity of creation. No tribal fictions need be rehearsed for us to realize, one fine day, that we do, in fact, love our neighbors, that our happiness is inextricable from their own, and that our interdependence demands that people everywhere be given the opportunity to flourish" (227). Hitchens's proposal for humanity was this: "Above all, we are in need of a renewed Enlightenment, which will base itself on the proposition that the proper study of mankind is man, and woman . . . The study of literature and poetry, both for its own sake and for the eternal ethical questions with which it deals, *can now easily depose the scrutiny of sacred texts that have been found to be corrupt and confected.*" (283) [italics added].

No disagreement is offered to the content of these quotations except to the wording in italics in the last statement presented. The New Atheists's earnestness and devotion to truth as they see it, as well as their respect for humanity, are applauded. However, having made the most serious charges against the practice of religion, they have failed to complement their negative attitudes with some concrete recommendations for positive change. Surely, some suggestions could have been made for actions by open-minded believers as well as by national governments, in order to minimize or reverse the hatred and violence generated by religious belief. Without these necessary additions, the substance of their final chapters is shallow and elementary. A strong attempt has been made to prevent that failing from being repeated here.

Hitchens's attack on the holy books, indicated by italics, was myopic. He demonstrated an inability to appreciate that discerning people, some believers included, understand the holy texts to be documents that reflect the culture of the times and places in which they were written. These discerning folk, not blinded by either fundamentalist or atheist ideology, are able to interpret the texts in a humanistic way for their meaning for today's world, can plumb the texts for "the eternal ethical questions," *and* can treat these texts as the poetry and literature that they are.

Premises Adopted

This book has been written with the understanding that all changes to our physical universe, from the time of the Big Bang, 13.73 billion years ago, until now, have occurred by the operation of the universe's physical laws, and not from any supernatural intervention. That implies that no human female was ever impregnated by a god to give birth to a human (invariably male) with supernatural powers; that edible food to sustain thousands of people in the desert for forty years was not provided supernaturally; and that Earth has never stopped rotating on its axis. Furthermore, this condition of no miraculous events will continue until the universe comes to a natural end, several billion years in the future. The universe will not end with a supernatural Day of Judgment, End of Days, or Coming of the Messiah (whether for the first or second time). Atheists would certainly agree with this particular understanding, as well as the assertion that prayer, by itself, cannot change the operation of the physical laws of the universe. However, atheists may not appreciate the psychological benefits for those doing the praying, which is really why prayer continues to be employed by rational humans.

It is understood that some changes to the physical universe have been caused by the volitional (even if instinctual) activities of animals on this Earth, including humans. For example, bees pollinate flowers that are naturally transformed into fruits that nourish other animals, beavers build dams that change the ecology, and predatory animals kill their prey. Humans have hunted some species to extinction, cut down many trees, built power plants and automobiles, paved fields, and domesticated certain animals, creating large herds of them. Enormous amounts of greenhouse gases have been generated as a result.

Biological and atomic warfare remain potential threats to all life. During the Cold War, the Soviet Union, in violation of its signature on an international treaty, continued production of anthrax that could have been mounted on ballistic missiles. This effort ended only when the USSR disintegrated. There is no guarantee that biological warfare will not be attempted again. Atomic weapons are in the possession of a number of nations; the possibility of hostile use continues. Dangerous atomic radiation has been released already. Humans have constructed and detonated atomic bombs and are not perfect in their ability to control nuclear power plants. Perfect control to eliminate all risk would require infinite resources, certainly not available. There is a possibility that humans will cause the end of their own species before that end would naturally occur, due to their innate aggressiveness, overreaching in proposed accomplishments, and individual egoism, combined with an inability to control these impulses and redirect them sufficiently to a communitarian spirit.

By the statement that "no miracles occur," a piece of the question of whether supernatural beings exist has been sliced away. The nonexistence of supernatural intervention implies that it makes no difference on Earth whether gods exist or not. This attitude may be identified as naturalism, in order to indicate clearly that only physical laws apply on Earth. It is reiterated, as stated in Chapter 1, that revelations—that is, the claimed receipt of the wishes or words of a god to the mind of a human—are not violations of physical laws. However, naturalism implies no opinion on the question of sacred values, so that it is not the sole "ism" of this presentation. Sacred values are considered below.

Another premise is that it is unknowable whether each person has a soul that does not die with the body; similarly, it is not possible to determine whether gods and an afterlife exist. It is asserted that there is no existing data on these subjects one way or the other, and it is not possible to collect any. A corollary is that "reality" is here among the living. With this addition, the separation between the world in which we live and some unknown world of the spirit is made more certain. This assertion is in disagreement with some theorists of religion as well as with theologians who believe in an Ultimate Reality or some Spiritual World that is the realm of God or other supernatural beings.

Believers in an Ultimate Reality might claim that, even if there is no supernatural intervention in this world, what individuals do while alive is important for their afterlife or their future reincarnations. A Spiritual World exists, they insist, and humans will be judged by their god and assigned appropriate rewards or punishments. The view presented here is that each person is entitled to his or her own beliefs, and is entitled to act on those beliefs within the laws of the nation in which one is residing. That is, religion is not proscribed, subject to an essential caveat: that religion must remain a private practice totally divorced from state involvement.

While the nonexistence of miracles is consistent with atheists' thinking, the unknowability of the existence of gods, the soul, and an afterlife is not. The New Atheists would insist that any conception of a Spiritual World is fiction, although they have no evidence. Thus the unknowability of a Spiritual World is an understanding that disagrees with the conclusions of both believers and atheists.

Adherents of naturalism should be comfortable with the views of those minimalist believers—typically called deists—who assert that God began the universe with the Big Bang but otherwise does not interfere in the natural world. How the material that formed the Big Bang was initially created is a fundamentally unanswerable question; some people believe that God or a god created it, and no person has any data to authoritatively disagree, at least not now. Additionally, the assertion that violations of physical laws by supernatural beings have never occurred should not discomfit many Muslims, whether peace-loving or terroristic, as their religion depends, almost wholly, on interpretations of revelations received by their Prophet.

THE IDEA OF THE SACRED

If no miracles occur, and the question of whether gods exist can't be answered, then there is an issue of what constitutes the "sacred" in such a world. "Sacred" is a term usually associated with religion, but a search has been undertaken to find nonreligious uses of the term. In Chapter 1, several likely nonreligious uses of "sacred" were noted. The youth of classical Athens were required to "fight for the ideals and Sacred Things of the City." The signers of the US Declaration of Independence agreed among themselves to "mutually pledge to each other our lives, our Fortunes and our sacred Honor." Albert Einstein noted that "The intuitive mind is a sacred gift." Gary Lamston felt that a sense of the sacred was with him as the coffin containing the body of his wife, Susan, was being lowered into the ground, but it was not a believer's hierophany.

Among the New Atheists, Sam Harris noted in *The End of Faith* that "There is a sacred dimension to our existence" (16), while Daniel Dennett, another atheist author, reported about himself in *Breaking the Spell* that "My sacred values are obvious and quite ecumenical: democracy, justice, life, love and truth (in alphabetical order)" (23). The uses of the term "sacred" by these atheists are clear and overt examples of its application in a nonreligious context.

In Chapter 3, "sacred" was shown to be used as a noun or an adjective employed in writings by anthropologist Clifford Geertz, religion-theorist Mircea Eliade, and sociologist Emile Durkheim. Geertz was primarily interested in understanding cultures, and he defined culture as a "historically transmitted pattern of meanings embodied in symbols." In his paper "Ethos, World View, and the Analysis of Sacred Symbols," also included in his book *The Interpretation of Cultures*, he stated that a religious system is made up of "a cluster of sacred symbols, woven into some sort of ordered whole" (129). It appears that Geertz used the concept of "sacred" solely in connection with religion. It may be noted, however, that the cultures he investigated were all traditional ones, in which modern secular humanity with a scientific outlook made no appearance.

Mircea Eliade envisioned only two types of humans: those who are religious and those who are not. In *The Sacred and the Profane*, he asserted that, for religious man, "there is an absolute reality, *the sacred*, which transcends this world but manifests itself in this world" (202). Earlier in the same book, he stated that religious phenomena involve occurrences of a "hierophany," that is, "the act of manifestation of the sacred" (11).

Using Eliade's definition, the experience of Gary Lamston might have been a hierophany if it was "religious," but it was not. Gary understood, in a flash of insight, that Susan's burial was a completion of her contributions to human civilization—one finality in a very long line of the same, extending back to the far-distant past when our ancient ancestors first mourned their dead and buried them with rituals. Gary's hierophany recognized the sacred character of human history, with its advance from the age of stone tools, absence of the rule of law, and limited knowledge of the workings of the physical world, to the present day, with its enormous advances in tools, law, and scientific understanding, as well as its dangers. Susan's contribution was to pass on to her children, students, and clients the knowledge and wisdom that she received, augmented with additional knowledge gained from her experiences.

The following passage by Eliade, discussing nonreligious man, is also from *Sacred and Profane:* "[Modern nonreligious man] accepts no model for humanity outside the human condition . . . Man *makes himself,* and he only makes himself completely in proportion as he desacralizes himself and the world. The sacred is the prime obstacle to his freedom. He will become himself only when he is totally demysticized. He will not be truly free until he has killed the last god" (203).

Thus Eliade saw the sacred as applying only to religious man and as an obstacle to nonreligious man. The following provides a different point of view. Modern nonreligious humans are not a uniform lot in their approaches to life, and it is certainly true that many live a totally profane existence. Some individuals may be egoists who live only for their self-interest, or sensualists who only pursue their own pleasures. However, there is another type of nonreligious human, totally ignored by Eliade. Members of the latter group, here called sacred humanists, take their roles in life very seriously; they have strongly held ideals for society in general, for their government, and for personal and group interactions among their fellow humans. They have sacred values, do not require a religion to hold these values firmly without doubt, and act on them as appropriate. Sacred humanists may reconsider these ideals often, and may refine their views based on the receipt of new information and on current happenings in the world around them. They keep their ideals in mind, promote them when the opportunity arises, and act accordingly in daily life. It is useless to hold sacred values if they are never acted upon.

Emile Durkheim defined religion as a social activity, requiring membership in "a single moral community called a church," but secular people with sacred values may not belong to a church and have no holy book. Durkheim also saw a civic celebration of national success as similar to a religious celebration. The implication is that "sacred" could be put into a nonreligious context as an element of a civic religion. It fits Durkheim's model, in which all the people of a community act together in a common ritual that may be sacred, whether its setting is secular or religious. (Durkheim's concept is not the same as the "civil religion" of philosopher Jean Jacques Rousseau [1712–78], presented in his *Social Contract* of 1762. Rousseau envisioned a civil government employing, for purposes of public cohesion and stability, the theological concept of an afterlife in which virtue was rewarded and vice punished by God.)

The concept presented here is somewhat different then either Durkheim's or Rousseau's. Religious people worship in many different types of holy structures—for example, churches, synagogues, mosques, and temples—but with a common aim, *To Connect with the Infinite*. In the most traditional setting, life is what has been established by God or the gods. In this religiously oriented culture, individuals participate in the group's connection with the Infinite, that is, in communal rites that are carried out in an approved manner. In such a society, it might be highly unusual or even dangerous for individuals to promote their own views that have implications for changing communal rites or interpersonal relationships in an unapproved fashion.

In modern times, religious people also involve themselves in what are sometimes referred to as "good works." For example, abolition of slavery before the US Civil War was championed by religiously oriented folk, but the idea was opposed by other believers, who cited Biblical passages that appeared to condone the practice. Subjects supported must be consistent with the theology of the religion. The difference of opinion on slavery resulted in a split among Baptists into northern and southern denominations. In recent times, if a churchgoing Roman Catholic or Southern Baptist supports the right of a woman to have an abortion or for two people of the same sex to form a legally approved personal partnership, he or she may have to be circumspect about it. These days, noncontroversial "good works" often includes providing direct aid to the poor, hungry, ill-clothed, or ill-housed.

Among Jews, the involvement in issues of social justice is encouraged, partly because it is in the service of "*tikkun olam*," meaning "repair of the world." This concept is derived from *kabbalah*, a Jewish mystical tradition. This particular idea was put forth in the writings of Isaac Luria (1534–72). He lived in Safed, now in Israel but then in the Ottoman Empire. In Lurianic *kabbalah*, a mystical creation myth is presented, very different from that of Genesis. In this myth, repair of the world is now required because, in the world's creation by God, an unintentional error occurred. This catastrophe involved, as reported by *The Encyclopedia of the Jewish Religion* (1966), "the breaking of the vessels, whereby the primordial light of creation [held in those vessels] spilled over . . . and its sparks fell into . . . demonic spheres" (243). Evil was thereby enabled to occur, and the human task is to heal this breach and repair the world. The conversion of this mystical idea into a practical program for people living today is an example of an effort, like "good works," for religion to retain meaning in a scientific age.

Unfortunately, there are humans who carry out "bad works" that are often religiously motivated. They have strongly held values that they consider sacred, but that are considered antisocial, fanatical, or even criminal by many others. It is important that public law be legislated such that all citizens have equal protection; that freedoms of speech, press, assembly, association, and the right to petition for redress of grievances are maximized while the ability of activists to perpetrate violence or tread on the rights of others is minimized. Separation of church and state is essential. This arrangement requires the implementation of a just rule of law that defines and is further legislated by a government that has been popularly elected and is of limited duration for its incumbents before another public referendum. Such a government will allow itself to be criticized and will be sensitive to public opinion.

In a modern, secularly organized society in which democracy prevails, citizens have the right to hold individual sacred values and act on them within the law. Nonreligious folk don't need the permission implied by "good works" that is secondary or even tertiary to belief, as well as to practice and promotion of a religion. With their individual sacred values, they typically divide themselves by subject matter according to their personal priorities, such as the environment, education, civil rights of minorities, research to find cures for particular diseases, improving the health of individuals, ending the death penalty, stopping drunk driving, ameliorating poverty and hunger, and promoting world nuclear disarmament.

It is asserted here that these secular carriers of the sacred also have a common aim, *To Maintain and Improve the World*, but their methods are more realistic than prayer. They contribute to or actually work for causes. Additionally, they attend meetings, distribute flyers, write letters to newspapers, contribute to online blogs, lobby their legislative representatives, vote for candidates who support their views, and occasionally demonstrate in front of offices of perceived offenders. They discuss their views with their family members, including children, and provide examples for them. Children are attentive to what is important to their parents.

"Meanings" of the Abrahamic Creation Myth

Differing Interpretations

A story of creation of the universe, using the terminology of Clifford Geertz, is an integral element of the ethos and world-view of the people who adopt it. Interpreting the real creation story summarized in Chapter 2 is essential, as that will yield the sacred values that are the intended output of this presentation. Naive individuals may believe that, since the real history of the universe and of the evolution of humanity have been determined by scientific research, there can be only one interpretation. That would be an incorrect conclusion. Only the facts are indisputable; possible meanings are multifold.

In advance of that discussion, it is useful to consider the one creation story that is most widely known and that is currently in use by much of the world. The creation myth of Genesis was briefly discussed in Chapter 1 and, for adherents of one of the Abrahamic religions, it can be included among the "sacred symbols" defined by Geertz. This preliminary analysis demonstrates that there can be more than one "meaning" assigned to a creation story, a concept that will be carried over to the later exposition. Where religion and the state are separate, there may be many interpretations, none of which requires permission to be expressed. An individual may accept the one that appears most reasonable and is endorsed by others that he or she admires for their perspicacity and understanding. Varying interpretations fuel controversies over public policies, which are made by a democratic process. On the other hand, when a religion has political power and controls a nation's official policy, its interpretation of its own creation myth applies nationwide; woe to anyone who disagrees.

A most significant occurrence in the creation myth of Genesis is called by some "the Fall of Man." It consists of the eating of the fruit of the Tree of Knowledge of Good and Evil by the first humans, Adam and Eve, contrary to the command of God. The decision to eat this fruit had extremely important consequences for all the descendants of the first couple. According to Genesis, humans could no longer live in the Garden of Eden. Death would now occur; people would have to work for a living, and women would have to bear the pain of childbirth. The incident is woven through the theology of the various religions and, in some, it is more important and central than in others.

In Roman Catholicism, this first sin of disobeying God's command was transmitted by Adam and Eve to all their descendants as "original sin." Baptism in the Church is believed to erase original sin, implying that non-Catholics continue to carry this stigma. Even for persons so baptized, the effects on the human condition remain; humans must bear pain and die. In the book *Original Sin and Everyday Protestants* (2009) by Andrew Finstuen, it is reported that three important Protestant public figures of the twentieth century, Reinhold Niebuhr, Billy Graham, and Paul Tillich, strongly believed in original sin, but it is likely that they had differences with the Roman Catholic interpretation and, as Finstuen notes, "the three men conceptualized original sin differently" (2). The Eastern Orthodox denomination rejects the idea that original sin is passed down through the generations.

In Judaism, which does not accept original sin, several passages in the Hebrew Bible are interpreted to imply that no human is without sin; the death of every person is due to his or her own failings, and is not connected with the sins of Adam and Eve. Islam, similarly, has not adopted the concept. The Koran states that the devil, called *Iblis* in Arabic, was the tempter of Eve. In Islam, the universal existence of evil in personal lives is experienced as a consequence of the devil as a personal agent. Thus in Islam, each individual struggles with sin, without any extra burden imposed by the sins of Adam and Eve.

Weber's Analysis

The impact of differing worldviews of Christian denominations was examined by Max Weber in articles published in 1904 and 1905. (Weber, who was briefly mentioned in Chapter 3, was often referenced in the writings of Geertz, whom he significantly influenced.) Some time after his death, the articles were collected and made available in English as *The Protestant Ethic and the Spirit of Capitalism* (1930).

Weber's thesis begins with a distinction that he believed existed between the way Roman Catholics and Protestants viewed secular work, following the social revolution begun by Martin Luther (1483–1548). According to Weber, the work of the laity to earn their living was considered less worthy in Roman Catholicism than the work of those with a religious calling, such as monks and priests. In Luther's differing conception, all persons are equal before God, and their work, even if secular, is just as important as any performed by persons of the cloth. Under medieval Catholicism, the attempt to acquire riches by those not endowed with them at birth was considered sinful. Under Protestantism, particularly those denominations influenced by John Calvin (1509–64), the profligate use of resources for worldly pleasures was still considered sinful, but not necessarily the acquisition of resources. Required were thrift, self-discipline, hard work, and the efficient use of time. Resources earned through a business were to be reinvested rather than used for pleasures, thereby building the assets of the business and creating a capitalist enterprise. Weber found that, from his investigations, those businessmen following this pathway of life in Western Europe were far more likely to be Protestant than Catholic. Those men (they were virtually all men) who achieved success under this "Protestant ethic" were admired. Becoming wealthy in this manner began to be seen as the result of God's favor for good habits, not as sinful. The previous interpretation was reversed.

Three Misinformed Interpretations of Humanity's Real History

1. Active Denial

Creationism
Persons who genuinely believe in a literal interpretation of the story in the first chapters of Genesis, or some variation thereof, are generally called "creationists." Opposition to the teaching of evolution by such people began to coalesce in the United States after World War I, probably because that subject began to be widely

taught in public schools at that time. An organization called the World Christian Fundamentals Association was founded in Minneapolis in 1919 by a Baptist minister. John Washington Butler (1875–1952), a State Representative in Tennessee, was its head in the middle 1920s. Butler lobbied state legislatures to enact laws that would forbid the teaching of evolution by natural selection, as described in Darwin's famous tome and further supported by the more recent research of other scientists, such as anthropologists, biologists, and geologists.

Butler was successful in his own state; the legislature adopted his concept in what was called the Butler Act. To force a test case, an offer to defend anyone accused of teaching the theory of evolution was tendered by the American Civil Liberties Union (ACLU). The cause was taken up by high school teacher John T. Scopes (1900–70) of Dayton, Tennessee. The famous trial in 1925, with former Democratic presidential contender William Jennings Bryan (1860–1925) arguing for the prosecution and nationally known attorney Clarence Darrow (1857–1938) countering for the defense, was used as the subject for a Broadway play *Inherit the Wind* in 1955 and a movie of the same name in 1960. The trial became a referendum on evolution, overwhelming the elementary question of whether, in fact, Scopes had taught the subject contrary to the law. Scopes was convicted and paid a fine. The Tennessee Supreme Court upheld the constitutionality of the Butler Act in 1927.

Laws restricting the teaching of evolution were enacted in a number of other states in the 1920s, for example, Arkansas and Louisiana. It was not until after World War II that organizations supporting the Constitutional principle of separation of church and state, as well as proscience groups, began to seriously counterattack. In 1948, in *McCollum v. Board of Education*, the US Supreme Court, in an 8-to-1 decision, declared unconstitutional the teaching of religion by clergy in public schools. A case specifically on evolution was *Epperson v. Arkansas*, decided by the US Supreme Court by a 9-to-0 vote in 1968. The court held that the Arkansas law forbidding the teaching of evolution violated the Establishment Clause of the First Amendment to the US Constitution. As a result, some states adopted legislation that permitted the teaching of evolution but required the teaching of "creation-science" whenever evolution was taught.

These "equal time" laws were similarly attacked in the federal courts. In *Daniel v. Waters*, a suit filed in Tennessee in 1975 in response to that state's law, the US Court of Appeals for the Sixth Circuit held that the law violated the Constitution, as in *Epperson*. In *McLean v. Arkansas Board of Education* in 1981, there was a similar outcome. The state law, declaring "creation-science" to be an equally credible alternative to "evolution-science," was struck down by the US District Court of the Eastern District of Arkansas. In 1987, in *Edwards v. Aguillard*, the US Supreme Court, in a 7-to-2 decision, ruled that a Louisiana law requiring that "creation-science" be taught alongside evolution was unconstitutional. (The dissenters were William Rehnquist and Antonin Scalia, two of the more conservative justices, both appointed by Republican presidents.) In the suit, amicus curiae (friend of the court) briefs in support of the plaintiffs were filed by many Nobel Prize–winning scientists and state academies of science.

Active Denial Redux: Intelligent Design
Having lost at the highest court in the nation, creationists tried a slightly different approach. A concept called "intelligent design" was devised. Funding and advocacy of this concept was carried out by the Discovery Institute and its Center for Science and Culture (CSC). This nonprofit organization, headquartered in Seattle, was founded in 1990. The institute's goal, according to its own literature, is to "reverse the stifling dominance of the materialist worldview, and to replace it with a science consonant with Christian and theistic convictions."

All the prominent proponents of intelligent design are Christians, and their underlying purpose is, apparently, to promote that religion, in agreement with the quote immediately above. They planned to accomplish this by requiring public school children to be taught explanations of the origin of the human species consistent with their interpretation of the creation story in Genesis, in addition to the facts of evolution discovered by science. One possible method was to leave their underlying purpose unstated, in order to hide their religious message. Thus the "designer" responsible for intelligent design was not to be named, even though all the proponents personally believed it was God as defined by Christianity. A supporter of intelligent design is mathematician/philosopher William Dembski (b. 1960). In *Intelligent Design: The Bridge between Science and Theology* (1999), he makes clear his orientation. Dembski writes that "Christ is indispensable to any scientific theory . . . The pragmatics of a scientific theory can, to be sure, be pursued without recourse to Christ. But the conceptual soundness of the theory can in the end only be located in Christ" (210).

A primary argument of proponents of intelligent design is called "irreducible complexity." The term was invented by Michael Behe (b. 1952), a professor of biochemistry at Lehigh University. Both Behe and Dembski are senior fellows at CSC. Behe defines an irreducibly complex system as one that is "composed of several well-matched interacting parts that contribute to the basic function, wherein the removal of any one the parts causes the system to effectively cease functioning."

The desire of Behe, Dembski, and likeminded individuals is to demonstrate that certain biological systems found in nature are irreducibly complex and could not have been produced by evolution via natural selection. Such systems would then require a "designer," as mentioned above.

The concept has antecedents that go back to writings by ancient Romans. In more recent times, the argument for an intelligent designer of the universe was put forward by the Rev. William Paley (1743–1805), an English theologian in his book *Natural Theology* (1802). Paley's view was that, if he found a pocket watch on the ground while walking in the fields, he would naturally assume that the watch had been made by a watchmaker and dropped by a previous walker. He would not assume that "the watch might have always been there." That is, it could not have grown there by itself. His conclusion was that anything that complex must have had a designer and, by extension, the universe and everything in it must have had an intelligent designer. Paley's exposition is called the "teleological argument," or argument by design for the existence of God.

Behe's nonbiological explanatory example is a mousetrap. He states that a mousetrap's mechanism consists of a certain set of necessary parts: a base, a catch, a spring, a hammer, and a hold-down bar. If any one of them is missing, the system cannot carry out its function. It meets the definition of irreducible complexity. Behe's fallacy is that he has used as an example a mechanism that either works fully or it doesn't work at all; there is no possibility of partial success. Evolution by natural selection doesn't work in that manner. A biological function begins with a limited capability, generated by random mutations, that is retained because it is advantageous to the organism. Additional capabilities are added slowly, by natural selection, until a complex, highly valuable function results.

A biological example is the evolution of the eye. Behe has cited the "development of the eye problem" as evidence for intelligent design. Darwin mentioned the evolution of the eye as a particularly challenging development, but he believed, with some evidence, that even that was accomplished through evolution by natural selection. Recent research has added justification to his early understanding. Different types of eyes have emerged in various organisms and, according to an exposition produced by the WGBH Educational Foundation (named for the Boston media outlet), the human eye isn't even the best one. The discussion includes the following: "Because blood vessels run across the surface of the retina instead of beneath it, it's easy for the vessels to proliferate or leak and impair vision. So, the evolution theorists say, the anti-evolution argument that life was created by an 'intelligent designer' doesn't hold water. If God or some other omnipotent force was responsible for the human eye, it was something of a botched design" (Espar 2001).

Scientists calculate that the first animals with the most elementary "eyes" lived about 550 million years ago. They had only small groups of photoreceptor cells that could detect light but not the direction from which it came. Later, these cells began to exist in a concavity, which protected them and began, as well, to provide some directional information. As time progressed, the opening to the concavity narrowed, so that light entered through a small, pinhole-like aperture. This change permitted the organism to make out shapes. The shelled marine creature called a nautilus has such an eye. Eventually, the light-sensitive area evolved into a retina at the back of the eye. Still later, a protective layer of transparent cells over the aperture was differentiated into a crude lens, and the interior of the eye was filled with material that assisted in the focusing of images. The previously cited presentation concludes that "eyes corresponding to every stage in this sequence have been found in existing living species. The existence of this range of less complex light-sensitive structures supports scientists' hypotheses about how complex eyes like ours could evolve."

Other examples of supposed "irreducible complexity" in biological systems have been identified by proponents of intelligent design, and each has been countered effectively by knowledgeable scientists. It has been noted that the intelligent design movement has yet to publish a properly peer-reviewed article in a scientific journal. Countering the claim that their papers have been rejected because of bias, a scientist named two others who have challenged Darwinian concepts and have not been shunned or persecuted. "They are doing science, not religion," he stated.

Intelligent Design Fails in Court
Dover is a small town in Pennsylvania, about 20 miles south of Harrisburg, the state capital. It is also located in York County and a few miles from York city, the county seat. That county's southern boundary is the Mason-Dixon line, the boundary with Maryland. In 2005, it became the focus of a lawsuit about the teaching of evolution, as the small town of Dayton, Tennessee, became, almost exactly eighty years earlier. The stakes were similar, although no nationally known celebrities came to Dover.

In October 2004, the school board of the Dover Area School District, on the initiative of two members who were creationists, voted 6-to-3 that the following statement would be made a part of the curriculum in biology: "Students will be made aware of the gaps/problems in Darwin's theory and of other theories of evolution including, but not limited to, intelligent design."

About one month later, the school board issued a press release supporting this position, including the following phrasing: "Darwin's Theory . . . is not a fact. Gaps in the Theory exist for which there is no evidence ... Intelligent design is an explanation of the origin of life that differs from Darwin's view."

The ACLU, along with Americans United for Separation of Church and State, filed suit against the Dover Area School District on behalf of 11 parents with children in its schools. The lead plaintiff was parent Tammy Kitzmiller, in whose name the suit is referenced. The trial began in September 2005 before Judge John E. Jones III (b. 1955) of the US District Court for the Middle District of Pennsylvania. (There was no jury.) Jones was appointed by President George W. Bush in 2002 and had been characterized as a conservative Republican.

Judge Jones's decision, in December 2005, was a strong blow to intelligent design and, as of 2011, no appeal has been filed. Some of the statements in the judge's opinion are as follows:

> ... the facts of this case make it abundantly clear that the Board's ID (Intelligent Design) Policy violates the Establishment Clause [of the First Amendment to the US Constitution] ...

> ... the writings of leading ID proponents reveal that the designer postulated by their argument is the God of Christianity.

> ID is not science. We find that ID fails on three different levels, any one of which is sufficient to preclude a determination that ID is science. They are (1) ID violates the centuries-old ground rules of science by invoking and permitting supernatural causation; (2) the argument of irreducible complexity, central to ID, employs the same flawed and illogical contrived dualism that doomed creation science in the 1980s, and (3) ID's negative attacks on evolution have been refuted by the scientific community.

We may not be done with Intelligent Design. Additional attempts to impose religious beliefs in this manner may occur in other states of the United States.

2. Survival of the Fittest/Social Darwinism

The first phrase of this pair of identifiers was invented by Herbert Spencer (1820–1903), British philosopher and writer on many subjects, such as anthropology, biology, economics, political theory, psychology, and sociology. Spencer had read Charles Darwin's *Origin of Species* and coined the term as his summary of Darwin's ideas of 1859 in his own book *Principles of Biology, Vol. 1* (1864). He wrote, "This survival of the fittest, which I have here sought to express in mechanical terms, is that which Mr. Darwin has called 'natural selection' or the preservation of favoured races in the struggle for life" (444–445).

"Survival of the fittest" was used as a concept in the late nineteenth and early twentieth centuries in controversies related to the provision of charity to the poor, the use of medicine and surgery to repair the health of the ill, and competition among groups such as races, nations, or capitalist firms. Spencer, who was an early expositor of libertarianism or absolute minimum governmental interference in the private sector, was opposed to the adoption of legislation that aided the poor, regulated the workplace with safety requirements, set maximum working hours per day or week, and limited children's employment while requiring compulsory education for them. Spencer's viewpoint on these issues demonstrates that he interpreted "survival of the fittest" to imply the desirability of maximum competition among individuals without government interference to ensure that the strongest, the most clever, or those with the most resources do better than others.

Darwin himself, in his later book *The Descent of Man* (2nd ed., 1874), equates "natural selection" with "survival of the fittest" (62), although he states that it is limited to "adaptive changes in structure." However, in a later section titled "Natural Selection as Affecting Civilized Nations," he goes much further. He states that, because of such societal actions as smallpox vaccinations and because "our medical men exert their utmost skill to save the life of every one to the very last moment," "the weak members of civilized societies propagate their kind" (138). It is "to be hoped for rather than expected," he continues, "that the weaker and inferior members of society do not marry so freely as the sound" (139). Here,

Darwin demonstrates interest in a new subject: breeding a stronger and superior class of humans; see below under "3. Eugenics."

Opponents of those who justify aggression in competition as "survival of the fittest" often characterize that aggression as "Social Darwinism." While the latter term was used in Great Britain as early as 1877, it was popularized in the United States by historian Richard Hofstadter (1916–70) in his book *Social Darwinism in American Thought* (1944). The newer term has basically the same meaning as the older one, that is, the belief that the concept of natural selection applies to human cultural systems.

In the United States, William Graham Sumner (1840–1910) filled a niche equivalent to that occupied by Herbert Spencer in Great Britain. While Spencer was 20 years older, both were active during the final 35 years of the nineteenth century. Like Spencer, Sumner wrote books and essays on several academic subjects, such as anthropology, American history, economic history, political theory, and sociology. Sumner held libertarian attitudes similar to Spencer's and would be characterized as a Social Darwinist. In fact, Sumner, as a professor of sociology at Yale, wanted to use a book by Spencer in his syllabus, but that decision was opposed by Yale's president.

The era from the end of the Civil War in 1865 to the end of the nineteenth century is known in American history as the Gilded Age, so named after the title of a book coauthored by Mark Twain. It was an era of great industrial expansion, but also one of an increase in the disparity between rich and poor and exploitation of workers by rapacious employers. Owners of the larger, most successful of these businesses were often identified as "robber barons," who certainly would have agreed that they professed Social Darwinism if it had been explained to them. The name "Gilded Age" seemed appropriate for the ostentatious opulence by the newly rich, called "conspicuous consumption" by a leading American economist of the period Thorstein Veblen (1857–1929). Sumner's book *What Social Classes Owe to Each Other* (1883) averred that public assistance to the poor actually weakened their ability to persevere. In true libertarian style, Sumner favored a hands-off policy by government toward private industry.

Soon after the turn of the century, the Gilded Age morphed into the Progressive Era. Social Darwinism had run its course in the economic sphere, and the views of Spencer and Sumner were successfully opposed. The new political consensus in the United States, headed by such men as Theodore Roosevelt and Robert LaFollette Sr., spearheaded the beginnings of government regulation. Activities of robber barons began to be restrained with the Sherman Anti-Trust Act, and trade unions began to achieve acceptance. The federal income tax was adopted with the Sixteenth Amendment to the US Constitution, direct election of US Senators was imposed by the Seventeenth, and women were guaranteed the right to vote with the Nineteenth Amendment. All three of these enactments were intended to reduce public corruption and increase equality among all citizens. However, Social Darwinism would remain popular in certain quarters through the end of World War II, not in economic activity, but in what can be broadly described as racialism that claimed a scientific basis.

3. EUGENICS: JUSTIFYING COERCION AND VIOLENCE AGAINST THE WEAK OR POOR

Francis Galton (1822–1911) and Charles Darwin were both grandsons of English physician Erasmus Darwin (1731–1802), although by different wives of this patriarch. Galton, in his lifetime, made important contributions to certain applied sciences. He constructed the first popular weather maps (meteorology), significantly added to knowledge about correlation and regression (statistics), and made important analyses of fingerprints (criminology). Additionally, his enthusiasm for his half-cousin's work led him to establish an organization in 1907 that eventually became known as the Eugenics Society. "Eugenics" was a word that he invented.

Galton was desirous of improving the human race through breeding, as indicated by statements derived from his writings published in a British magazine called *MacMillan's* of 1864 and 1865. He later expanded his ideas in a book *Hereditary Genius* (1869). He proposed that human mating be given the same thought and deliberate action that animal husbandry applies to cattle, racehorses, and foxhounds. Perhaps he didn't realize the implications of his proposals: that people were to be figuratively put into kennels and stables and forced to couple with mates selected by some unnamed others serving as breeders. Later, he would agree that his proposal was unrealistic for implementation.

However, a group in the United States would work to implement coercive public policies consistent with Galton's concepts. This movement had widespread support from the turn of the twentieth century until World War II demonstrated where such views would lead. Descriptions of the situation, for example, in *War against the Weak* (2003) by Edwin Black, have revealed that eugenics had strong backing by certain wealthy and influential persons throughout the United States as well as in other countries. It was, to a large extent, in the United States, a supremacist movement favoring those with northwest European ancestry. Its prevalence strongly affected social policy in those years. Adolf Hitler praised the movement and incorporated eugenic ideas in *Mein Kampf* (1925). Eugenics lost favor after it was adopted by the Nazis in their program of killing individuals with mental and physical disabilities who were declared to be "life unworthy of life." The Nazi program, which began in 1939, was code-named "Aktion T4." Most of those killed in this manner were Christian, and the protests of relatives, as well as those of Roman Catholic Bishop Clemens von Galen, stopped this type of killing by 1941. (It appears that as many as 350,000 persons were forcibly sterilized in Nazi Germany but not killed.)

In the decades of its popularity, eugenics was promoted as a social philosophy for the improvement of human hereditary traits. One of its most influential supporters was Charles B. Davenport (1866–1944), who taught biology at Harvard, later at the University of Chicago. He founded a eugenics laboratory at Cold Spring Harbor, New York, with the support of the Carnegie Foundation and with funds from the widow of railroad magnate E. H. Harriman and from the Rockefeller Foundation. Davenport hired Harry H. Laughlin (1880–1943) to manage one part of the facility, the Eugenics Records Office. Davenport wrote in 1916 that "the general program of the eugenicist is clear—it is to improve the race... It also includes the control by the state of the propagation of the mentally incompetent."

A supporter of Davenport, Madison Grant (1865–1937), was a wealthy New York lawyer. He penned *The Passing of the Great Race: Or, the Racial Basis of European History* (1916). In his book, filled with ethnic and racial disparagements, he described his solution to crime and poverty. He wrote,

> A rigid system of selection through the elimination of those who are weak or unfit—in other words social failures—would allow [us to] solve the whole question in one hundred years, as well as enable us to get rid of the undesirables who crowd our jails, hospitals, and insane asylums... [S]terilization... is a practical, merciful, and inevitable solution of the whole problem, and can be applied to an ever widening circle of social discards, beginning always with the criminal, the diseased, and the insane, and extending gradually to types which may be called weaklings rather than defectives, and perhaps, ultimately to worthless race types. (46, 47)

Franz Boas, the German-American anthropologist mentioned in Chapter 3, and others with a similar understanding, opposed this program. They deserve commendation, but they were not the only ones. Nobel Prize–winning geneticist Thomas Hunt Morgan (1866–1945) of Columbia University was opposed, as was Clarence Darrow, counsel for the defense in the Scopes trial.

State-level legislation mandating sterilization of "unfit" members of society was adopted first in Indiana in 1907 and then in Connecticut in 1909. By 1914, 12 states had passed sterilization laws. However, some laws were ambiguous and were carelessly written so that they might be subject to Constitutional challenge. Harry H. Laughlin drafted a model law for compulsory sterilization and published it in his study *Eugenical Sterilization in the United States* (1922). Potential subjects for mandatory sterilization, according to Laughlin, were the feebleminded, the insane, criminals, epileptics, alcoholics, blind, deaf and deformed persons, and the indigent. By the end of the decade of the 1920s, some 18 additional states had adopted such laws, including Virginia in 1924. The right of the State of Virginia to sterilize a poor woman involuntarily was upheld by the US Supreme Court in *Buck v. Bell* (1927). Part of the insensitive and inhumane decision, written by Justice Oliver Wendell Holmes, Jr. (1841–1935), is quoted by Black (402). Laughlin, who had testified for the state in the state-level trial, also supported passage of Virginia's Racial Integrity Act of 1924, which outlawed interracial marriage. That law was overturned by the US Supreme Court in *Loving v. Virginia* in 1967. Mandatory sterilization laws began to be repealed after World War II, but some enforced sterilization continued into the 1970s. One source states that the last sterilization occurred in 1981. The total number of Americans thus violated was said to be about 60,000. Of these, about 20,000 sterilizations were performed in California. Other countries in which enforced sterilization was enacted include Canada, Japan, and Sweden. In the latter nation, a process of victim compensation has been implemented.

The eugenics movement also had an important impact on immigration into the United States, through its effect on passage of the Immigration (Johnson-Reed) Act of 1924. The law limited the number of immigrants who could be admitted from any country to 2 percent of the number of people from that country who were already living in the United States in 1890, based on the national census of that year. Much sentiment for passage was influenced by Madison Grant's book, identified earlier.

Enactment had been aided also by testimony from Harry H. Laughlin. His data was arranged to show that there was a difference in criminality between immigrants who came from northwest Europe compared to those who came from southern or eastern Europe. That is, he claimed that those from the northwest, such as Germans and English, were more law-abiding, while those who came from the south or east, such as Italians and Russians, were less so. Later, analysis of Laughlin's statistics by Johns Hopkins geneticist Herbert Spencer Jennings (1868–1947) showed that the conclusions were specious. Laughlin had not properly classified the Irish, who came from northwest Europe but were apparently more similar to the Italians than others from their home region. The concept that these national groupings were genetically distinct and that they differed in the prevalence of inherent criminality among them was totally incorrect.

The effect of the law was to strongly reduce the number of immigrants from southern and eastern Europe, in particular, Italians, Greeks, and Jews from Russia. These people had begun to come to the United States in great numbers in the 1890s, but their ability to immigrate for a better life was now diminished. Many American Jews believed that the law was discriminatory against Jewish immigration; Emanuel Celler (1888–1981), a US Representative who voted against the law, was one of those. However, Samuel Gompers (1850–1924), who was also Jewish and headed the American Federation of Labor at the time, favored the legislation. It could be said more generally that the law discriminated against immigrants who were not of the majority faith practiced in northwest Europe. The act also discriminated against Asians, for example Chinese and Japanese. The law stated that no alien ineligible to become a citizen (as Chinese and Japanese were at the time) could be admitted to the United States as an immigrant. Following World War II, US immigration laws were revised to eliminate the quota system of the Johnson-Reed Act of 1924.

Much more is now known about heredity since the double-helix form of DNA was determined in 1953. This work has led to significant increases in the area of knowledge known as molecular biology. It is now generally understood that social conditions do not have a genetic basis. This finding undercuts the basic premise of the eugenics movement. "Eugenics," as a term, is no longer used. Additionally, "weak" and "feebleminded," both widely applied during the heyday of the eugenics movement to persons to be sterilized, are subjective and pejorative terms with no generally accepted technical or scientific meaning. However, there is evidence that certain diseases or medical conditions have a genetic basis, at least in part, but a full understanding is not known. Other diseases are known to be fully genetically caused. Genetic counseling and screening by biomedical experts are now used to inform prospective parents of the likelihood of their offspring's having certain fatal or seriously debilitating diseases.

Diseases with a genetic basis include color blindness, cystic fibrosis, Down syndrome, hemophilia, Klinefelter's syndrome, phenylketonuria, progeria, and sickle-cell disease. Rare conditions may be difficult to diagnose. A child born in Frederick, Maryland, in 2002 was not properly diagnosed with Cohen's syndrome (named for the physician who first described it) until 2008 at the Kennedy Krieger Institute in Baltimore. Certain genetic disorders may be more common in specific populations. Cohen's syndrome appears primarily in persons of Amish and Finnish descent.

In the nation of Cyprus, a screening process is required before marriage to reduce the incidence of thalassemia, a hereditary blood disorder. Since the start of the screening, the incidence of children born with the condition has been reduced from one out of 158 births to near zero. In Israel, screening programs are run at state expense in order to reduce the incidence of a number of inherited diseases, such as Tay-Sachs. If both parties to an expected marriage have the gene generating this disease, marriage is not advised. Children of such a marriage are likely to be victims of Infantile Tay-Sachs disease, and may die by the age of 4. A father who lost several children because of this condition was instrumental in establishment of the government program.

A Humanistic View of the Real Creation Story

Human Life: Its History and Value

As pointed out in Chapter 2, the development of humanity has taken 13.73 billion years from the Big Bang and 4.56 billion years from the formation of the Earth. We know that all humans now living are members of the same subspecies, *homo sapiens sapiens*. The basic physical and mental makeup of each of us at the time of birth (excluding those with birth defects, who, according to true believers, must have been born with God's permission, if not approval) is very similar every other, within a very narrow range. If you prick any of us, we bleed human blood; Shakespeare implied something similar in *The Merchant of Venice* in having his protagonist make the point that Jews were no different from Christians in this regard.

An important book that attempts to reconcile belief in God with personal experience of inexplicable suffering is *When Bad Things Happen to Good People* (1981) by Rabbi Harold S. Kushner. The author fathered a child with a severe genetic disorder (progeria), resulting in an early death. His chapter heading "God Can't Do Everything, But He Can Do Some Important Things" (113) is a rare admission by a clergyman. His book has been popular, for good reasons.

Each of us has feelings, that is, we are sentient. We hurt if attacked physically or emotionally. We may laugh or cry, become angry or ecstatically happy. Each of us has a large repertoire of such feelings; they show themselves at different times but may not last long at each occurrence. However, simmering anger that is retained can be disastrous. The first person each of us knows is our mother, who is usually loving, but not in every case. We form attachments to other humans in our local group, usually our close family, but sometimes others. Additionally, we have memory and intelligence, implying that we can learn and store what we learn. In general, we can retrieve from memory what we have learned, but not necessarily everything and, of that which we can retrieve, some of it may be distorted or incomplete. We have developed the use of language and its extensions, such as rhetoric, poetry, and literature, as well as a large variety of music and an enormous number of tools, some of incredible complexity.

An essential value judgment expressed here is that human life is both precious and sacred. Each human life has equal value, and that means all human life, not just the life of our family, ethnic group, religion, nationality, or race. For believers to accept this statement, they would require the approval of their god, who often denigrates nonbelievers. Among the function of gods is to provide simple answers to very fundamental and difficult questions. What is asserted here, without resorting to the supernatural, is the following:

- It has taken billions of years for humanity to evolve and, if not unique in the entire universe, we are rare enough that, so far, no other example has been found. Life like ours, if found on a planet of another star, may be hundreds or even millions of light-years away. Consequently, exchange of communications between living persons in the two separate worlds is likely to be impossible. Each world would know the other only as it was many years before, because any information transmitted could not travel faster than the speed of light.

- Therefore, our life is only here on Earth, and it is very special; there are no superior beings from other worlds who can provide us with extraterrestrial wisdom. As Walt Kelly said some years ago in his comic strip *Pogo*, "We have met the enemy and he is us." We are responsible for ourselves and must ensure that life here is preserved and enhanced.

- Humans are enormously creative, and the nurturing of human life may lead to additional intellectual creations in the sciences, the humanities, and in worldwide political arrangements that could improve the quality of life, or at least make it more fulfilling and less dangerous. Retention of current knowledge is essential so that it can be built upon.

- Human life involves suffering, and each human is similar to every other. The reciprocity formulated as the Golden Rule applies to each of us: do not do unto others what you would not want done to you.

- Humans are a social species; each human is related to a family or family-like group that provides support; the hurt applied to one human affects the members of that family or group. The Golden Rule should apply to groups as well as to individuals, although this is rarely stated and even less applied. Human divisiveness, some of it fostered by religions, has prevented its widespread application.

Modern Humanism and Its Significant Documents

World War I (1914–18) marked the beginning of a new era in the history of Western civilization. Besides the fact that its outcome resulted in the fall of four important monarchies and other significant political changes, it was the first mechanized land war, fought with tanks, machine guns, and poison gas, none of which had been used previously. About eight million soldiers were killed, all of them from overwhelmingly Christian nations, except those from Turkey and Japan. Several million soldiers were killed in the trench warfare on the Western Front. Even before the even-worse slaughter of World War II (1939–45), thoughtful people must have wondered why the Christian God, if such an entity really existed, would have permitted such a thing to happen.

One outcome of the international slaughter was a greater interest in ethical action within a matrix of humanism. By this term is meant a philosophy that, without supernaturalism, affirms each person's ability and responsibility to lead an ethical life that contributes to the greater good of all humanity. An organized humanistic movement began following World War I. The Humanist Fellowship was founded in the United States in 1928 and by 1941 was called the American Humanist Association. This idea was not new; certainly the rationalism of the late eighteenth century tended in that direction.

Some significant humanist documents, intended for worldwide distribution, are described immediately below. The presentation of praiseworthy materials from each of these documents does not imply agreement with certain other items contained within them and not reported here. Such items, such as calls for major changes in our economic system and implementation of world government, have little merit as written in the original documents.

Humanist Manifesto of 1933

The Humanist Manifesto was written in 1933 by Raymond B. Bragg, secretary of the Western Unitarian Conference, and Roy Wood Sellars, professor of philosophy at the University of Michigan. The 34 signers, all from the United States, included nine persons identified with the Unitarian or Universalist Church, one rabbi, and 11 professors associated with universities. Psychologist and educational reformer John Dewey was one of the latter.

The authors of this document appear not to be sure whether they want to be known as "humanists" or "religious humanists." Both terms are used. Later manifestos would drop "religious." Within their 15 numbered statements, they wrote the following:

Humanism asserts that the nature of the universe depicted by modern science makes unacceptable any supernatural or cosmic guarantees of human values.

The individual born into a particular culture is largely molded by that culture.

Religious Humanism considers the complete realization of human personality to be the end of man's life and seeks its development and fulfillment in the here and now.

... the humanist finds his religious emotions ... in a cooperative effort to promote social well-being.

Nonsupernaturalism, fulfillment of human aspirations on Earth and not in heaven, respect for others, and cooperation among all humans are all hallmarks of the humanist philosophy.

Humanist Manifesto II of 1973

The Humanist Manifesto II was signed by 114 individuals in 1973. Among the signers were 14 from the United Kingdom, three from Canada, two from Belgium, two from the USSR, and one each from India, Netherlands, and Yugoslavia. The remaining 90 were from the United States. Of the Americans, eight identified themselves as associated with the Unitarian or Universalist Church and two identified themselves as Jews. The latter were Mordecai M. Kaplan, founder of the Jewish Reconstructionist Movement, and Sherwin T. Wine, founder of the Society for Humanistic Judaism. One of the two from the USSR was physicist and future Nobel Peace Prize–winner Andre Sakharov. A signer from Canada was Kai Nielsen, professor of philosophy, University of Calgary, the author of *Ethics without God* (1972), later revised in 1990 and further cited below. A large number of signers, besides Nielsen, were associated with universities, for example, B. F. Skinner (Harvard), Lionel Able (SUNY-Buffalo), Brand Blanshard (Yale), Herman Bondi (University of London), and Sidney Hook (New York University). Other well-known names included author and professor Isaac Asimov, poet John Ciardi, Nobel Prize recipient Francis Crick (mentioned in Chapter 2), psychologist Albert Ellis, and Planned Parenthood executive Alan Guttmacher. The manifesto categorizes its 17 numbered paragraphs into five topics. Quotes from each topic are provided here.

- Religion: "We find insufficient evidence for belief in the existence of a supernatural; it is either meaningless or irrelevant to the question of survival and fulfillment of the human race."
- Ethics: "We affirm that moral values derive their source from human experience . . . Human life has meaning because we create and develop our futures . . . We strive for the good life, here and now."
- The Individual: "The preciousness and dignity of the individual person is a central humanist value . . . We believe in maximum individual autonomy consonant with social responsibility . . . The right to birth control, abortion, and divorce should be recognized . . . Short of harming others or compelling them to do likewise, individuals should be permitted to express their sexual proclivities and pursue their lifestyles as they desire."
- Democratic Society: "To enhance freedom and dignity, the individual must experience a full range of civil liberties in all societies . . . The separation of church and state [is] imperative . . . We are concerned for the welfare of the aged, the infirm, the disadvantaged, and also for the outcasts—the mentally retarded, abandoned, or abused children, the handicapped, prisoners, and addicts."
- World Community: "War is obsolete. So is the use of nuclear, biological, and chemical weapons . . . The planet Earth must be considered a single ecosystem. Ecological damage must be checked by international concord."

THE SECULAR HUMANIST DECLARATION OF 1980

In 1980 a Secular Humanist Declaration was issued by the Council for Secular Humanism, headquartered in the United States. It was signed by 58 individuals, 36 of whom were from the United

States, 11 from the United Kingdom, and 11 from six other countries. Some of the signers had also signed Humanist Manifesto II.

Among its declarations in its 11 paragraphs are the following quotes:

> Separation of church and state: Clerical authorities should not be permitted to legislate their own parochial views . . . for the rest of society. Nor should tax revenues be enacted for the benefit or support of sectarian religious institutions.

> . . . we consistently defend . . . minority rights and the rule of law.

> The right to private property is a human right without which other rights are [inoperative].

> . . . ethical judgments can be formulated independently of revealed religion.

> [We understand] the requirements of social justice and the individual's obligations and responsibilities toward others.

> We . . . conclude that the ethical life can be lived without the illusions of immortality or reincarnation.

Humanist Manifesto III of 2003

This document, titled "Humanism and Its Aspirations," was published by the American Humanist Association. There were 99 signers, including 18 Nobel laureates in physics, chemistry, and medicine. New, well-known signers included film director Oliver Stone, author Kurt Vonnegut, and biologist Edward O. Wilson.

This declaration does not provide ideals that are significantly different than any of the texts previously described. However, the emphasis is slightly different, as demonstrated with the following quotes:

Humans are an integral part of nature, the result of unguided evolutionary change.

We work to uphold the equal enjoyment of human rights and civil liberties in an open, secular society, and maintain that it is a civic duty to participate in the democratic process and a planetary duty to protect nature's integrity, diversity and beauty in a secure, sustainable manner.

Three Other Recent and Important Documents on Ethical Action

The following texts were intended for worldwide application and did not exclude believers in the supernatural.

Universal Declaration of Human Rights

This document was adopted by the United Nations in 1948. A US delegate to the United Nations, Eleanor Roosevelt, widow of President Franklin D. Roosevelt, chaired the committee that drafted the declaration. The document adopts the type of explicit civil rights given US citizens under Constitutional Amendments 1, 4, 5, 6, 7, 8, 13, and 19, as well as the "due process" and "equal protection" concepts of Amendment 14. Additionally, the declaration includes the following statements, which are implicit in the US Constitution and expressed in subsequent federal or state laws:

- All persons have a right to their privacy.
- Free and full consent of persons to be married to each other is to be required.
- Freedoms of thought, conscience, and religion are essential.
- The authority of government is to be obtained by the will of the people through free and fair elections carried out by "secret vote or by equivalent free voting procedures."
- A recognized principle is that everyone has duties to the community.

The Geneva Spiritual Appeal of 1999

Buddhist, Roman Catholic, Orthodox Christian, Protestant Christian, Jewish, and Muslim leaders signed the Geneva Spiritual Appeal document at Geneva, Switzerland, in 1999, a full 50 years after the signing of the Geneva Conventions. Also present at the signing were heads of secular groups, including the International Committee of the Red Cross, the World Health Organization, and the UN Commissions on Human Rights and Refugees.

The signers appealed "to the leaders of the world . . . to strictly adhere to the following three principles:

1. "A refusal to invoke a religious or spiritual power to justify violence of any kind"
2. "A refusal to invoke a religious or spiritual source to justify discrimination and exclusion"
3. "A refusal to exploit or dominate others by means of strength, intellectual capacity or spiritual persuasion, wealth or social status."

The Charter for Compassion of 2009

A Charter for Compassion was developed and signed in 2009, with the primary impetus of Karen Armstrong, the author of books on religion and quoted in Chapter 1. She had won a prize calling for her to make a wish important enough to change the world. As of May 2011, over 70,000 people have signed the charter online.

The charter is short, less than one double-spaced typewritten page. It is, perhaps, the Gettysburg Address of all the documents cited. The following is from the charter:

- "The principle of compassion lies at the heart of all religious, ethical and spiritual traditions, calling us always to treat all others as we wish to be treated ourselves."
- "It is also necessary in both public and private life to refrain consistently and empathetically from inflicting pain."
- ". . . any interpretation of scripture that breeds violence, hatred or disdain is illegitimate."

Imperatives for Individuals

Facts Brought to Light

The text of this book, including the quotes above from seven manifestos and declarations, has provided guidance for actions in support of sacred ideals that are intended to preserve and enhance human life. The facts supporting the guidance includes the following:

- Events on Earth occur according to physical laws only, never because of supernatural interference.
- The practice of religion is unlikely to end as long as humans continue to die; religion is as old as humanity, and it has some inherent value, as evidenced by continuing membership by many rational individuals who demonstrate a humane outlook on life.
- A Spiritual World may or may not exist; humans are entitled to act according to their beliefs, within the context of reasonable local law.
- Religion, more so when it can exercise state power, has been responsible for extensive violence and discrimination against nonbelievers.
- The Golden Rule is an essential guideline for human interpersonal interaction. An enlightening exposition on this general subject is *The Power of Kindness; The Unexpected Benefits of Leading a Compassionate Life* (2007), by Italian psychologist Piero Ferrucci.

Actions Called for by Each Human

Actively Support Separation of Church and State

This concept, stated explicitly in the First Amendment to the US Constitution, is an essential buttress against interfaith strife and totalitarian domination; it must be actively protected and enforced. Fundamentalists are continually attempting to find ways to minimize its effect and to oppose its intent, for example, by promoting public subsidies to religious schools, by erecting religious symbols on public property, and by proposing prayers to "God" during public functions. In 2010, about $80,000 of public money was used to support an event sponsored by the Billy Graham Evangelistic Association at a US military base in North Carolina. Citizens accepting the sacred ideals presented here should join and contribute to organizations whose function is to preserve the First Amendment guarantee of separation through voter mobilization and active political pressure on public executives, legislatures, and the judiciary.

Work to Eliminate Hateful Characterizations of Nonbelievers

The three principles of *The Geneva Spiritual Appeal of 1999*, although directed to "the leaders of the world," should be actively supported by individual members of religious organizations. Individual adherents of a religion should review prayer books, other documents of their respective religions, and public statements of their leaders to identify bigotry and hateful characterizations. (Note also the third quote from the *Charter for Compassion of 2009*.) Believers should join with others of their particular denomination to have these statements eliminated or satisfactorily altered. Statements in holy books that cannot be changed should be reinterpreted to make clear that characterizations of nonbelievers that were made many centuries ago do not apply to persons living today.

Celebrate Each Person's Life Passages

Discrete passages from one phase of life to another, that is, birth, coming of age, marriage, and death, are the most significant steps in an individual's human journey. It is symbolic of the sacredness of human life to recognize these events in each human, and to carry out appropriate celebrations. Even those who do not fully subscribe to the particular theologies of their respective denominations may find the rites of those denominations appropriate to use in these important events in the presence of family and close friends. Atheists who cannot abide any religious rite should find a method of invoking the sacred, that is, humanity's highest ideals, in marking these occasions.

Evaluate Ethical Issues with Scientific Information and Compassion

Issues such as end of life, abortion, the beginning of life, and circumcision should be resolved with the aid of expert medical opinion and respect for human life and not with the ideology of religion or of atheism. The following text presents information for rational, ethical decision-making.

End of Life

The cessation of brain activity generally indicates death. The physician attending a dying person and any medical consultants the physician employs should be the ones to pronounce a person as deceased with the cessation of brain activity. The human body can be kept "alive" with the aid of a machine even when a person has brain activity that is minimal or absent. If the deceased person is a pregnant woman, life-support may be appropriate to attempt to save the fetus. (This has been done in some recent cases.) Other than that exception, maintaining life of a body when the brain is dead or in a "persistent vegetative state" is a ghoulish procedure and is disrespectful of the deceased. Every competent person should execute a "living will" to prevent this from happening at some indeterminate future time.

Abortion and the Beginning of Life

As a human fetus is not an independent entity and depends on the woman bearing it for providing its sustenance, almost all rational people believe that human life begins at birth, and not before. For most people, certainly including many religious folk as well as humanists, if there is competition between the life of the pregnant woman and the life of the fetus due to a medical emergency, the life of the woman, a genuinely living human being, takes precedence. For most of us, the idea that the life of the fetus has priority is inhumane and untenable. (Note that *Humanist Manifesto II of 1973* calls for the right to birth control and abortion.) In Phoenix, in 2010, an administrator in a hospital associated with the Roman Catholic Church decided, in agreement with the patient's doctors, to save the life of a pregnant but critically ill woman by aborting the fetus. For this action, she was severely disciplined by the hospital management. Nevertheless, she should have a clear conscience, understanding that whoever saves a single life saves the whole world (a viewpoint originally expressed in the Talmud, tractate Sanhedrin 37a, and widely appreciated in modern times).

Thus "a woman's right to choose" whether or not to have an abortion has primacy. The idea that abortion is murder and should never be undertaken is a religious ideology that is unmerciful and irrational. If any fetus is not to be aborted, a woman who is impregnated by rape or been taken in incest must endure nine months of hell. That is where rigid religious ideology leads. Furthermore, those who oppose abortion in any situation are promoting the birth of children who are unwanted, adding unnecessarily to overpopulation and subjecting the community to additional and unnecessary costs of care.

Given recent advances in medical technology that permit the successful delivery of a late-term fetus, a woman who must abort due a medical condition, or who wishes to abort, may be willing to have a survivable fetus born instead (possibly by C-section), if that is medically feasible without harming her. This suggests a possible reasonable change in public policy toward very-late-term abortions. The mother could willingly give up the child, if born alive, to the care of the state, which assumes all costs.

Male Circumcision
Jewish and Muslim males are circumcised as a religious commandment. Jewish infant boys are required to have the procedure done on the eighth day of life (with delay permitted for health reasons). Muslim males are typically circumcised on the seventh day of life or at a later time often connected to the number seven. In both religions, the respective holy scripture implies the particular day following birth on which the circumcision is to be performed. Consider the possibility that the sages of many centuries ago who instituted the procedure may have begun to realize the health benefits, but made it a religious requirement because of understandable resistance by parents. The founders of Christianity eliminated the circumcision requirement to attract believers from the Greco-Roman world where the procedure was not done and, since then,

Christians have avoided it as a practice of a religion that they believe their own religion replaced.

Christopher Hitchens, in *god is Not Great,* wrote a diatribe against male circumcision (225, 226), calling it "a hideous procedure" and "a mutilation of a powerless infant with the aim of ruining its future sex life." Hitchens wrote also that "Medicine has exploded . . . claims" that circumcision has health benefits. He did not understand why "Christian doctors began to adopt ancient Jewish folklore in their hospitals." His palpable hostility that displayed an embarrassing ignorance was severely misplaced.

It is likely that these Christian physicians cited by Hitchens are not blinded by the same ideology that has caused him to ignore facts readily available. As a matter of course, many infants in the US are circumcised, regardless of the parents' religion because of general recognition by physicians that it is a healthful procedure. Hitchens should have been aware of studies, publicized around the year 2000, which demonstrated that, in Africa, uncircumcised, primarily Christian men, were far more likely to contract the AIDS virus than circumcised, primarily Muslim men. Correct information is easily available in many places, for example, on the Internet. At the International Circumcision Information Reference Centre (http://www.circinfo.com/benefits/bmc.html), a presentation dated March 2004 (before publication of Hitchens's book) by British physician David Hawker provides several benefits of circumcision. Among these are the following:

- "Cancer of the cervix in women is due to the Human Papilloma Virus. It thrives under and on the foreskin from where it can be transmitted during intercourse. An article in the *British Medical Journal* in April 2002 suggested that at least 20 percent of cancer of the cervix would be avoided if all men were circumcised."
- "Another *British Medical Journal* article in May 2000 suggested that circumcised men are 8 times less likely to contract the HIV virus;"
- "Lots of men, and their partners, prefer the appearance of their penis after circumcision. It is odour-free, it feels cleaner,

and they enjoy better sex." (Compare with Hitchens's assertion on circumcision ruining a man's sex life.)
- "Balanitis is an unpleasant, often recurring, inflammation of the glans. It is quite common and can be prevented by circumcision."
- "Urinary tract infections sometimes occur in babies and can be quite serious. Circumcision in infancy makes it ten times less likely."

A similar set of benefits is reported at Medscape (http://www.medscape.com/viewarticle/714553). This webpage consists of an article dated January 2010 titled "New Data Support Long-Term Health Benefits of Male Circumcision." The data were developed by Aaron A. R. Tobian, MD, and colleagues. Tobian is associated with Johns Hopkins University School of Medicine, Baltimore, one of the nation's premier medical research facilities. The studies revealed that "Male circumcision significantly decreased male heterosexual HIV transmission." It "decreased herpes simplex virus type-2 acquisition" and decreased infections in female partners. "Because of the new evidence, the World Health Organization (WHO) together with the Joint United Nations Program on HIV/AIDS (UNAIDS), recommended that male circumcision be provided as an important intervention to reduce heterosexually acquired HIV in men."

There is no reason that circumcision should not be added to the many immunization and anti-infection procedures already recommended for newborns and infants by the American Academy of Pediatrics and American Academy of Family Physicians.

Important Issue (1)—Just Governance Is a Sacred Value

Humanist Manifesto III of 2003 specified that it is a "civic duty to participate in the democratic process," and the *Universal Declaration of Human Rights* stated that "everyone has duties to the community." Two often-cited quotations with a similar viewpoint are these: "Eternal vigilance is the price of liberty" and "All that is necessary for the triumph of evil is for good men to do nothing."

Both quotations imply that involvement to ensure just governance is a sacred duty for citizens. Government is the primary way that all citizens act together as one community. Areas of governance that could benefit from additional citizen concern are the following

Personal Education

Citizens need to understand public issues so that they can effectively evaluate candidate and officeholder statements, and vote intelligently. Government actions affect all of us; participation in determining government's direction is a civic duty.

Equitable Tax Policy

Fairness requires that those with higher disposable incomes should pay a proportionately increasing percentage of their incomes as taxes. Related items are "Fiscal Responsibility" and "Social Justice," below.

Fiscal Responsibility

While the extension of the human life-span in the past several decades may require changes in the parameters of social security, pensions, and health benefits, it is the elimination of the threat from the former Soviet Union that should bring about further savings in US national expenditures. Individual terrorists carrying bombs hidden in their clothing cannot be fought with supersonic aircraft, nuclear-driven aircraft carriers, and intercontinental ballistic missiles. Significant reductions in US Department of Defense expenditures for development and deployment of advanced weapons systems should be possible, providing a major aid to federal budget balancing.

Election Administration

The basic requirement for fair elections is for suffrage that is universal for all adult citizens, with minimal exceptions (such as for incarcerated felons), and a voter-friendly secret ballot used by citizens who cannot be coerced, bribed, intimidated, or prevented from voting. Those entitled to vote should be able to do so by obtaining the necessary documentation of identity with ease and free of cost. Requiring a payment or an involved procedure in order to vote is contrary in the United States to the intent of the Twenty-Fourth Amendment, which eliminates poll taxes. Election administration at every level should be carried out by a bipartisan commission that hires an operating executive by merit only. Partisan election administration in Florida in the 2000 presidential election was a disgrace to the United States and a travesty of a fair election process. Additionally, better data systems that do not impose difficulties on citizens are needed to ensure that noncitizens cannot vote and that citizens cannot vote twice in the same election. A national, interstate voter-identity databank might assist this effort.

Funding of Elections

The US Supreme Court decision in *Citizens United v. Federal Election Commission (2010)* has opened the door to unlimited private expenditures to influence elections, an outcome that is dangerous to democracy. Citizens should ask their members of Congress to work actively to reverse or ameliorate this decision. The Court's ruling that corporations have the same civil rights as individuals is puzzling, as a corporation is a legal artifice to provide owners with limited liability, a boon not available to real flesh-and-blood persons.

Criminal Justice

The assurance of equal justice under the rule of law is a sacred value. Penalties for various crimes should be consistent with the severity of the crime with respect to impact on the victims. An efficient and well-funded police force and prosecutorial staff should ensure that the actual criminals are arrested and prosecuted, and that innocent persons are not incorrectly prosecuted or convicted. Certainly, the systems in democratic nations are far more equitable than those of either China or Russia. In China, incarceration of dissidents without trial is common. In Russia, there is a more reasonable process but, for political prosecutions, a guilty verdict is preordained; as an example, whistleblower Serge Magnitsky was imprisoned and tortured to death. The failure to identify and prosecute the murderers of outspoken critics such as Natalya Estemirova and Anna Politikovskaya is a black mark against any Russian claim of a just society. In the United States, prosecutors need to resist pressures that call for someone's conviction, regardless of whether it is justified. False imprisonment is a serious crime, and horrendous if done through lawful procedures in a democratic nation.

A specific example of this type of malfeasance (and there are many others) was the conviction of Martin Tankleff of Suffolk County, New York, for the murder of both his parents in 1988. Immediately after the crime was discovered, the boy, then 17, was brought to a police facility where he was interrogated without benefit of counsel by a detective for several hours. With the aid of a lie, that the boy's father, then in a coma preceding his death in a hospital, had accused his son of the crime, the detective was able to coerce the boy to falsely admit guilt. The "confession" was almost immediately repudiated and no physical evidence against the boy whatsoever (such as blood on his clothing or a murder weapon) was found. Additionally, there was circumstantial evidence connected to a visitor to the house the previous evening, who owed the father a substantial amount of money. The district attorney of Suffolk County ignored the lack of evidence and obtained a conviction. Tankleff served 17 years in prison, but was eventually exonerated with the help of family, another detective acting in a pro bono capacity, the voluntary confessions of associates of the probable mastermind, and a special judicial panel formed by the governor of New York.

Among the many exonerated persons who spent significant time in prison are Roy A. Brown of Cayuga County, New York; Clarence Elkins of Barberton, Ohio; Joshua Kezer of Jefferson City, Missouri; and Julie Rea Harper of Lawrenceville, Illinois. Clarence Brandley of Conroe, Texas, a black man whose prosecution involved racism, spent nine years on death row before exoneration. The story of Randall Dale Adams was told in the 1988 movie *The Thin Blue Line*. According to his obituary in *The Washington Post* of June 27, 2011, "Mr. Adams became a symbol of a fallible criminal justice system that—aided by perjured witnesses and overzealous prosecutors—could convict the wrong man."

The function of a prosecutor should be to pursue justice ("justice, justice shalt thou follow," states Deuteronomy 16:20), not simply work to jail whoever is easily convictable without the effort of a full investigation. Belated DNA testing has freed hundreds of innocents, many with the help of *The Innocence Project*.

SOCIAL JUSTICE

A goal of a humane and civilized society should be to make it possible for each individual to achieve his or her potential. A "safety net" for those unable to care for themselves is an ever-present requirement. An increasing income gap, as is now occurring in the United States, may indicate the presence of a problem of social justice. A 2005 report by well-qualified financial analysts showed that America is composed of two distinct economic groups: the rich and the rest. The richest 1 percent earns as much as the bottom 60 percent put together, and they possess as much wealth as the bottom 90 percent (see bibliographic reference by Don Peck).

ILLEGAL IMMIGRATION

The presence of approximately 11 million illegal immigrants in the United States in 2011 is an indication that the existing legislation is ineffective. Disrespect for government and legal inequities have been generated. A solution is needed in the very near future. The interpretation of the Fourteenth Amendment that guaranteed citizenship to newly freed slaves in 1865 may not be appropriate to be applied to newly born infants of illegal immigrants in the twenty-first century.

PUBLIC INTEGRITY

There must be an absence of bribery or conflict of interest in public decision-making.

Merit-Based Staffing

Civil servants performing professional or clerical duties that have no political content should be hired and retained on merit, not on political or family connections or other nonmerit factors.

Important Issue (2)—Ending Organized Violence against Women Is a Sacred Cause

While men commit far more violent crimes than women, men are also more often the victims of violence. Almost all the soldiers killed in wars have been men. However, females have a special vulnerability, and there are certain crimes and violent actions against females that deserve heightened concern. While the majority of these activities do not occur in First World countries, some actually have occurred in countries such as the United States, primarily due to immigration from undeveloped nations. Individuals with sacred values need to be aware of these types of violent activities, in order to make their voices heard in helping to eliminate them everywhere.

Female Genital Cutting

At some time in the past, "female circumcision" was used to describe this process. However, it is generally understood now that, in whatever form it is practiced, female genital cutting is not at all analogous to male circumcision. Christopher Hitchens wrote that "little girls can be Jewish without genital alteration; it is useless to look for consistency in the covenants that people believe they have made with god" (223). Hitchens, in his concern for consistency, forgot or ignored Ralph Waldo Emerson's maxim that "a foolish consistency is the hobgoblin of little minds."

Both the World Health Organization (WHO) and the United Nations have resolved to oppose female genital cutting (FGC). A study by the WHO raised concern for the safety of any type of genital cutting. The study showed that if an FGC procedure had been done on a prospective mother, an increased risk of death was passed on to the baby. The UN Population Fund has stated that FGC "violates the basic rights of women and girls." Neither Jewish or Muslim law requires FGC. It was made illegal in the United States in a law adopted in 1996. One immigrant was convicted of it in 2006.

FGC appears to be most prevalent in a band across central Africa, from Benin on the west coast to Somalia on the east, plus Sudan and Egypt. These cases continue to occur despite the adoption of the African Union of the Maputo Protocol in 2003 calling for an end to FGC. The procedure is also practiced in the Arabian peninsula and in Kurdish regions of several nations.

Honor Killings

This crime involves the murder of a relative who supposedly has brought dishonor on the family. Reasons for such killings of a young women can include refusing to marry a preselected spouse, being raped, or becoming more modern in lifestyle. A large majority of such crimes are against women or girls, but some young men are also killed. In a documented case, a gay Turkish man was shot by his brother.

In some countries such as Pakistan, where honor killings have a long history, leniency for perpetrators is common. In the United States, murder is almost always prosecuted severely; an honor killing should be classified as murder in the first degree, as it is certainly premeditated. There have been such killings in the United States and other Western nations such as Germany, perpetrated within immigrant families from Muslim countries. Respect for other cultures must not include passive acceptance of this type of genuine crime.

Human Trafficking

The felononious practice of human trafficking involves the coerced activities of innocent persons by criminal gangs for the purpose of earning money from commercial sexual exploitation, forced labor, or debt bondage. With increased ease of travel around the world, such crimes have become more frequent. In sexual exploitation, virtually all the victims are female. The increased prevalence of trafficking across national boundaries has resulted in national and international efforts to stamp it out. The United Nations, in 2000, adopted the Protocol to Prevent, Suppress and Punish Trafficking in Persons, especially Women and Children, often identified as the UN Trafficking Protocol.

In 2000, the United States adopted a law entitled the Trafficking Victims Protection Act. There have been subsequent reauthorizations that continue the act in force. Each year since the passage of the act, the US Department of State has published a Trafficking in Persons Report. The report covers the extent of the problem for each nation on which it has done research, and it includes the efforts of those national governments to resolve the problems and prosecute offenders. In 2010, the report included such a country report for the United States, an effort not previously undertaken. Domestic examples of human trafficking may exist, and citizens should make available to law enforcement any information about this activity that they have obtained.

Human trafficking typically involves "source countries" from which individuals are taken, and "destination countries" to which the victims are transported. Major source countries are, in Asia, Thailand and China; in Europe, Albania, Bulgaria, Belarus, Moldova, and Ukraine; and in Central America, Guatemala and El Salvador. These countries typically have very low standards of living and have suffered from war or natural disasters Women in the source countries are lured by promises of legitimate jobs, but soon find out, too late, the functions intended for them by their captors. Major countries of destination include Belgium, Germany, Israel, Italy, Japan, Netherlands, Turkey, and the United States.

It has been estimated that about 15,000 persons are trafficked to the United States annually. The US Federal Bureau of Investigation (FBI) has undertaken an initiative on this subject. The agency works with other local, state, and federal law enforcement agencies and national victim-based advocacy groups in joint task forces. The FBI also participates in the Human Smuggling Trafficking Center, created in 2004 by the US Departments of State, Justice, and Homeland Security. Clearly, the issue is one that is not being ignored. Persons with any relevant information should not hesitate to speak with law enforcement authorities.

Hope—It Keeps Us Going

In Chapter 3, the story of Hugo Gryn was related. While he and his father were incarcerated at Auschwitz, his father told him that you can't live three minutes without hope—an important lesson. The younger Gryn survived.

Kai Nielsen (b. 1926), in *Ethics without God* (190), cites a famous trio of questions asked by philosopher Immanuel Kant (1724–1804). The first was "What can I know?" The answer given here includes the nonexistence of miracles and the evolution of humans by natural selection in a universe that began billions of years ago. Furthermore, all humans are sentient beings of one subspecies, with all the implications for equal and reciprocal treatment that may be drawn from that fact. Kant's second question was "What ought I to do?" This chapter has tried to provide some proposed actions that each of us can carry out, based on sacred values. Working toward just governance and ensuring total separation of religion from the state are two important areas of involvement. Another is striving to end denigration of nonbelievers in whatever religious denomination we know best. The Golden Rule is unsurpassed as a brief description of appropriate ethical action.

Kant's third question was "What may I hope?" It has been proposed that, if one works toward improving humanity, perhaps some additional success may be achieved. While there are reversals—for example, the twentieth century was a barbarous era of mechanized murder—perhaps humanity can do better than Sisyphus. We may be able to prevent the stone from rolling back all the way down the mountain if we have learned from the past. Then we can start again from a higher point than before.

To conclude on a positive note, some nonfundamentalist people continue to cite the Hebrew Bible because, among other reasons, it contains a number of impressive metaphors, some involving hope for a better world. My favorite, from Micah 3 and 4, is well-known for its majestic imagery that also displays immense literary power.

It is up to ourselves—all of humanity—to work to implement these soaring hopes as, certainly, no god has delivered them to us.

> And they shall beat their swords into plowshares,
> And their spears into pruning-hooks;
> Nation shall not lift up sword against nation,
> Neither shall they learn war any more.
> But they shall sit every man under his vine and under his fig tree,
> And none shall make them afraid.

References

Alhazen and A. I. Sabra. (1021) 1989. *The Optics of Ibn Al-Haytham*. London: Warburg Institute, University of London.

Armstrong, Karen. 1993. *A History of God*. New York: Ballantine Books.

———. 2009. *The Case for God*. New York: Knopf.

Atran, Scott. 2002. *In Gods We Trust: The Evolutionary Landscape of Religion*. New York: Oxford University Press.

Benson, Herbert, et al. 2006. "Study of the Therapeutic Effects of Intercessory Prayer (STEP) in Cardiac Bypass Patients." *American Heart Journal* 151 (4): 934–42.

Berger, Peter L. 1967. *The Sacred Canopy: Elements of a Sociological Theory of Religion*. Garden City, NY: Doubleday.

Black, Edwin. 2003. *War against the Weak: Eugenics and America's Campaign to Create a Master Race*. New York: Four Walls Eight Windows.

Boyer, Pascal. 2001. *Religion Explained*. New York: Basic Books.

Calaprice, Alice, ed. 2011. *The Ultimate Quotable Einstein*. Princeton: Princeton University Press.

Campbell, Joseph. (1968) 1992. *The Masks of God*. 4 vols. Reprint, New York: Penguin Arkana.

———. 2001. *Thou Art That: Transforming Religious Metaphor*. Novato, CA: New World Library.

Campbell, Joseph, with Bill Moyers. 1988. *The Power of Myth*. New York: Doubleday.

Carroll, James. 2001 *Constantine's Sword: The Church and the Jews*. New York: Mariner Books.

Clendinnen, Inga. 2003. *Ambivalent Conquests: Maya and Spaniard in Yucatan, 1517–1570*. 2nd ed. New York: Cambridge University Press.

Copernicus, Nicolaus. (1543) 1995. *On the Revolutions of Heavenly Spheres*. Amherst, NY: Prometheus Books.

Dalley, Stephanie, ed. 1989. *Myths from Mesopotamia*. New York: Oxford.

Dalrymple, William. 2009. *Nine Lives: In Search of the Sacred in Modern India*. New York: Alfred A. Knopf.

Darwin, Charles. (1859) 1993. *Origin of Species*. Reprint, New York: Random House.

———. (1874) 1998. *The Descent of Man*. 2nd ed. Reprint, Amherst, NY: Prometheus Books.

Dawkins, Richard. 2006. *The God Delusion*. New York: Houghton Mifflin.

Dembski, William. 1999. *Intelligent Design: The Bridge between Science and Theology*. Downers Grove, IL: InterVarsity.

Dennett, Daniel C. 2006. *Breaking the Spell*. New York: Penguin.

Durkheim, Emile. (1912) 2001. *The Elementary Forms of Religious Life*. Reprint, New York: Oxford University Press.

Edmundson, Mark. 2007. *The Death of Sigmund Freud: The Legacy of His Last Days*. New York: Bloomsbury USA.

———. 2007. "Defender of the Faith?" *New York Times*, September 9. http://www.nytimes.com/2007/09/09/magazine/09wwln-lede-t.html.

Ehrman, Bart D. 2000. *The Historical Jesus*. DVD course. Chantilly, VA: The Teaching Company.

———. 2008. *God's Problem*. New York: HarperCollins.

Eisenhower, Dwight D. (1948) 1997. *Crusade in Europe*. Baltimore: Johns Hopkins University Press.

Eliade, Mircea. (1949) 1963. *Patterns in Comparative Religion*. Reprint, New York: World Publishing.

———. (1949) 2005. *The Myth of the Eternal Return*. Reprint, Princeton: Princeton University Press.

———. (1959) 1987. *The Sacred and the Profane*. Reprint, New York: Harcourt.

Espar, David, and Susan K. Lewis. 2001. *Evolution: Darwin's Danger Idea*. DVD. Boston: WGBH Boston.

Ferrucci, Piero. 2007. *The Power of Kindness: The Unexpected Benefits of Leading a Compassionate Life*. New York: Jeremy P. Tarcher/Penguin.

Finstuen, Andrew. 2009. *Original Sin and Everyday Protestants*. Chapel Hill: University of North Carolina Press.

Firth, Raymond. 1996. *Religion: A Humanist Interpretation*. New York: Routledge.

Frazer, James G. (1890) 2010. *The Golden Bough*. Reprint, Charleston, SC: Nabu.

Fredriksen, Paula. 2000. *From Jesus to Christ*. 2nd ed. New Haven, CT: Yale University Press.

Fredriksen, Paula, and Adele Reinhartz, eds. 2002. *Jesus, Judaism & Christian Anti-Judaism: Reading the New Testament after the Holocaust*. Louisville, KY: Westminster John Knox Press.

Freedom House. 2005. *Saudi Publications on Hate Ideology Invade American Mosques*. Washington, DC: Center for Religious Freedom.

Freud, Sigmund. (1913) 1946. *Totem and Taboo*. Reprint, New York: Random House.

———. (1927) 1961. *The Future of an Illusion*. Reprint, New York: Norton.

———. (1939) 1953. *Civilization and its Discontents*. London: Hogarth.

———. (1939) 1967. *Moses and Monotheism*. Reprint, New York: Knopf.

REFERENCES

Friedman, Thomas L. 2011. "Israel: Adrift at Sea Alone." *New York Times Sunday Review*, September 18, 13.

Geertz, Clifford. (1973) 2000. *The Interpretation of Cultures*. Reprint, New York: Basic Books.

Gibson, Charles. 1967. *Spain in America*. New York: Harper Torchbooks.

Gilbert, Martin. 1993. *The Dent Atlas of Jewish History*, 5th ed. London: J. M. Dent.

Grant, Madison. (1916) 1970. *The Passing of the Great Race; or, The Racial Basis of European History*. Reprint, New York: Arno.

Gryn, Hugo, with Naomi Gryn. 2000. *Chasing Shadows*. New York: Penguin Putnam.

Hakakian, Roya. 2005. *Journey from the Land of No*. New York: Crown Publishing Group.

Harris, Sam. 2006. *The End of Faith*. New York: Norton.

Hertzberg, Hendrik. 2011. "Words and Deeds." *New Yorker*, January 24.

Hinde, Robert A. 2010. *Why Gods Persist: A Scientific Approach to Religion*, 2nd ed. New York: Routledge.

Hitchens, Christopher. 2007. *god Is Not Great: How Religion Poisons Everything*. New York: Hachette.

Hofstadter, Richard. (1944) 1971. *Social Darwinism in American Thought*. Reprint, Boston: Beacon.

The Holy Bible. 1940. Philadelphia: A. J. Holman.

The Holy Scriptures. 1944. Philadelphia: The Jewish Publication Society of America.

Huntington, Samuel P. (1996) 2002. *The Clash of Civilizations and the Remaking of World Order*. Reprint, New York: Free Press.

Kroeber, A. L., and Clyde Kluckhohn. 1952. *Culture: A Critical Review of Concepts and Definitions*. Cambridge, MA: Peabody Museum of American Archaeology and Ethnology.

Kushner, Harold S. 1981. *When Bad Things Happen To Good People*. New York: Schocken Books.

Laughlin, Harry H. (1922) 2009. *Eugenical Sterilization in the United States*. Whitefish, MT: Kessinger Publishing.

Lewis, Bernard. 1984. *The Jews of Islam*. Princeton: Princeton University Press.

———. 1990. "The Roots of Muslim Rage." *Atlantic Monthly*, September, 47–58.

Levine, Amy-Jill. 2002. "Matthew, Mark, and Luke: Good News or Bad?" In *Jesus, Judaism & Christian Anti-Judaism*, edited by Paula Fredriksen and Adele Reinhartz. Louisville, KY: Westminster John Knox.

Lieberman, Philip. 1991. *Uniquely Human*. Cambridge, MA: Harvard University Press.

Lipstadt, Deborah. (1994). *Denying the Holocaust: The Growing Assault on Truth and Memory*. Reprint, London: Penguin.

Maimonides, Moses. (ca. 1185) 1963. *The Guide of the Perplexed*. Translated by Shlomo Pines. Chicago: University of Chicago Press.

Malinowski, Bronislaw. (1922) 2008. *Argonauts of the Western Pacific*. Reprint, Whitefish, MT: Kessinger.

———. (1948) 1955. *Magic, Science and Religion; and Other Essays*. Garden City, NY: Doubleday.

Marx, Karl. (1867) 1996. *Das Kapital*. Washington, D.C.: Regnery Gateway Editions.

Micklethwait, John, and Adrian Wooldridge. 2009. *God is Back*. New York: Penguin.

Moses, Jeffrey. (1989) 2002. *Oneness: Great Principles Shared By All Religions*. New York: Ballantine.

Nielsen, Kai. 1990. *Ethics without God*. Rev. ed. Amherst, NY: Prometheus Books.

Newberg, Andrew, Eugene D'Aquili, and Vince Rause. 2001. *Why God Won't Go Away: Brain Science and the Biology of Belief*. New York: Ballantine Books.

Newton, Isaac. (1687) 1999. *The Principia: Mathematical Principles of Natural Philosophy*. Translated by I. Bernard Cohen and Anne Whitman, with assistance from Julia Budenz. Berkeley, CA: University of California Press.

Noriega, Roger. 2011. "Is There a Chavez Terror Network on America's Doorstep?" *Washington Post*, March 20, A21.

Otto, Rudolf. (1923) 1958. *The Idea of the Holy*. Reprint, New York: Oxford University Press.

Paley, William. (1802) 2006. *Natural Theology*. New York: Oxford University Press.

Pals, Daniel L. 2006. *Eight Theories of Religion*. 2nd ed. New York: Oxford University Press.

Peck, Don. 2011. "Can the Middle Class Be Saved?" *The Atlantic*, September, 60–78.

Pedahzur, Ami, and Arie Perliger. 2009. *Jewish Terrorism in Israel*. New York: Columbia University Press.

Rappaport, Roy A. 1999. *Ritual and Religion in the Making of Humanity*. New York: Cambridge University Press.

Remnick, David. 2011. "A Man, a Plan." *New Yorker*, March 21, 19.

Renard, John. 2002. *The Handy Religion Answer Book*. Canton, MI: Visible Ink.

Rousseau, Jean-Jacques. (1762) 1988. *The Social Contract*. Translated by G. D. H. Cole. Amherst, NY: Prometheus Books.

Sanders, E. P. 2002. "Jesus, Ancient Judaism, and Modern Christianity: The Quest Continues." In *Jesus, Judaism, & Christian Anti-Judaism*, edited by Paula Fredriksen and Adele Reinhartz. Louisville, KY: Westminster John Knox.

Smith, Huston. 1995. *The Illustrated World's Religions: A Guide to Our Faith Traditions*. New York: HarperOne.

Smith, W. Robertson. (1889) 1972. *The Religion of the Semites: The Fundamental Institutions*. New York: Schocken Books.
Smoot, George. 2007. *Wrinkles in Time: Witness to the Birth of the Universe*. New York: HarperCollins.
Souli, Sofia. 2007. *Greek Mythology*. Attiki, Greece: Toubis Publications.
Southwood, T. R. E. 2003. *The Story of Life*. New York: Oxford University Press.
Spencer, Herbert. (1864) 2002. *Principles of Biology*. Vol. 1. Honolulu, HI: University Press of the Pacific.
Sumner, William Graham. (1883) 2008. *What Social Classes Owe to Each Other*. Caldwell, ID: Caxton.
Tylor, Edward Burnett. (1871) 2010. *Primitive Culture*. Charleston, SC: Nabu.
Wade, Nicholas. 2009. *The Faith Instinct: How Religion Evolved and Why It Endures*. New York: Penguin.
Weber, Max. (1930) 2001. *The Protestant Ethic and the Spirit of Capitalism*. Los Angeles: Roxbury.
Wegener, Alfred. (1915) 1966. *The Origin of Continents and Oceans*. Mineola, New York: Dover.
Werblowsky, R. J. Zwi, and Geoffrey Wigoder, eds. 1966. *Encyclopedia of the Jewish Religion*. New York: Holt, Rinehart and Winston.
Yalom, Irvin D. 2008. *Staring at the Sun: Overcoming the Terror of Death*. San Francisco, CA: Jossey-Bass.
Zakaria, Fareed. 2011. "Where Netanyahu Fails Himself and Israel." *Washington Post*, May 25, A23.
Zeitlin, Solomon. 1969. *The Rise and Fall of the Judean State: A Political, Social and Religious History of the Second Commonwealth*. Vol. 2. Philadelphia, PA: Jewish Publication Society.

Index

Abd al-Wahhab, Muhammad ibn, 166
Able, Lionel, 228
abortion, 173, 206, 229, 235–36
Account of Things in Yucatan (Landa), 140
active denial, 210–16
Adams, Randall Dale, 241–42
Afghanistan, 13, 163, 168–69, 172, 194
agnostics and agnosticism, 1, 18, 35, 83, 103
Ahmadinejad, Mahmood, 119
Alexander the Great, 7, 10
Alhazen, 45–46
Alpher, Ralph, 49–50
al-Qaeda, 146, 163–64, 169–70
Ambivalent Conquests: Maya and Spaniard in Yucatan (Clendinnen), 139
American Humanist Association, 227, 230
Americans United for Separation of Church and State, 14, 216
anti-abortion violence, 173–74
anti-Judaism, 120–36
anti-Semitism, 112, 153–54, 164, 176, 186–94
apocalypse. *See* End of Days
Apollonius of Tyana, 9–11
Arab League, 156
Arafat, Yasser, 177–81, 183
Argentina, 152, 164
Argonauts of the Western Pacific (Malinowski), 97

Aristarchus of Samos, 44
Aristotle, 43–44, 46
Armenia, 151–52
Armstrong, Karen, 3–5, 232
Asimov, Isaac, 229
Ataturk, Mustafa Kemal, 150
atheists. *See* New Atheists
Atran, Scott, 194
Augustine of Hippo, 133–34, 136

Baha'i Faith, 158–61
Banna, Hassan al-, 167
Barak, Ehud, 180
Begin, Menachem, 178
Behe, Michael, 213–14
Benson, Herbert, 20
Berger, Peter L., 85
Bethe, Hans, 52
Bible. *See* Hebrew Bible; New Testament
Big Bang, 48–53, 61, 71, 200, 202, 224
Bill of Rights, 14, 194. *See also* Constitution, US
bin Laden, Osama, 164, 168–69
Black, Edwin, 220
Black, Hugo, 14–15
Blanshard, Brand, 228
blood libel, 134, 153
Boas, Franz, 90, 221
Bondi, Herman, 228
Boutros-Ghali, Boutros, 180
Boyer, Pascal, 87, 98
Bragg, Raymond B., 227

Brahe, Tycho, 45
Brandley, Clarence, 241
Breaking the Spell (Dennett), 28, 203
Breivik, Anders Behring, 171
Breuer, Josef, 94
Brown, Roy A., 241
Bryan, William Jennings, 211
Buddhism, 85, 87–88, 96, 159, 232
burial, human, 33–36, 83–84, 109, 199, 204
Bush, George W., 216
Butler, John Washington, 211
Butler Act, 211

Calaprice, Alice, 26
Caligula, 122
Calvin, John, 210
Campbell, Joseph, 40–41
Carroll, James, 121–22, 128, 136
Casablanca (film), 154
Case for God, The (Armstrong), 3–4
Catholicism. *See* Roman Catholic Church
Celler, Emanuel, 223
Charcot, Jean-Martin, 94
Charter for Compassion, 232
Chasing Shadows (Gryn), 105
Chavez, Hugo, 119
Chernomyrdin, Viktor, 180
children and religion, 106–10
Christianity and Christians
  as Abrahamic religion, 1
  anti-abortion violence and, 173–74
  anti-Judaism and, 120–36
  baptism and, 107, 147–48, 209
  circumcision and, 236–37
  creation myth of, 40–41, 43
  early history, 7–13, 118, 143–44
  evangelical, 6, 170, 176–77
  Hebrew Bible and, 111–12, 133–34
  holidays, 80–81, 93, 108–9, 132, 135
  impact of no miracles on, 21–23
  linear view of time of, 100
  Maya subjugation and, 136–41
  Muslim rule and, 143–44, 147–51, 163–64
  origin of, 6, 8
  prejudice and violence against Muslims, 170–73
  proselytizing and, 174–77
  violence against, 130, 157
  winter solstice and, 79
  See also Copts; New Testament; Protestantism; Roman Catholic Church
Christmas, 93, 108–9
Chrysostom, John, bishop of Antioch, 12, 133
Churchill's War (Irving), 193
Church of Jesus Christ of Latter-day Saints, 22
Ciardi, John, 229
circumcision, 107, 128, 130, 235–37
City of God (Augustine), 133
Clash of Civilizations and the Remaking of World Order, The (Huntington), 117
Clendinnen, Inga, 139–41
Clinton, Bill, 174, 179–80
Clinton, Hillary, 160–61
Communist Manifesto, The (Marx), 29
Confessions (Augustine), 133
Confucianism, 87
Constantine, 11, 13, 79, 131–32, 154
Constantine's Sword: The Church and the Jews (Carroll), 121
Constitution, US, 3, 13–14, 85, 173, 194, 211–12, 221
  Eighth Amendment, 231
  Fifth Amendment, 231
  First Amendment, 13–14, 173, 211, 216, 231, 233–34
  Fourteenth Amendment, 231, 242
  Fourth Amendment, 231

Nineteenth Amendment, 219, 231
Seventeenth Amendment, 219
Seventh Amendment, 231
Sixteenth Amendment, 219
Sixth Amendment, 231
Thirteenth Amendment, 231
Twenty-Fourth Amendment, 240
Copernicus, Nicolaus, 25, 44–45
Copts, 156–58
cosmic microwave background (CMB) radiation, 50–51
court cases. *See* lawsuits
creationism, 18, 210–12, 215
creation myths, 2, 40–42, 83, 206, 208–10
Crick, Francis, 55, 229
criminal justice, 240–42. *See also* lawsuits
Crusade in Europe (Eisenhower), 127
culture
  distant, 136–41
  Frazer on, 93
  Geertz on, 203–4
  Humanist Manifesto and, 228
  of humans, 71–73
  religion and, 25, 41, 84, 89, 103–10, 117, 198, 200
  Tylor on, 91
  use of the term, 102–3
Culture: A Critical Review of Concepts and Definitions (Kroeber and Kluckhohn), 102

Dalley, Stephanie, 76
Dalrymple, William, 106, 167
Daoism, 87
D'Aquili, Eugene, 24
Darrow, Clarence, 211
Darwin, Charles, 16, 71, 91–92, 211, 214–19
Darwin, Erasmus, 219
Das Kapital (Marx), 29
Davenport, Charles B., 220–21

da Vinci, Leonardo, 25
Dawkins, Richard, 2, 15–20, 29, 103–7, 114–15, 134, 197–99
Day of Judgment. *See* End of Days
death. *See* life passages; religion and religious
Death of Sigmund Freud: The Legacy of His Last Days, The (Edmundson), 96
Declaration of Independence, US, 26–27, 29, 166, 203
Dembski, William, 213
Denmark, 145, 165
Dennett, Daniel C., 28, 110, 203
Dent Atlas of Jewish History, The (Gilbert), 8
Descartes, Rene, 46
Descent of Man, The (Darwin), 91, 217
Dewey, John, 227
dhimma, 24, 143–50, 157
DNA, 2, 25, 54–55, 58–60, 69, 190, 223, 242
Doppler, Christian, 48
Durkheim, Emile, 90–91, 95–97, 203, 205

Earth, 1, 5–6, 18–21, 39, 41–46, 51–65, 77–78, 81–83, 91, 110, 200–201, 224, 226–29, 233
Easter, 80–81, 93, 108–9, 132, 135
Edmundson, Mark, 95
Egypt, 4, 8, 10, 13, 20, 44, 95–97, 124, 131, 146, 149–50, 153–60, 166–69, 177–81, 187, 244
Egyptian Islamic Jihad (EIJ), 168–69
Ehrman, Bart D., 10, 17, 103
Eid ul-Adha, 109
Eid ul-Fitr, 109
Eight Theories of Religion (Pals), 91
Einstein, Albert, 25–26, 47–48, 52, 203
Eisenhower, Dwight D., 127

election administration, 239–40
elections, funding of, 240
Elementary Forms of Religious Life, The (Durkheim), 96
Eliade, Mircea, 26, 98–101, 203–5
Elkins, Clarence, 241
Ellis, Albert, 229
End of Days, 19, 29, 120, 125–26, 200
End of Faith, The (Harris), 15–16, 27, 29, 105, 203
Ethics without God (Nielsen), 228, 246
eugenics, 192, 219–23
evangelicals, 6, 170, 176–77

Faith Instinct, The (Wade), 141
female clergy, 22–23
female genital cutting, 243–44
Ferrucci, Piero, 233
Festival of Lights, 78. *See also* Hanukkah
Finstuen, Andrew, 209
Firth, Raymond, 88
fiscal responsibility, 239
Franklin, Benjamin, 85
Franklin, Rosalind, 55
Frazer, James G., 93–94
Fredriksen, Paula, 12, 122, 125, 128
Free Inquiry (magazine), 2
Freud, Sigmund, 93–99
Friedman, Thomas L., 181
From Jesus to Christ (Fredriksen), 122
funerals, 31, 33–35, 109, 144
Future of an Illusion, The (Freud), 94–95

Galilei, Galileo, 25, 44–45
Galton, Francis, 219–20
Gamow, George, 59
Gaza Strip, 163, 165, 178, 181
Geertz, Clifford, 71, 101–3, 203–4, 208–9

Geneva Spiritual Appeal, 232, 234
Gibson, Charles, 138
Gilbert, Martin, 8
Gingrich, Newt, 173
God Delusion, The (Dawkins), 15, 18, 29
God Is Back (Micklethwait and Wooldridge), 112
god Is Not Great: How Religion Poisons Everything (Hitchens), 15, 86, 94, 237
God's Problem (Ehrman), 103
Golden Bough, The (Frazer), 93
Goldstein, Baruch, 179, 182
Gompers, Samuel, 223
Graham, Billy, 175, 209
Grant, Madison, 221
Great Britain and United Kingdom, 77–78, 91, 106, 127, 135, 150–51, 154–55, 164–65, 167, 176, 187, 190, 193, 197, 218–19, 228, 230
Greek Mythology (Souli), 9
Gryn, Hugo, 105–6, 246
Gryn, Naomi, 105–6
Guide of the Perplexed, The (Maimonides), 4
Guttmacher, Alan, 229

Hakakian, Roya, 145
Hamas, 165, 181, 188
Hamidian massacres, 151
Hamlet (Shakespeare), 25
Handy Religion Answer Book, The (Smith), 87
Hanukkah, 8, 78, 82, 105, 108–9
Harper, Julie Rae, 241
Harris, Sam, 15–16, 27–29, 104–5, 115, 197, 199, 203, 215
Hawker, David, 237
Hebrew Bible
 Christian interpretations of, 111–12, 133–34

Daniel 7:13–14, 125
Deuteronomy 13, 111–12
Deuteronomy 21:18, 111
Deuteronomy 24:16, 129
Exodus 13:4, 80–81
Exodus 21:23–25, 113–14
Genesis 1–2, 40
Genesis 15:18, 5
Genesis 22, 114–15
Joshua 10:12, 21
Judges 11:39, 115
Leviticus 20, 111
mashiach in, 124–25
Micah 3–4, 246–47
Micah 6:7–8, 115
Muslims and, 23
New Atheists and, 16–17, 110–15, 197
original sin and, 209
Psalms 23, 33
Psalms 106:37–40, 115
Song of Songs, 113
See also *midrash/midrashim*; *Septuagint*
Heracles, 9, 11, 84
Hereditary Genius (Galton), 219
Herman, Robert, 49–50
Herod Agrippa, 122–23
Herod the Great, 79, 121
Herschel, William, 46
Hertz, Heinrich, 50
Hertzberg, Hendrick, 179
Heschel, Abraham Joshua, 20
Hezbollah, 164–65, 181
Hillel the Elder, 17
Hinde, Robert A., 17
Hinduism, 10, 76, 102, 106, 119, 159, 165
Historical Jesus, The (video course), 10
History of God, A (Armstrong), 3–4
Hitchens, Christopher, 15–17, 86, 94, 106, 114–15, 197, 199–200, 237–38, 243

Hitler, Adolf, 47, 105, 152, 154–55, 189, 193, 220
Hitler's War (Irving), 193
Hofstadter, Richard, 218
Holmes, Oliver Wendell, Jr., 222
Holocaust, 105, 130, 188, 193
Homo sapiens sapiens, development of, 68–71, 75
honor killings, 244
Hook, Sidney, 228
Hooper, Simon, 15
Hoyle, Fred, 53
Hubble, Edwin, 46, 48
humanism
  actions called for by, 233–38
  hope and, 246–47
  just governance and, 238–43
  significant documents of, 226–32
  view of human life, 224–26
  violence against women and, 243–46
Humanist Manifesto, 227–28
Humanist Manifesto II, 228–30
Humanist Manifesto III, 230–31
human trafficking, 244–45
Huntington, Samuel P., 117
Hurricane Katrina, 6
Husayni, Amin al-, 155
Hussein, King, 180
Hussein, Saddam, 168

Idea of the Holy, The (Otto), 26
immigration, 106, 149, 165, 171, 187, 189, 192, 222–23, 242–44
India, 67, 69, 81, 89, 98, 106, 110, 119, 160, 165, 228
In Gods We Trust: The Evolutionary Landscape of Religion (Atran), 194
Inherit the Wind (play), 211
intelligent design, 18, 212–16
Interpretation of Cultures, The (Geertz), 71, 101, 103–4

Iran, 23, 81, 111, 118–10, 145–46, 152–53, 156, 158–61, 164–65, 169–70, 181, 184, 188
Iraq, 8, 42, 45, 146, 154–56, 163, 168–69, 172, 177
irreducible complexity, 213–16
Irving, David, 192–93
Islam and Muslims
  as Abrahamic religion, 1
  anti-Judaism and, 187–88
  Armenian persecution and, 151–52
  Baha'i Faith and, 159–60
  Christianity prejudice and violence against, 170–73
  dhimma and, 24, 143–50, 157
  Hajj of, 106
  impact of no miracles on, 23–24
  jihad and, 5, 15–16, 169
  linear view of time in, 100
  Maimonides influenced by, 4
  New Atheists and, 16, 197–98
  original sin and, 209
  origin and rise of, 12, 118–19, 141–43
  Salafi Islam, 157, 166–70
  science and, 46
  sharia and, 150, 157, 168–70, 173
  Shi'a Islam, 118, 145, 159–60
  slavery and, 136
  Sufi Islam, 167
  Sunni Islam, 118, 157, 159, 166
  Wahhabi Islam, 166–67
Islamism, 157, 163–64
Israel, 70, 112–15, 124, 149, 152, 155–56, 159–60, 165–66, 169, 177–89, 192, 224

Jefferson, Thomas, 166
Jews and Jewish
  ancient Rome and, 7–13, 120–34
  Augustine and, 133–34, 136
  Bethe and, 52
  conservative, 191
  cultural, 37, 191
  customs, funeral and burial, 31–37
  Einstein and, 47
  exodus from Arab countries and Iran, 152–56
  Freud and, 93
  Gryn and, 105
  Hasidic, 191
  homes, 108
  humanist, 191
  Muslim rule and, 141–48
  Nazism and, 47, 52, 105
  New Atheists and, 16, 105
  New Testament and, 126–30
  non-Orthodox, 21, 108, 180
  Orthodox, 108, 179–80, 191–92
  as "people of the book," 23–24
  Reconstructionist, 191
  Reform, 33, 36, 181
  September 11, 2011 and, 164
  social justice and, 206
  See also anti-Judaism; anti-Semitism; Israel; Judaism
Jews of Islam, The (Lewis), 119, 145–46
jihad and *jihadis*, 5, 15–16, 169
Jones, John E., III, 216
Jordan, 9, 75, 146, 177–78, 180
Journey from the Land of No (Hakakian), 145
J Street, 185
Judaism
  as Abrahamic religion, 1
  in ancient Rome, 8–13
  Baha'i Faith and, 159
  Christianity's origin and, 6, 8
  creation myth of, 2, 40
  festivals and holidays, 8, 78, 80–82, 105, 108–9
  impact of no miracles on, 20–21
  linear view of time in, 100
  midrash/midrashim and, 3, 113–15
  national laws and, 112–13

New Atheists and, 16–17, 104, 197–98
original sin and, 209
See also anti-Judaism; anti-Semitism; Hebrew Bible; Jews and Jewish
Jung, Carl, 98
just governance, 238–43, 246

kabbalah, 206
Kant, Immanuel, 246
Kaplan, Mordecai M., 228
Karzai, Hamid, 172
Kennedy, Eugene, 41
Kenya, 164
Kepler, Johannes, 45–46
Kezer, Joshua, 241
Khomeini, Ayatollah, 145–46
Kitzmiller, Tammy, 216
Kluckhohn, Clyde, 102
Koran, 5, 8, 23, 111, 118, 143, 166, 172, 197, 209
Kristof, Nicholas, 177, 184
Kroeber, Alfred, 102
Kushner, Harold S., 225
Kuwait, 168

LaFollette, Robert, Sr., 219
Lamston, Gary, 30–37, 174–77, 203–4
Lamston, Susan, 30–37, 174–77, 199
Landa, Diego de, 140–41
Laughlin, Harry H., 220–22
Lausanne Committee for World Evangelization (LCWE), 175–76
Laval, Pierre, 127
lawsuits
  Buck v. Bell, 222
  Citizens United v. Federal Election Commission, 240
  Daniel v. Waters, 212
  Edwards v. Aguillard, 212
  Epperson v. Arkansas, 211–12
  Gitlow v. New York, 14
  Gore v. Harris, x
  Kitzmiller et al v. Dover Area School District, 216
  Loving v. Virginia, 222
  McCollum v. Board of Education, 211
  McLean v. Arkansas Board of Education, 212
  Torcaso v. Watkins, 15
Lebanon, 146, 154, 164–65, 177, 180–81
Levine, Amy-Jill, 129
Levi-Strauss, Claude, 85
Lewis, Bernard, 117, 119, 144–45, 153, 155
Libya, 8, 150, 155
Lieberman, Philip, 83–84
life passages, 30–37, 89, 234–35
Lipstadt, Deborah, 193
London, England, 94–95, 98, 170, 193
Luria, Isaac, 206
Lyell, Charles, 91

MacDonald, Kevin B., 190–94
Madrid, Spain, 170
Magic, Science and Religion, and Other Essays (Malinowski), 85, 97
Maimonides, 4
Malinowski, Bronislaw, 85, 97–98
Malmo, Sweden, 165, 171, 187
Manila Manifesto, 175–76
Marr, Wilhelm, 187
Marx, Karl, 29, 99
Masks of God, The (Campbell), 41
Maya, 42–43, 82, 136–41
Mendel, Gregor, 55
Merchant of Venice, The (Shakespeare), 224
merit-based staffing, 243
Messiah, 19, 23, 124–28, 159, 192, 200
Michelson, Albert, 47

Micklethwait, John, 112
midrash/midrashim, 3, 113–15
miracles, 6, 9, 11, 15, 17–24, 30, 89–90, 101, 106, 201–3, 246
Morgan, Thomas Hunt, 221
Mormon Church. *See* Church of Jesus Christ of Latter-day Saints
Morocco, 101–2, 147, 153–56, 163
Moses, Jeffrey, 4
Moses and Monotheism (Freud), 95
Moyers, Bill, 41
Mozart, Wolfgang Amadeus, 25
Mubarak, Hosni, 157, 169, 180–81
Muhammad, 23, 90, 141–42, 145, 159
Muhammad, Mahathir bin, 187
Muslim Brotherhood, 157, 167
Muslims. *See* Islam and Muslims
Mussolini, Benito, 154
Myth of the Eternal Return, The (Eliade), 100

Nasser, Gamal Abdul, 178
natural disasters, 6, 245
Netanyahu, Binyamin, 184–86
Netherlands, 144, 164, 187, 228, 245
New Atheists, 2, 15–19, 25–30, 77, 88, 94, 98, 101, 109–12, 117, 197–200, 202–3
Newberg, Andrew, 24
New Testament
    anti-Judaism of, 126–30, 198
    1 Thessalonians 4:15–17, 125–26
    Greek as original language of, 9
    literalist approach to, 5
    Luke 2:8, 79
    Luke 8:26–39, 10
    Matthew 1:21, 125
    Matthew 7:12, 17
    Matthew 16:17–28, 126
    Matthew 27:25, 129
    Muslims and, 23, 111
Newton, Isaac, 45, 47

Nicene Creed, 7, 21, 132
Niebuhr, Reinhold, 209
Nielsen, Kai, 228, 246
Nine Lives (Dalrymple), 106
Norway massacre, 171

Obama, Barack, 164, 185
Olmert, Ehud, 182
On the Revolutions of the Heavenly Spheres (Copernicus), 44
Oneness: Great Principles Shared by All Religions (Moses), 4
Optics (Alhazen), 46
original sin, 2, 133, 209
Original Sin and Everyday Protestants (Finstuen), 209
Origin of Species (Darwin), 91, 217
Origin of Continents and Oceans, The (Wegener), 61
Oslo Accord, 178–79
Otto, Rudolf, 26, 98
Ottoman empire, 144, 146, 148–59, 206
oxygen catastrophe, 58–59

paganism, 6–7, 11, 13, 78–81, 93, 102, 118, 130–32, 136, 141–42, 146
Pakistan, 23, 118–19, 163–69, 104, 244
Palestine Liberation Organization (PLO), 177
Palestinian Authority (PA), 179
Paley, William, 213
Pals, Daniel, 91, 102
Passover, 21, 80–82, 108–9, 132
Patterns in Comparative Religion (Eliade), 99
Pedahzur, Ami, 182
Pentateuch, 17
Penzias, Arno, 50
Perliger, Arie, 182
Petraeus, David, 172

INDEX

Philippines, 163–64, 175
Plato, 7, 12
Pompey the Great, 8, 120
Power of Kindness, The (Ferrucci), 233
Power of Myth, The (Campbell and Moyers), 41
prayer, 1, 20–21, 33–35, 84–85, 107–8, 167, 199–201, 207, 233–34
Primitive Culture (Tylor), 91
Principia Mathematica (Newton), 45
Protestantism, 16, 22, 36, 197, 209–10
Protocols of the Elders of Zion, 154, 190
Ptolemy, Claudius, 44
public integrity, 242
Putin, Vladimir, 188

Qaradawi, Yusuf al-, 187
Quakers. *See* Religious Society of Friends
Quisling, Vidkun, 127
Qutb, Sayyid, 168

Rabin, Yitzhak, 178–80, 182
Ramayana, 10
Rappaport, Roy, 84
Rause, Vince, 24
Rees, Martin, 104
Rehnquist, William, 212
Reinhartz, Adele, 128–29
Religion: A Humanist Interpretation (Firth), 88
religion and religious
  advanced symbolic thinking and, 75–77
  children and, 106–10
  continuation of, 103–6
  as a cultural system, 101–3
  death and, 84–87
  early spiritual thinking and, 83–84
  moderation, 29–30, 198–99
  modern thought and, 87–91
  terminology and, 227–28
  theories and theories of, 91–101
  universe and, 77–83
  See also individual religions
Religion Explained (Boyer), 87, 98
Religion of the Semites, The (Smith), 92
Religious Society of Friends, 25, 91
Remnick, David, 185
Rise and Fall of the Judean State, The (Zeitlin), 123
Ritual and Religion in the Making of Humanity (Rappaport), 84
Robertson, Pat, 170
Roman Catholic Church, 21–22, 36, 80, 105, 107, 119, 128, 138, 157, 174, 191, 206, 209–10, 232, 235
Rommel, Erwin, 155
Roosevelt, Eleanor, 231
Roosevelt, Franklin D., 231
Roosevelt, Theodore, 219
Roth, Sid, 177
Rousseau, Jean-Jacques, 205
Rushdie, Salman, 145
Russia, 29, 135, 150–51, 180, 188, 22–23, 240–41
Russo-Turkish War of 1877–78, 151

Sacred and the Profane, The (Eliade), 26, 101, 204
sacred and the sacred
  Dennett on, 28, 203
  Durkheim on, 205
  Eliade on, 99–101, 203–5
  Geertz on, 102–3, 204, 208
  Harris on, 27, 203
  holy vs., 26–27
  human life as, 109–10, 225, 234
  just governance as, 238–43
  languages, 108
  life passages as, 30–37, 89, 234–35
  magic and, 97

sacred and the sacred (*continued*)
  naming events as, 76
  nonreligious uses of, 203–7
  profane vs., 26, 96
  symbols, 102–3, 177, 208
  texts, 96, 199
  totem, 92–93
  use of the term, 26–28, 203–7
  values and ideals, 6–7, 27–28, 195, 202, 233–34, 238–43
  violence against women, as sacred cause to prevent, 243–46
Sacred Canopy: Elements of a Sociological Theory of Religion, The (Berger), 85
Sadat, Anwar, 168, 178
saints, 21, 79, 133–34
Sakharov, Andre, 228
Salafi Islam, 157, 166–70
Sanders, E. P., 129
Saud, Muhammad ibn, 166
Saudi Arabia, 111, 118, 141, 164, 166–70
Scalia, Antonin, 212
Scholem, Gershom, 98
Scopes, John T., 211, 221
Sellars, Roy Wood, 227
separation of church and state, 13–14, 34, 120, 161, 191, 207, 211, 216, 229–30, 233–34
September, 11, 2001, 15, 164
Septuagint, 9
Shakespeare, William, 25, 224
sharia, 150, 157, 168–70, 173
Sharon, Ariel, 181
Shi'a Islam, 118, 145, 159–60
Shinto, 87
shiva services, 36
Shvetashvetara Upanishad, 89
Six-Day War, 177–78
Skinner, B. F., 228
Slipher, Vesto, 48
Smith, Huston, 87

Smith, William Robertson, 91–93, 96
Smoot, George, 40, 46, 50–51
Social Darwinism, 92, 217–19
Social Darwinism in American Thought (Hofstadter), 218
social justice, 28, 206, 230, 242
Socrates, 7, 12
Somalia, 194, 244
Souli, Sofia, 9
Southwood, T. R. E., 56, 60, 63, 65
Spain in America (Gibson), 138
Spencer, Herbert, 217–19
Spiritual World, 1, 18, 24–26, 73, 90, 175, 202, 233
Staring at the Sun (Yalom), 86
Stone, Oliver, 230
Story of Life, The (Southwood), 56
Sudan, 168–69, 244
Sufi Islam, 167
Sukkot, 108–9
Sumner, William Graham, 218–19
Sunni Islam, 118, 157, 159, 166
survival of the fittest, 217–19
Sweden or Swedish, 78, 165, 171, 182, 187, 222
symbolic thinking, 75–77
Syria, 8, 120–23, 125, 132, 146, 151, 153–55, 177–78, 180

Taliban, 13, 144, 167
Tankleff, Martin, 241
terrorism, 163–71, 179–84
Theodosius, 13, 132–33
They Thought for Themselves: The Story of Ten Amazing Jews (Roth), 177
Thou Art That: Transforming Religious Metaphor (Campbell), 40–41
tikkun olam, 206
Tiller, George, 173
Tillich, Paul, 209

Tobian, Aaron A. R., 238
Torcaso, Roy, 15
Totem and Taboo (Freud), 94–95
trafficking. *See* human trafficking
Tunisia, 150, 153–55, 163
Twain, Mark, 218
Tylor, E. B., 90–93, 102

Uniquely Human (Lieberman), 83–84
United Kingdom. *See* Great Britain and United Kingdom
United Nations, 156, 183–84, 231, 238, 243, 245
United States
    anti-abortion violence in, 173
    anti-Semitism in, 189–94
    Baha'i Faith and, 160–61
    Boas in, 90
    Chaco Canyon, 82
    coinage of, 79
    creationism and intelligent design and, 210–16
    eugenics and, 220–22
    honor killings and, 244
    human trafficking and, 245
    immigration to, 135, 152, 223, 242
    income gap in, 242
    Israel-Palestine conflict and, 183–86
    modern humanism and, 227–29
    prejudice and violence against Muslims in, 170–73
    social Darwinism and, 218–19
    state constitutions, 14
    tax benefits for religious institutions in, 130
    terrorism in, 164–67
    violence against women in, 243–44
    World War II and, 127
    See also Constitution, US; Declaration of Independence, US
Universal Declaration of Human Rights, 231–32
Ussher, James, 91

van Leeuwenhoek, Anton, 54
Veblen, Thorstein, 218
violence
    Christian anti-abortion, 173–74
    against Christians, 130, 157
    eugenics and, 219–24
    against Jews, 129, 134–36, 148, 156, 180–82, 187–89
    against Muslims, 170–73
    religious extremists and, 29, 117, 121–24, 197–200
    responding to, 194–95
    against women, 243–46
Vonnegut, Kurt, 230

Wade, Nicholas, 141
Wahhabi Islam, 166–67
Watson, James, 55
Weber, Max, 99, 209–10
Wegener, Alfred, 61
West Bank, 5, 177–79, 182–86, 192
What Social Classes Owe to Each Other (Sumner), 218
When Bad Things Happen to Good People (Kushner), 225
Why Gods Persist (Hinde), 17
Why God Won't Go Away: Brain Science and the Biology of Belief (Newberg, D'Aquili, and Rause), 24
Wilkins, Maurice, 55
Wilson, Edward O., 230
Wilson, Robert, 50
Wine, Sherwin T., 228
Winston, Robert, 104
women, violence against, 243–46

Wooldridge, Adrian, 112
World Organization of Jews from Arab Countries (WOJAC), 152, 156
World War I, 97, 150–51, 154, 210, 226–27
World War II, 47, 98–99, 127, 154–55, 188, 211, 219–20, 222–23, 227
Wrinkles in Time: Witness to the Birth of the Universe (Smoot), 46

Xenophanes, 12

Yalom, Irvin, 86–87
Yemen, 69, 155–56, 194
Yom Kippur, 109, 178

Zahar, Mahmoud al-, 188
Zakaria, Fareed, 186
Zawahiri, Ayman al-, 168–69
Zeitlin, Solomon, 123
Zoroastrianism, 81, 143, 159